Yes! I Will! I Do!

*Your Step-by-Step Guide
to Creating a Wedding Ceremony
as Unique as You Are*

by Maureen Burwell Pollinger

Purple Plume, a division of Inkwell, Ltd. New York

Yes! I Will! I Do!
Your Step-by-Step Guide to Creating a Wedding Ceremony as Unique as You Are

Published by Purple Plume, a division of Inkwell, Ltd.

ISBN: 978-0615510439

First Edition

Printed in the USA.

September 23, 1939 ∞ Leeds, Yorkshire England.
(Adapted from article in The Yorkshire Post, Wedding Section)

"The bride, who was given away by her father, wore a beautiful gown of white satin. The long train, cut in with the skirt, was quilted, and a panel of quilted satin also trimmed the bodice and long sleeves. Her long veil of fine net, embroidered with lovers' knots, fell from a coronet head-dress of seed pearls, and she carried a double sheaf of white lilies. The bridegroom was in the uniform of the Royal Artillery. After the reception, the bridal party went to the Leeds Cenotaph. Here the bride laid her bouquet, while the bridegroom stood at the salute."

When my mother passed away recently, we placed her funeral flowers—an arrangement of trumpet lilies and violas—at The Cenotaph; the violas were woven into the arrangement in honor of her name, Violet. What a fitting tribute to a life fulfilled. As we placed the flowers at the foot of the monument, we knew this gesture was the perfect completion and conclusion of her life of service to us, her family and to a loving marriage that spanned more than sixty years.

This book is a tribute to the infinite possibilities and the great majesty of a marriage born of love, built in love and dedicated to love.

Therefore I dedicate this book to my parents:
John Edmund and Violet Burwell.

TABLE OF CONTENTS

<u>PREFACE</u>

I grew up in England and was raised in the branch of the Church of England known as the High Church, or Anglo-Catholicism. I am deeply thankful for those early years and for their continuing influence on my spiritual life today as an ecumenical minister. Through my own spiritual journey, I became aware of other religious paths, leading me to the realization that regardless of one's religious, ethical, or spiritual beliefs, ultimately we must all forge our own relationship and dialogue with The Divine within our own hearts. For me, without this personal relationship with the sacred, I would be disconnected, unguided and alone.

I knew the decision to become a minister was right for me. I was unshakable in that conviction: this was my destiny; I felt it at my very core. Yet I didn't quite know where I fit. I knew the work of a church pastor was not for me and I wondered where I could best use my gifts. I prayed that I would be led to the perfect niche—if indeed, there was one for me.

As the process began to unfold, the pieces began snapping into place like connecting Legos. I was led to key people through a series of related and unrelated events. Then I was on my way. My dear friend Reverend Jon Mundy's generous role in my life was significant. He served as my advisor and mentor. Jon started out as a Methodist minister and expanded into the interfaith ecumenical movement, co-founding a seminary and a church fellowship. It was comforting to learn from him that I was not alone in my beliefs and convictions, that there were other ministers who represent and honor many religious traditions. Some ministers focus primarily on many or all of the Christian denominations, while others specifically represent the interfaith ministry, but one thing they have in common is that they all fit the category of ecumenical ministers. According to Merriam-Webster Online, "ecumenical" means promoting or tending toward worldwide Christian unity or cooperation, while according to *Webster's New World Dictionary*, "ecumenism" refers to the principals or practice of promoting cooperation and understanding among differing religious faiths. Ecumenical ministers share a belief in religious tolerance and honor the right of each individual to find and practice the spiritual path of their choice.

I remember feeling exhilaration upon finding my spiritual niche. I made a commitment to give it my all—which was not difficult because I felt such passion about this work. In over twenty years, nothing has changed in that regard. I still experience the same joy for the work I do, such that it hardly feels like work at all.

As an ecumenical minister and wedding celebrant, I am doubly blessed to have the opportunity not only to help create and write a ceremony but in addition, to be the person who officiates that wedding. This I consider such an honor. Regardless of the number of weddings I officiate, I am always in awe of the atmosphere of anticipation and excitement in those moments just before each ceremony. The collective hush is filled with emotion. I feel truly fortunate and blessed to be a part of each ceremony.

The writing of the ceremony, the creation of all manner of ceremony components for specific couples, and, of course, the legal officiating of the ceremony are the main functions of the celebrant, yet these duties comprise only a part of the ministry.

I remember working with a lovely couple whose grandparents were Buddhist and whose Asian parents had converted to Christian denominations. Though they did not follow the religious paths of their parents and grandparents, this couple wished to honor their relatives—without compromising their own spiritual ethics. Finding an appropriate benediction was impossible, so I wrote one myself. This example illustrates the unique needs of the many couples that do not fit, or do not wish to fit, into any one religious or spiritual category.

Over the years, I have had the honor and privilege to officiate many wonderful and unique weddings, from the minimally planned, informal, and quirky, to the deeply moving. Looking back, I remember a last-minute ceremony I officiated for a couple. They were strolling around a street fair here in Nyack, New York. The French bride-to-be was facing deportation in a few days, due to an expired visa. They sought me out and approached me with license in hand. Two random witnesses were chosen on the spot, and the ceremony commenced with the couples' newborn infant in tow. During the brief ceremony, the bride cradled and nursed her infant. The final pronouncement was punctuated with the baby's burp, prompting peals of laughter from us all.

Then I think back to September 11, 2001, the events of which shook us all, both at home and abroad. In New York, we watched the towers disintegrate into clouds of acrid black smoke. For weeks afterward, celebrations seemed frivolous and many weddings were postponed; most of us didn't have the heart to celebrate. But I recall one bride who was to be married three days after the tragedy; she informed me that she and the groom were expecting the cancellations of many guests, some of whom were still awaiting the fate of their loved ones. What I did not know until I arrived at the ceremony was that the bride had been in one of the towers that day. She had a slight disability, which made it difficult for her to navigate the stairs in order to escape quickly. In order to help move the human traffic along, a fire fighter had carried her to the ground floor. When she turned to thank him, he was already heading back up the stairwell to assist others. Very shortly thereafter, the tower collapsed. She barely made it through the rubble. We can only imagine the fate of the dear and courageous soul who assisted her. The ceremony was dedicated to that unknown and unnamed fire fighter whose heroism we honored. Though we were all on the brink of tears, we reminded ourselves that this was also a celebration of a marriage ceremony, and of the life of the bride. It is one ceremony I will never forget.

Every wedding is precious to me. Every couple offers me the opportunity to improve my own creativity and skills, and further my own spiritual growth as I help them create an authentic, meaningful, unique, and memorable ceremony.

When I began my wedding ministry more than twenty years ago, I often felt frustrated at the lack of resources available for the construction of a marriage ceremony. I was at a loss as to how to customize elements for the singular, unusual, and vastly diverse needs of the couples with whom I worked. The few books available were predominantly reference works and compilations of quotations, mostly poetry and readings, from the writings of others. The only exception I found was a small booklet written by my friends Rev. Jon Mundy and Rev. Diane Berke, Ph.D., which became an enormously helpful and precious resource.

However, as my ministry expanded, I needed specific benedictions and blessings, and I was not finding exactly the right words that reflected the needs of the individuals who were getting married. With no other option available, I began writing them myself. One day, my husband Kenneth took a look at some of my work and said, "Maureen, do you realize you have a book here?" *A book?* Until that moment, the idea of writing one had never occurred to me. Starting as a list of necessary wedding components, my book evolved more by default than by intention, and with the encouragement of my dear husband, who always supports my varied (and sometimes incongruous) endeavors. As the manuscript developed, I realized how tremendous an undertaking composing their own wedding ceremony can be for couples. The research and gathering of information can be overwhelming and the lack of helpful resources is discouraging. My hope is that this book will serve as both an informational resource and as a systematic, step-by-step guide to simplify the non-traditional ceremony creation process.

My ministerial journey began many years ago; while sitting quietly in meditation, I was unmistakably called or touched by the Spirit. Within the mysterious inner world of the soul, often beyond our ordinary understanding, the power of the Spirit makes known its Presence. For some, it is a quiet whisper amid all the mental chatter. For others, it is like the crack of thunder in the depths of stillness. The spiritual "tap on the shoulder" that prepares us for future spiritual service is truly mysterious.

Often, it can appear that this awakening comes far too soon; when mine occurred, I still had young children to raise. In that regard, it felt as though the timing was not quite in sync with the call. However, appearances can be—and often are—deceptive. I knew I had experienced an "inner calling" and from that moment, for me, an invisible switch was turned on; I became aware. Thus, I began the pursuit and development of all things spiritual.

Much of my early inner work involved self-evaluation and awareness techniques, and the exploration of many spiritual paths. It was at this time in my life that I read *The Seven Story Mountain,* the biography of Thomas Merton. Merton was a Trappist monk, poet, peace activist, prolific writer, and a leading advocate of interfaith dialogue. In his book, he describes his conversion to Catholicism and the need for interfaith understanding. Merton saw and expressed appreciation for the truth and beauty that lie at the core of all time-honored traditions. He spoke and corresponded with spiritual leaders of all faiths. In the later years of his life, he traveled through Asia to meet with leading Hindus and Buddhists. During his stay in India, he met the Dalai Lama, exiled leader of Tibetan Buddhists. They had daily meetings and developed a warm personal relationship. What an amazing man and a pioneer in the nascent interfaith movement that fully emerged many years later. This remarkable man's story left a great impression on me.

My personal ministerial journey has included spiritual support groups and classes, a hospital chaplaincy, a counseling practice, and a healing ministry. However, it has been my choice in recent years to function primarily as a wedding celebrant. For the celebrant, each wedding is a new adventure, since each couple is unique. Creating a marriage requires merging and interweaving diverse characteristics and qualities. Each couple will describe and express their own relationship in their own words and in their own way, and the celebrant needs to listen carefully to each word, with deep respect for the speakers both as individuals and as a couple. Sometimes when I meet my client couples and I begin asking questions, they surprise me by expressing deep feelings that they have never before revealed and verbalized to one another. These precious words are woven into the ceremony to create the core or theme. Words are powerful. When spoken from the heart and witnessed by God and loving individuals, they become transformed into prayers of intention and support for the couple and their rite of passage into their marriage.

About The Title of This Book

My ideas for the title of this book lived very briefly through a few unpublished incarnations. First, in an attempt to describe its contents clearly, I tried to squeeze an explanation of the entire project into one line. That was pretty futile! Then I struggled with a few insipid generic titles, to no avail. Finally, I threw up my hands and decided to pursue a simpler course. I thought about all of my wonderful wedding clients and of the many enjoyable conversations we have shared. I realized that there was one thing— something fun and catchy—that left an impression and that was repeated time after time.

Most grooms rarely concern themselves with wedding ceremony particulars until the last minutes—and in many cases, *seconds*—before the ceremony. Often, as I do a "run through" of final details with the couple, the groom starts to panic, particularly regarding the exchange of wedding vows. The following is a typical last-minute conversation:

"What do I say?" asks the groom.

I respond, "Whenever the celebrant asks, 'Will you take...?' you answer, 'I will!' Whenever the celebrant asks, 'Do you take...?' you answer, 'I do!' If you forget either of the above, then just answer 'Yes!'"

"Okay," says the groom, "but if I forget and freak out, I'll say

'Yes! I will! I do!'"

Therefore, I dedicate the title of this book to every person I know who has experienced last-minute pre-ceremony jitters.

INTRODUCTION

During more than twenty years as a minister, it has become increasingly clear to me that many couples are no longer inspired by the conventional wedding ceremony. This book was written primarily for those couples, as a guide to designing their own unique custom ceremonies.

In addition, however, it can also serve as a ceremony manual for celebrants. As more and more couples opt for personally designed wedding ceremonies, many wonderful, open-minded, independent wedding celebrants are emerging, some of whom are ecumenical ministers who are willing to help couples design their own ceremonies. This guide offers helpful resources for both newly ordained and seasoned celebrants who wish to expand their inventory of ceremony ideas and choices.

To be asked by a friend to officiate their wedding is one of the greatest honors imaginable. Depending on where a potential celebrant resides, it may actually be possible to officiate the wedding even if you are not a legally registered wedding celebrant. A recent phenomenon is the "one-day minister." For a small fee, some states or counties offer a "one-day minister-celebrant license." Of course, the only drawback to engaging a novice celebrant is her or his lack of experience. In such cases, this easy-to-follow text can guide the one-day celebrant in the areas of ceremony ideas and construction, structuring and organizing the order of procession, marriage license information, setting up the altar, and other topics.

As this book was evolving, I tried to imagine the predicament couples find themselves in when planning a ceremony that truly speaks to their hearts. When I envisioned stepping into their shoes, I realized that what they needed was an organized and easy-to-follow resource guide for designing their ceremony. During the busy weeks leading up to the wedding day, the last thing a couple needs is a complicated, mind-numbing writing project. Bearing this in mind, I focused intently on keeping this guide simple and easy to follow. In the end, all that is required from the couple is carefully selecting the desired text and weaving it all together. In addition, I considered all the couples who are of different religious denominations, traditions, and spiritual ethics, who choose to express their diverse values in a ceremony that is uniquely their own. Therefore, I have done my best to offer numerous and diverse choices of ceremonial elements, addressing and honoring many religious and cultural traditions.

Each couple planning to marry brings to their union their own personal life journey, drawn from all they have experienced in the past and who they are becoming in the present. This is their still-evolving life story, filled with their own experiences, preferences, values, hopes, and dreams. It makes perfect sense that they envision a ritual that reflects their own individual spirituality yet honors their equally distinct relationship. Today, brides and grooms are often a little older, perhaps a little more mature, and generally financially independent. Rarely do we see the coy brides of the past. So veering from a typical and predictable ceremony to a personalized ceremony is the perfect opportunity for these modern brides to express their love in language that is authentic and unique to them.

Most couples don't feel that being of different denominations or faiths, or even having no faith at all, is an obstacle to a spiritual ceremony or an impediment to the marital union. I agree. Every marriage represents an entirely new life, beginning with the ceremony itself, which marks the ancient rite of passage into the marriage. In their union, the couple works together not only for the greater good of themselves and each other, but also for the actual marriage itself. Therefore, the wording of the ceremony needs to express the intentions of the couple truthfully and clearly. I ask each couple to describe their individual spirituality and how they envision the ceremony. I also ask them to think about specific words that they do not want in the ceremony. Every celebrant needs to listen very carefully to the individual wishes and preferences of each member of the couple. Often a word can elicit a negative response, not necessarily because of its actual definition but rather by an association it triggers.

Writing a book is similar to a construction project, only the building blocks already exist within the author's mind. For the storyteller or fiction writer, this material is stored in the author's prolific imagination. There are characters and stories lurking in their minds just waiting to be coaxed or plucked out and then brought to life in the pages of a book. For the author of an informational book such as this one, the building material is the life experience already stockpiled in the author's memory. My own particular experience as a wedding celebrant has provided me with a collection of rich and wonderful experiences—a mental Rolodex to draw upon when working with couples, and while creating this book.

Personally, I tend not to be very linear in my thinking and find that images are essential to my own thought processes. Likewise,

I hope the reader will benefit from the following images:

Think of a great circular hall surrounded by small rooms. The Great Hall represents the wedding ceremony. Each adjoining small room serves as an information-gathering resource room, and each has a door leading and funneling information into the Great Hall. These rooms are broken down into three departments. Part One deals with all the countless details and information for beginning the ceremony planning process. Part Two serves as the advice and information manual, which I have gathered from over twenty years of hands-on experience. Part Three, the ceremony text handbook, brings us to the final stages of ceremony designing and constructing. We are now ready to enter the Great Hall: the actual ceremony. The entire process is an enlightening learning adventure for the bride and groom, culminating in the most significant day of their lives: their unique and special wedding ceremony.

The information, ceremony text, and samples in these pages include interfaith and multicultural ceremonies, yet this book cannot be categorized as an interfaith and multicultural ceremony book, as these traditions comprise just one segment of the information contained in the text. Within this category, I have purposely chosen to include Jewish, Celtic, Quaker, Latin American/Hispanic/Filipino, and Greek ceremonies. In the section on Standard–Traditional Vows, which includes most Christian denominations and Judaism, I have also included the Muslim and Hindu exchange of wedding vows. This choice of traditions is based on my twenty-plus years' experience as a celebrant in the New York tri-state area, which is rich in ethnic diversity. Living and working in this location has brought me to the following realization:

Regardless of their religious affiliation, what most couples want is a wedding ceremony that is unique and meaningful to them, even if that simply means a few personal words about the couple woven into the sermon by the officiating celebrant. Whether they are an interfaith, intercultural, or same-faith couple, the common thread they share is that they want a service that speaks to and of them. When I meet specifically with interfaith couples, their overriding desire is for a unique ceremony, with minimal religious elements and overtones, that subtly honors each of their own traditions. The bride and groom are each trying to please their own family while not offending their new family. The most common interfaith ceremonies I officiate are Jewish–Christian, though I have served other religious combinations, including Muslim–Christian, Hindu–Jewish, Greek Orthodox–Jewish, Sikh–Christian (I have officiated one), and Hindu–Christian (I have officiated three). Usually I represent the Christian partner, but I act as a neutral representative for each partner when the ceremony style allows. Either way, as a liberal Christian ecumenical minister, I can fully bless the union. While there are interfaith wedding compendiums on the market, the focus of this book is on the creation of a unique personalized ceremony—from procession to final pronouncement—for couples within all faith traditions.

Part One

Getting Started – Participants, Particulars, Places, and Plans

Chapter One:
The Celebrant

Before you begin your committing
To a wedding officiant, it's fitting
That she cares from the start
That she speaks from the heart
That she listens, is also befitting.

As a celebrant, I have been privy to hundreds of weddings, yet I continue to be awestruck by the flurry of active participants involved in the overall production of the wedding celebration. I find it truly amazing that such magic can emerge from orchestrated chaos.

The planning of a wedding and reception requires the products and services of a team of many experts, but the ceremony is the very heart and core of the celebration. The ceremony sets the tone and impression for the festivities that follow. For most of us, when we recall a particularly memorable wedding, we generally remember the special moments during the actual ceremony.

With very few exceptions, every wedding ceremony requires a celebrant's services. It makes so much sense to regard the celebrant as the primary person to consider and consult when planning a wedding. In many cases, however, she or he is the last person contacted and often at the last minute, resulting in dissatisfaction on the part of the bride and groom.

For couples planning a typical or traditional wedding, little thought is given to the celebrant, since the celebrant is often assigned to the couple by their own church, temple or place of worship. On the other hand, there are couples that already have a close relationship with a beloved family priest or rabbi with whom they are perfectly satisfied. For them there is no need to search further.

It is for those who prefer a personalized or nontraditional ceremony that I make the following suggestion: Start thinking about the wedding celebrant in an entirely new way. Consider the celebrant as someone you choose, interview, and hire, just as you choose all the key players who play a vital role in your wedding celebration. Research and interview the celebrant as you would the banquet hall manager, florist, musicians, and photographers. She is no less important than the aforementioned; in fact, without the celebrant there is no ceremony.

Be sure that you feel a mutual rapport and that she listens to you. And remember, if you are dissatisfied, providing you give her enough notice you can dismiss her, though I suggest that you do so politely.

The celebrant has two primary roles. Her principal function is to legally solemnize your union. The second function is the creative work of ceremony construction. She guides the couple in writing and creating their ceremony. Creating a ceremony outline is done at the initial consultation. Even before the meeting, I ask the couple to begin considering the type of ceremony they would prefer and if they wish, to bring samples and ideas they have collected to the consultation. We may incorporate these into the ceremony. Generally, the couple becomes aware of the value of their own unique words while answering the ceremony questionnaire. These answers form the ceremony theme, since these are the couple's own special words, thoughts, and expressions from the heart.

The Role of Questionnaires

Included in Chapter 2 are two questionnaires: the Ceremony Questionnaire and the Spirituality Questionnaire. In addition a third questionnaire, the Vows Renewal Ceremony Questionnaire, included in Chapter 10, is designed specifically for couples planning on renewing their vows. As a celebrant, I cannot imagine working without these valuable tools. A ceremony questionnaire is a priceless resource when beginning ceremony planning; it helps couples to identify what their preferences are, and determine whether or not they are in agreement on key issues and choices. Without a couple being clear on their individual preferences and choices, moving forward to actual ceremony completion is challenging. Planning this way protects against last-minute arguments, even if compromises need to be made along the way.

The Celebrant Search

My advice is that the safest way to choose the celebrant is through the time-honored method of personal relationship or recommendation. In fact, my wedding ministry is based on recommendation, particularly from couples whose weddings I have performed.

When searching for a celebrant, couples may be astonished to discover that some celebrants refuse to officiate their wedding ceremony. There are a number of reasons for this. Some clergy-persons refuse based upon the general beliefs, guidelines, and policies of the religious organization with which they are affiliated, particularly if the couple requesting their services is of different Christian denominations or of different faiths altogether. Some priests, ministers, and rabbis decline because the bride and groom are not active members of that celebrant's particular congregation, or because only one person in the couple is a member. In addition, they may refuse because the ceremony is to take place at a wedding hall, private home, or site other than the church or temple where that celebrant presides. In some cases, a celebrant may agree to officiate at the church or temple at which she or he presides, with the stipulation that the couple become regular congregants. Some celebrants may be willing to officiate at their church, temple, or even at an outside wedding location, but they may not be open to officiating a personalized ceremony. Some celebrants do not object to officiating a Christian interdenominational ceremony, but they do object to officiating or co-officiating an interfaith ceremony. In the case of an interfaith ceremony representing two different religious traditions, Conservative rabbis, evangelical Christian pastors, Greek Orthodox priests, and Muslim clergypersons will most likely not be willing to co-officiate with another clergyperson, nor will they be open to officiating a ceremony outside of their church or temple. For any of the above reasons, you may want to seek out an independent celebrant, a nondenominational or interdenominational, ecumenical or interfaith minister-celebrant.

If the ceremony is scheduled to take place at a wedding location or banquet hall, the wedding coordinator or banquet manager will have a list of celebrant referrals. These lists are generally valuable because the wedding location will rate the celebrants in terms of reliability and positive feedback from their clientele. There are other referral services listed in the phone book and on the Internet. A couple who recently asked me to officiate their ceremony had seen a recommendation for my services on the chat board of a wedding-related website. I had never advertised on that site; apparently another couple over whose wedding ceremony I had presided had graciously placed an endorsement there.

What Type of Celebrant?

With a few exceptions, most couples constructing some or all of their own ceremony and vows will be working with one of the celebrant types outlined below. Keep in mind that some categories overlap. The term "ecumenical" broadly covers both "Christian nondenominational" and "interfaith or multi-faith."

- An independent minister-celebrant

- A nondenominational, interdenominational, or ecumenical minister-celebrant

- An interfaith, multi-faith, or ecumenical minister-celebrant

- A Unitarian Universalist, Science of Mind, or Unity minister-celebrant

- A Reform or Liberal rabbi-celebrant

- A cantor-celebrant

- A minister of a mainstream church or a rabbi of a mainstream temple who is willing to officiate the ceremony at a non-church or non-temple location, or even allow the couple ceremony construction freedom. Note that some of the celebrants listed above also fit this category. (Generally, a rabbi affiliated with a Reform or Reconstruction temple is often, although not always, open to officiating your ceremony.)

- A liberal married or unmarried Catholic priest. (In New York City, there exists an organization of Catholic priests who have stepped out of the hierarchical structure of the church, some of whom are married. They are legally credentialed to officiate wedding ceremonies.)

- A judge, mayor, justice of the peace, or secular person licensed to perform civil wedding ceremonies

Celebrant Essentials

- *The legal requirements* for a secular celebrant who performs civil ceremonies may vary from state to state. However, weddings are generally officiated by judges. In some states, county clerks, mayors, or other government officials may conduct civil ceremonies.

- Most states require one or two witnesses to sign the marriage certificate. Even when only one witness is legally required, the license may reflect a two-signature requirement.

- The celebrant who officiates the marriage ceremony has a duty to send a copy of the marriage certificate to the county or state agency that records marriage certificates. Failure to send the marriage certificate to the appropriate agency does not necessarily nullify the marriage, but it may make proof of the marriage more difficult.

- Most states consider a couple to be married when the ceremony ends, or at the final pronouncement. For this reason it is preferable that the celebrant and witnesses do not sign the license until after the final pronouncement, thereby concluding the ceremony.

- A marriage performed in another jurisdiction—even overseas—is usually valid in any state as long as the marriage was legal in the jurisdiction where it occurred.

- Contrary to common belief, a ship's captain is not automatically qualified to officiate marriages. If you are planning a wedding aboard a ship, check with your local clerk of marriages.

- Some licensed celebrants will be agreeable to working with a personalized ceremony that the bride and groom have written themselves, while others may use a prewritten, standardized state format. You should ask whether the celebrant would be flexible and accommodate you in working with your own personalized ceremony.

- Remember also that there are questions included in the ceremony that the celebrant is legally obligated to ask you.

- *Important note:* Marriage license requirements not only differ from state to state, they change over time. It is vital that you verify all information with your local registrar or clerk of marriage licenses at your local town or city before making any wedding plans.

Wedding Words and the Consultation

Writing most or all of the wedding ceremony may seem like an overwhelming task. However, when the ceremony is broken down into smaller parts, the couple can construct the whole ceremony more easily. Again, it is important to remember that there are statements and questions that the celebrant must ask by law. Therefore, I recommend working with an experienced celebrant, if one is available, whose ministry is based on personalized ceremony construction. With the invaluable help of this celebrant, the process of putting together the ceremony can be quite simple. A necessary and essential part of the process is a *leisurely* consultation appointment. Ideally, this initial meeting should take place in person. However, if geographic circumstances don't allow for this, email or a phone consultation can work as well. During the consultation, the couple will:

- Talk about their own ideas and preferences

- Answer the questions on the questionnaire—(answers to these questions create the core wording and theme for the ceremony

- Listen to ideas offered by the celebrant

- Read and review samples

- Reach mutual agreements with one another

- Make choices

At this meeting, the celebrant will:

- Listen carefully to the needs and preferences of the couple

- Ask questions and record the answers if the couple has not already given the celebrant a completed questionnaire

- Offer ideas and samples

- Advise and guide the couple, if necessary, to reach an agreement

- Construct the ceremony outline

- Make sure the couple leaves the consultation appointment with a copy of this outline

The creation of an exceptional ceremony is dependent on the three elements of ceremony construction: *meaning, authenticity, and flow.* We'll go into this more thoroughly in Chapter 2.

The Phone Interview

Of course, you really want to have a sense of who your celebrant is. If I were searching for the person who was to preside over the most important day of my life, I would without a doubt want to speak to her. Most of us can glean volumes about a person by the way they conduct themselves over the phone, particularly if that celebrant is thrown a few unpredictable or pointed questions. For example, you may want to ask a couple of the questions outlined in the "Credentials, Essentials, and Legalities" interview below. Be attentive as to how she responds. I suggest that this brief initial interview be conducted over the phone for the following reasons:

- Hearing the celebrant's voice and listening to her spontaneous answers to your questions affords a sense of who she is and whether her personality is simpatico with yours

- You can save both the celebrant and yourselves time by conducting a phone interview before the in-person consultation

- The phone interview will allow you to focus your consultation time on the reason you are there—the construction of your ceremony.

The Information Package

Once the phone interview is completed, the celebrant may ask the couple if they would like an information package, which she may mail or email to them. I generally prefer to send the package by mail, as email attachments can be difficult to open. Either way, this correspondence generally offers the couple more information about the services of the celebrant. My typical package includes a cover letter, my fee, newspaper and magazine articles about weddings I have officiated, and ceremony sample ideas based on information the bride and groom have shared with me during the phone conversation. My package also includes the ceremony questionnaire, which is important both for ceremony wording and determining the core theme of the ceremony. After receiving and reviewing the package, the couple may then contact me again, this time to set up a consultation appointment.

The Personality Interview

I cannot emphasize enough the importance of empowering yourselves in the selection of the celebrant. The wrong celebrant can spoil an otherwise perfectly planned wedding. I recently watched a TV reality show that featured a couple and followed their wedding plans from the time of their engagement to the actual ceremony. In this instance, the celebrant and the couple were not compatible. The bride and groom were extremely shy and reserved. They conversed almost in whispers. The celebrant was loud and raucous, and cracked unnecessary jokes. His personality was overbearing. I would not have recommended this minister for this couple. At the culmination of months of tireless planning, on the most important day of your life, imagine dealing with an irritating celebrant who triggers feeling of annoyance and frustration. For this reason, it is important to question or interview the celebrant.

Determining the right personality fit is quite subjective.

During the telephone interview, be aware of how you feel about the celebrant and always trust your intuition. Be sure that you are comfortable with her personality and demeanor. Bear in mind that she is *serving you,* therefore please seriously consider interviewing her.

Credentials, Essentials, and Legalities Interview

Once you feel confident and satisfied with your choice of celebrant, there is the extremely important matter of legalities. Ask yourself, "How do I know if this celebrant is legally registered to officiate weddings?" Indeed, how *do* you know? On a few occasions my services have been requested to legally solemnize marriages for "married" couples who discovered, after their original ceremony, that they were not in fact legally married, thanks to an uninformed, unregistered minister celebrant and an unscrupulous clergyperson with doctored credentials. Therefore, once you have one or more recommendations, I suggest that you ask the celebrant the following questions:

- *How long have you been a celebrant?*

- *Are you legally registered?*

- *In what state are you registered?* If the celebrant is registered in a state other than the one in which you are to be married, ask whether that registration is reciprocal throughout the US. (A New York minister registration is reciprocal in most states.)

- *What is your registration number?* You can check a celebrant's registration status in the city where the registration was issued. (In New York City, clergy registration is issued at City Hall on Centre Street.)

- *How much time do you spend working with a couple at the consultation?* Ceremony construction takes time. Generally, one and one-half to two hours will be adequate at the initial consultation, where the outline of the ceremony is constructed.

- *What time do you arrive at the wedding location site? Will you get there early?* The celebrant needs to arrive in ample time for a number of reasons: to allay any concern on the part of the couple, to meet the family and the wedding party, to familiarize herself with the location staff and the location site if it is new to her, to set up and check the altar or ceremony site, to be alerted to any last-minute changes, and to avoid tardiness due to unpredictable traffic conditions.

- *What happens if you are ill the day of the wedding and cannot officiate? Do you have someone to cover for you?* This is a valid question. I have never found myself in a situation like this. However, I am fortunate to have my husband available most of the time to cover for me if necessary.

- *Can we stay in touch with you during the interval between the consultation and the ceremony in case we have questions or changes in the ceremony?* Make sure the celebrant is agreeable to staying in touch with you.

- *How much do you charge and when is payment expected?* An independent celebrant's fee will vary. A minister of a mainstream church generally reduces the fee for tithing congregants and charges non-congregants a substantially higher fee. To reduce the fee, some churches will offer the couple the option of becoming regular congregants for a specified period of time before the scheduled ceremony, with the hope that they will remain congregants after the ceremony. For nonmembers, one church in my local area charges $1,200 to $1,800, whereas another nearby church charges $500 to $600. I was recently informed by clients that a particular church in New York City charges $3,000 per wedding.

- *Could we speak to some of your past clients?* If you are unsure about the celebrant, ask if you may speak to a couple whose ceremony she or he has officiated.

- *Would you be prepared to be responsible for the order of procession?* In most cases, the order of procession is the responsibility of the banquet manager or bridal assistant at that location. However, in less formal ceremonies or in locations where such assistance is not available, the celebrant can be invaluable.

- Finally, and most importantly, ask yourself, "How do I feel about this celebrant?" Stop thinking for a moment and rely on your intuition. Listen to that small, still voice within.

Avoiding an Inefficient Officiant

Do not consider any celebrant who will not furnish you with the appropriate answers to the questions listed above. Do not make a commitment to a celebrant who responds in the following manner:

- She avoids or is vague in answering the questions you ask.

- She will not or cannot give you her registration information.

- She is not willing to spend the necessary time to get to know you, to listen to you, and to construct the ceremony with you.

- She attempts to talk you into a pre-formatted ceremony outline, simply inserting your names in the questions and vows section.

- She intends to show up at the wedding location just minutes before the actual ceremony.

- She refuses to be clear and forthright about her fee.

- She is coercive concerning the ceremony style, the religious content of the ceremony, the fee, or any other issue that makes you feel uncomfortable.

Do not be afraid of or intimidated by the celebrant. Her job is to minister to you. If you are unhappy or have doubts regarding this celebrant, be honest and speak up about how you feel. Your input and critique could prove helpful. If the celebrant takes offence, it may be time for an ego check. Priceless opportunities are often lost to a stubborn ego.

The Reverend's Regalia

Think of the exhaustive search for the perfect wedding outfits, not only for the bride and groom, but also for the attendants. Indigenous cultures place great emphasis upon the ceremonial attire as a way of paying homage to those involved, to the actual ritual itself, and of course, to the presence of the Spirit. Throughout time immemorial, special rituals have marked life passages. It is customary and respectful to honor such rituals by wearing the appropriate ceremonial dress. Since the celebrant maintains a visible role in the ceremony, the question of what she will wear is certainly a valid one.

In the case of a church wedding, the celebrant will wear the appropriate vestments or clothing that conforms to and befits the dictates or preferences of that particular religious body. However, in the case of an independent celebrant, what is the protocol? Obviously, there is more latitude. I feel that a robe is not only appropriate but also necessary. An informal wedding is still a significant occasion. For the celebrant to dress formally is respectful to the bride and groom as well as to those attending the wedding, and, in addition, it confers a sense of reverence and dignity to the ceremonial ritual itself. Since the parameters for an independent celebrant are much broader, I own more than one robe; my choice is generally driven by the ceremonial requirements of the individual couple. I keep in mind that, in spite of the celebrant's purpose and visibility, she or he needs to remain a somewhat neutral presence—visible yet barely noticed—even while wearing a robe and stole. This may be an entirely feminine perspective or simply my own. For this reason I no longer wear white. White competes with the bridal gown, particularly in photos. I have seen wedding photos in which a white ministerial robe and the bridal gown blur into one fuzzy, indistinguishable blob. Some brides ask me what I will wear; others don't think of asking. In any case, I personally choose not to wear the same color as the bride. Nor do I wear colors that are too vivid, with the exception of the stole. I often check with the bride regarding the color of the bridesmaids' dresses, so that I may avoid unnecessary color clashes. Please bear in mind, this is my own choice and is not considered a general rule. When it comes to my role in the aesthetics of a wedding ceremony, I confess, I tend to be rather a perfectionist. I know the care and consideration that can go into each detail of planning a ceremony, so I do my best to dress sensitively and appropriately.

Generally, I prefer to wear a rich brown-black brocade robe, a black silk robe, or a deep plum robe. I own a black silk, antique, hand-embroidered Japanese kimono that works beautifully as a ceremony robe. In addition, it is appropriate for couples of Asian origin. Beneath the robe, I wear a black or dark-colored suit and accessorize with the appropriate stole. I attempt a look of dignified, elegant neutrality. Religious insignia is minimized or neutralized in the case of an interfaith wedding, in deference to the non-Christian partner.

Final Advice

In conclusion, here is a little advice: *do not be coerced by someone regarding your choice of celebrant, regardless of his or her good intentions. Please be direct with that person right from the start.*

The following story is a perfect example.

I was asked by my friend Phyllis to officiate the wedding of her dear friends, whom she had introduced to one another. When she phoned me, she bubbled over with excitement at having played the role of matchmaker.

Generally, after making contact with prospective clients, I then inform them that if they decide to use my services, they should contact me themselves, at which time we will arrange for a consultation appointment.

However, since Phyllis is a friend and one of the most effervescent and positive people I know, I bent my own rules and met with her to discuss this couple's wedding ceremony. The plan was that I would give my information package to Phyllis, who would pass it on to the couple. My intention was to do the ceremony pro bono because of our wonderful mutual friend, Phyllis. Over lunch, I outlined possible ceremony ideas and styles, while dear Phyllis breathlessly narrated her role in the introduction as Mamma Phil, the maternal matchmaker. The next step in the process would be the consultation appointment.

I then went on vacation to England. Upon my return, I had received no word from the couple. However, I had—predictably—received a call from another couple for a ceremony on the same date at the same time. So, I called the first couple—but they never returned my call!

What do you do in a ticklish situation like this one? This raises some very interesting issues. I never relish the idea of phoning couples once I have emailed or mailed my package to them. Most couples call me immediately after they receive the package. Some couples even send me a deposit *before* the consultation to secure my services. If they want me, they contact me. In all honesty, who wants to be pursued and harassed by a minister? I would feel as though I were annoying or embarrassing them by calling. But in this case, I left the couple a message to please call me if they wanted to proceed with the consultation, and added that if they did not contact me, I would assume that they did not want my services. Because of my friendship with Phyllis, who is always so kind, I felt an obligation to contact them; I didn't want to stand them up nor disappoint Phyllis.

In the end, it became apparent that the couple had hired someone else and were uncomfortable coming clean to Phyllis. They probably felt indebted to her or perhaps did not want to cause her disappointment. Consequently, they felt unable to be direct.

Remember that the selection of the celebrant is *your choice.*

Review Checklist

- ❑ Decide on the type of celebrant you want to officiate your wedding.
- ❑ Make an appointment for a phone interview with the celebrant.
- ❑ Note her personality and professionalism.
- ❑ Check her credentials.
- ❑ Ask any pertinent questions.
- ❑ Note her efficiency. Is she knowledgeable? Is she coercive?
- ❑ Ask her what she is planning to wear to the ceremony.
- ❑ Request, receive, and review the information package and questionnaire.
- ❑ Fill out the questionnaire.
- ❑ Make an appointment for a consultation.
- ❑ Email or mail the completed questionnaire along with your ceremony ideas and preferences, or bring them to the consultation.
- ❑ Write down the ceremony outline.
- ❑ Be prepared to give the deposit to the celebrant at the consultation.

Chapter Two:
Ceremony Details

laborate wedding books cram the shelves of bookshops. These missals of information on producing an overall wedding include checklists and workbooks that are packed with helpful, well-organized, itemized details on wedding clothing, caterers, banquet halls, photographers, hotels, invitations, hair styles, and event planners, to name just a few.

In contrast, this wedding ceremony guide focuses specifically on all matters of the ceremony itself and addresses all essential issues of ceremony organizing, planning, and creating. Remember, the actual ceremony begins the moment the wedding party sets foot onto the ceremony site and ends the moment they exit, directly after the final pronouncement given by the celebrant.

As this guide continues, I recommend that couples take notes, particularly while working with the questionnaires. Having a written record will prove helpful, even enlightening.

A Question of Spirituality

One of the first questions I ask my clients is, "What type of ceremony would you like?" Though the answers may vary a little, over the years I have noticed similar themes. Most couples want a somewhat personalized ceremony. They may say, "We want it to be about us" or "We want it to be about love" or "We would like a ceremony that is meaningful to us." They wonder, "Could you help us put together something personal?" Sometimes they say "We want to write our own vows" or ask "If we write our own vows, could you help us or edit them?" I remind my clients that the actual vows, though pivotal, are still a relatively small part of the overall event. I then continue to question them about their preferences and vision for the ceremony, particularly concerning the question of spirituality. Often I find that I need to help them clarify where they fit with regard to this category. When a couple answers that they want a civil ceremony, I suggest that they find a justice or secular celebrant. Often though, when questioned 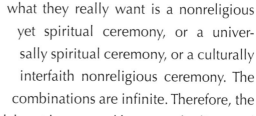 more deeply, it becomes clear to me that what they really want is a nonreligious yet spiritual ceremony, or a universally spiritual ceremony, or a culturally interfaith nonreligious ceremony. The combinations are infinite. Therefore, the celebrant has to read between the lines and then delve a little deeper. Interfaith, multi-faith, interdenominational, nondenominational and ecumenical wedding ceremonies are recent phenomena. That being so, many couples have not yet grasped the concept, let alone the language. So, their answers to the question, "Where are you spiritually?" are key in designing the structural theme, onto which, like a canvas, we weave the couple's unique words and story. Couples who actually fit the "universally spiritual" category listed in the questionnaire below often say, "We are freethinkers, but we believe in God or a Higher Power" or "We don't attend a church but we are spiritual" or "My spirituality is a private, personal, and important part of my life, but I am not affiliated with any religious body."

The following questions are similar to those I ask my couples. However, this list is rather basic, and I may go into greater detail at the consultation. (For example, those affiliated with the "Liberal Progressive movement"—a relatively new phenomenon in some Christian denominations—fit into all of the categories below except for the last one.) Being clear on where you fit in the following categories can be enormously helpful to the celebrant as well as revealing to you as a couple, and will prove important to the choices you make in constructing the actual ceremony.

The Spirituality Questionnaire

How would you describe yourselves in terms of your spirituality and religious beliefs?

- Religious—Those who would prefer a Catholic ceremony but are not eligible because one or both parties are divorced.

- Nonreligious spiritual—Those who believe in God and whose lives, ethics, and values reflect a deep spirituality, yet who do not participate regularly in religious ritual and community.

- Religious spiritual—Those who are practicing members of the religious affiliation of their choice, yet who respect and honor the rights and choices of others to practice their own religious affiliation.

- Universally spiritual—Those who say they believe in a spiritual presence that guides and protects them. This is the largest of groups. Some in this category explore and practice more than one religious denomination or path at different times in their lives. Others combine religious practices in an interdenominational or Unitarian approach to spirituality. Some do not necessarily perceive a spiritual Presence as the God who is worshipped through the rituals of religious bodies, although they nonetheless experience this Presence personally, fully, and actively guiding their lives. Many perceive this Presence more clearly in the magnificence and splendor of nature. The ethics of those who fit in this category are generally impeccable and their actions and daily lives reflect and manifest a reverence for all of nature and for all beings. A common thread is honor and respect for the rights of others to practice the path of their choice. They are deep believers in religious freedom and tolerance.

- None of the above—A ceremony that is nonreligious and non-spiritual is, in a word, atheist. In this case, I will decline to officiate the ceremony and suggest a secular, civil ceremony officiated by a justice of the peace, a judge, or a secular person licensed to officiate weddings. However, I will make exceptions in the case of a couple where one partner fits this category while the other fits one of the categories listed above. Bear in mind that in terms of the ceremony content and style, a minister celebrant, a rabbi celebrant, or any celebrant who represents one or more religious bodies, will be catering to the non-atheist partner. Interestingly, on a number of occasions, I have received requests from couples who claim to be staunch atheists. Their reason for calling me is that they have heard that I create and officiate unique, customized ceremonies. Their only alternative to a religious ceremony is a pre-formatted civil ceremony, but their preference is for a unique, customized ceremony. I refuse them, noting that—despite my very liberal views—as a minister I am a representative of God.

As such, if I am to officiate, I require that God, or Spirit, be acknowledged. Some couples have subsequently contacted me again; after reviewing their spirituality, they have come to the realization that they are not atheists after all. They want to utilize my services, but prefer the absolute minimum reference to God or Spirit in their ceremony.

The Ceremony Questionnaire

The ceremony:

- What do you want your ceremony to express?
- How would you envision and describe your ideal ceremony?
- How would you envision and describe your ideal ceremony if money were no object?
- How can you create your ideal ceremony while maintaining your budget?
- Why choose a public ceremony?
- Do you envision a public ceremony that includes your own private sentiments and statements?
- Do you feel pressured to create a ceremony that pleases parents and family?
- If so, is it possible to please yourselves and still please parents and family?
- Who will participate in the ceremony?
- Do you want readers?
- How many readers would you like?
- How many members will be in the wedding party?

- How many guests will you invite?

- Do you wish to include parents in the procession?

- Do you wish to include parents in the ceremony at the altar?

- What is the marital status of your parents?

- If parents are divorced and are with or without partners, do you wish to include them in the procession?

- How long (or short) would you prefer the ceremony to run?

- Are there any traditions you would like to include in your ceremony?

- Are there any traditions or words you would like to avoid?

The ceremony location:

- Have you visited the ceremony site?

- If this site is distant and a visit is not possible, can you obtain a photo?

- Is there room for a procession? Where will you enter and exit?

- How and where will the guests be seated?

- Is there a permanent altar?

- If not, where will the altar be located?

- If an altar needs to be created, what will constitute the backdrop for the altar?

- If the ceremony site is outdoors, is there an alternate site in case of rain?

- Where will the rehearsal take place?

Personal words: Will your celebrant be willing to personalize your ceremony by including the answers to the following questions?

- What qualities do both of you require in order to create a strong and lasting marriage? (Answer jointly)

- (To the groom) How would you describe the bride's greatest characteristics and qualities that she will contribute to the marriage?

- (To the bride) How would you describe the groom's greatest characteristics and qualities that he will contribute to the marriage?

- How and when did you meet?

- Was there a defining moment when you realized you were in love?

- What made you decide to marry?

- How would you describe the proposal?

- Were you introduced?

- Who introduced you?

- Is that person attending the ceremony?

- Do you wish to honor her or him in the ceremony?

- Do you wish to honor parents during the ceremony?

- Do you wish to honor or dedicate the ceremony to a loved one who has passed on?

So We Finally Meet: The Consultation

Working on the order of the ceremony occurs at the consultation. Before we begin, I always hand a pen and paper to the bride so she can write down the ceremony outline. Occasionally the groom will do so instead, but very rarely. For the couple, making a written ceremony outline is an essential part of the consultation, for four important reasons:

- Before the consultation, it will be unclear how the order of the ceremony will unfold.

- Having a written record gives a clear outline and timeline of the ceremony.

- Having a clear outline will provide the couple with all the information necessary to print a program, should they wish to do so.

- The couple will now have a tangible outline to refer to whenever they speak to the celebrant.

The Three Essentials of Ceremony Construction

When constructing a wedding ceremony, the three essentials to remember are:

- Meaning

- Authenticity

- Flow

Meaning: The meaning of the overall ceremony is conveyed through the eloquence with which the words and rituals express your intention. If you simply like a ritual but have no understanding of what it represents or conveys, it probably will not work. If you like a ritual but it does not represent or express a truth that has meaning to you, it definitely will not work.

Authenticity: Rituals are symbolic rites that focus toward an intention; therefore, the intention needs to be authentic. Though a ritual may be meaningful, it may not be an authentic expression of your personal beliefs and intentions regarding your unique marriage. A good rule of thumb is to listen carefully to the words with your *heart* as well as your mind. Ask yourselves how these words affect you, how you *feel* about them, and whether or not they really *speak* to you.

Flow: Creating a flowing ceremony is like composing music or writing poetry. There is an organic quality, a harmony, which unfolds effortlessly as the ceremony progresses. This is due in part to the *meaning* and *authenticity* of the content. At the most basic level of ceremony construction, harmony and flow can be achieved simply by correct selection and placement of the ceremony components. But at the deepest level, there is the issue of the actual words. When you ponder the magnitude and significance of a wedding ceremony, you begin to appreciate the power of words, particularly when those spoken words convey a profound truth. Truth is an outpouring and direct expression of Spirit. Spiritual truth lies at the heart of all time-honored traditions and at the heart of all beings. Words of spiritual truth, like poetry, flow in perfect harmony.

The Relevance of Readings

A reading may add or detract from the overall flow of the ceremony. The position and placement of a reading is vital, as is its content. The following rule, which I generally follow in my own wedding ministry, may be helpful:

If there are to be two readings, the first is placed *before* the exchange of vows.

The second reading follows directly or shortly *after* the exchange of vows.

The first reading is generally informational, containing advice pertaining to love and marriage. Appropriate first readings could include, the Navajo Prayer, "A Sacred Space" by Lau Tzu or the First Epistle to the Corinthians: 13. There are numerous choices. If there is to be one reading, decide upon the content of that reading and place it accordingly.

After the wedding vows have been exchanged, any second reading should convey acceptance, blessings, and benedictions rather than advice. At this point, the ceremony is moving toward completion. A Native American Wedding Blessing offers a perfect example:

"Walk together hand-in-hand upon life's unpredictable journey. For your two lives are now woven together as one life and your love will live forever in the heart of The Great Spirit."

An Irish wedding blessing also serves as a perfect second reading choice.

More Ceremony Details, from Paraphernalia to PA

- Do not trust a group of people to bring your ceremony necessities and paraphernalia: entrust them to one or two persons only. When many people are given incremental responsibilities, at least one will disappoint you.

- Select a person to pin boutonnières on the groom and his attendants. The fathers of the bride and groom should also be appropriately honored with a boutonnière. In addition, having a boutonnière assigned to them may also honor grandfathers, godfathers, favorite uncles, cousins, or friends, and even male readers. If there is no bridal assistant to pin the boutonnière properly, select someone with a little artistic ability and nimble fingers to do the honors. Please think twice about leaving it up to the groom's attendants.

- The groom should carry the marriage license to present to the celebrant before the ceremony or when she asks for it.

- The groom or a reliable person should carry monies—preferably checks. At a recent ceremony, the groom entrusted the best man to carry a number of envelopes containing payment designated for various service fees totaling thousands of dollars in cash. The best man left his jacket in the men's room and ten minutes later, when he retrieved it, the cash was missing. Please be careful.

- The groom should carry the rings until shortly before the ceremony, at which time they should be passed to the best man. Leave the rings in their boxes; loose rings have been known to slip through pocket seams. The best man should check the rings to be sure they are not anchored too tightly in the boxes.

- One trustworthy person should bring the unity candle set, memory candles, chalice for the wine ceremony, loving cup, altar flowers, and any other altar or ceremony items. When responsibility for these items is "divvied up" among many people, one person will surely forget their item. Generally, the designated person should be the bride herself, the bride's mother, or a trusted friend or relative.

- You have taken the time and effort to create a unique and personalized ceremony, so why not ensure that every word is heard? Working without a PA system can be a strain on the vocal chords. A loudly raised voice can become raucous and irritating, and it still may not be audible to many guests. A microphone allows the celebrant to maintain a natural vocal style and, when appropriate during the ceremony, to softly modulate her voice to express a feeling of intimacy. Without the PA system, an otherwise perfect ceremony can take on a shrill and strained tone.

• Certain circumstances and locations preclude the use of a PA system; when conditions do not allow for this luxury (or necessity), the celebrant has to be creative, confident, and spontaneous. When a PA system is unavailable or unfeasible, I will often position myself at the starting point of the aisle, facing the backs of the guests. I face and address the bride and groom from this location, so that the bride and groom turn to face the celebrant and the guests head-on. I am throwing my voice towards the altar, so most guests will be able to hear quite well. Sometimes I need to move my position during the ceremony, depending on what is required. Eventually, in this configuration, I bring the bride and groom into the middle of the aisle for the exchange of marriage vows, thus allowing the surrounding guests to hear at least part, if not all, of the vows. An experienced celebrant can work under these conditions; however, without a doubt, working with a PA system is far superior.

Making It Legal: The License

Consider the intense planning that goes into your wedding, one of the most significant and unforgettable days of your life. As with all rites of passage, the wedding ceremony honors and prepares you for entry into an entirely new phase of life. But being married also necessitates that certain legal requirements be fulfilled.

If you ignore them, you will have planned, created, and paid for a rather expensive *party*. It may resemble a wedding ceremony, but legally it is nothing more than a party.

Marriage license laws vary from state to state. However, despite differences among the state requirements, any marriage between a man and a woman performed in one state must be recognized by every other state, under Article IV, Section 1 of the United States Constitution, commonly known as the Full Faith and Credit Clause. Some of the requirements set by state laws include:

- Proof of ID.

- Proof of termination of a previous marriage. Both applicants need to produce proof of the termination of any previous marriage or marriages by death or judgment of dissolution (divorce or annulment).

- Sufficient mental capacity. This is defined as the ability to enter into a contract. Marriage requires two consenting people. If either person cannot or does not understand what it means to be married—due to mental illness, drugs or any other reason that affects judgment—that person does not have the capacity to consent to a marriage; therefore, that marriage is not valid.

- Kinship. In most states, close blood relatives cannot marry. Some states do allow first cousins to marry; a small number of those states also require that one of the cousins is no longer able to conceive children.

- Blood test for venereal disease. A small number of states require a blood test, or a blood test and physical examination, before marriage to establish whether either party is infected with a venereal disease. In some states, the clerk of marriages is forbidden to issue a marriage license until both parties present the results of the blood test to that clerk. Therefore, you should check with the local clerk of marriages in your municipality before applying for a marriage license.

• The waiting period. Many, but not all, states require a waiting period, generally one to six days, between the time the license is issued and the time of the marriage ceremony. The waiting period can be waived for good reason by a judge or clerk of a court. I have not listed the waiting periods required by various states, since there are so many variables. Check with the local clerk of marriages before applying for a marriage license.

I suggest that you review the legal requirements for a marriage license with the local clerk of marriages in the municipality in which you are to be married. Here in New York, the bride and groom must apply for the license together. The license will be issued while they wait. A representative cannot apply for the license on behalf of the bride or groom, nor can notarized marriage license affidavits signed by the bride or groom be substituted for their personal appearance. Bypassing the waiting period in New York requires a judicial waiver, and valid forms of ID.

Once you have your license, you must bring it to the ceremony to give to the celebrant. Most celebrants will ask for the license immediately upon arrival. This may allow the couple sufficient time to send someone to get this document in the event that they have forgotten to bring it. Once the celebrant has the license, it is her responsibility to fill it out, sign it, have witnesses sign it, have the bride and groom sign it (where applicable), and then mail it. The celebrant will mail the license to the clerk at the municipality where it was issued. It will be recorded and filed by the clerk at that municipality. In New York, the bride and groom will then receive an official license by mail. In New Jersey, and possibly in other states, the license is mailed back to the municipality of the town or city where the wedding took place. It then becomes the responsibility of the couple to contact this municipality to request an official copy of their license; in New Jersey, an official copy of a marriage license is not routinely sent to the newlywed couple without their request. There will also be a fee to that township for this document.

Marriage License Essentials: Questions and Answers

- *For how long is a marriage license valid?* A marriage license is valid for sixty days from the day of issuance.

- *How much does a marriage license cost?* The fee for a marriage license in New York is $25 to $30, depending on where it is issued. The fee may be different in other states.

- *In the event that the applicants are younger than eighteen years of age, is permission required and from whom?* If the applicants are fourteen or fifteen years old, the written consent of both parents is required, along with the consent of a justice of the Supreme Court or a judge of the Family Court having jurisdiction over the town or city in which the application is made. If either applicant is sixteen or seventeen years old, such applicant(s) must present the written consent of both parents. If both applicants are eighteen years of age or older, no consent is required. One parent alone may consent to a minor's marriage if the other parent has been missing for one year preceding the application or if the parents are divorced and the consenting parent was given sole custody of the child when the divorce decree was awarded.

- *Will my name automatically change after the ceremony?* A person's last name (surname) does not automatically change upon marriage, and neither party to a marriage is required to change his or her last name. The bride and groom need not take the same last name. One or both parties to a marriage may elect to change the surname by which he or she wishes to be known after the marriage by entering the new name in the appropriate space provided on the marriage license. The new name must consist of one of the following options:

  - The surname of the other spouse

  - Any former surname of either spouse

  - A name combining into a single surname all or a segment of the premarital surname or any former surname of each spouse

  - A combination name separated by a hyphen provided that each part of such combination surname is the premarital surname, or any former surname, of each of the spouses

The marriage certificate containing the new name, if any, is proof that the new name is lawful. The local Social Security Administration office should be contacted so that the records and your Social Security card reflect the name change. There is no charge for this service.

Review Checklist

❑ Decide where you fit spiritually.

❑ Review the worksheet and answer the questions.

❑ Meet the celebrant and construct the ceremony outline.

❑ Consider possible readings that you may wish to include.

❑ Decide who carries the rings, who carries checks to pay vendors, and who brings items for the altar. Assign these responsibilities to the parties you have chosen.

❑ Select a person to pin the boutonnières on the male wedding party attendants.

❑ Arrange for a PA system for the ceremony, if needed.

❑ Check with the clerk of marriages in your municipality for information and requirements for the marriage license.

Chapter Three:

Ceremony Locations and Settings

When planning your special occasion
Choos wise a well traveled location
For by thru-way or fair-way
Your guests must find their way
To get to this blessed celebration.

Choosing the ceremony location and setting is a significant decision. Couples need to allow sufficient time to search out their perfect ceremony location and setting. I recommend a preliminary guest list be worked on to help determine the right location in terms of the numbers of guests that can be accommodated. Be aware that guest lists tend to keep expanding.

If the ceremony is to be held at the banquet hall of a highly credentialed, well-referred venue, it will most likely work wonderfully. The benefit of a banquet hall ceremony is the easy transition from the ceremony service to the reception dinner and festivities. If the couple opts for one of the ceremony sites listed in this chapter, being mindful of travel time and distance between the ceremony and reception location is vital, particularly if directions are difficult for the guests to navigate. The ceremony setting, whether indoors or outdoors, needs to be fully optimized. For example, if the ceremony location is a large home porch, indoors by a vast window, or by a garden gazebo, and the ceremony time is at sunset, the sunset should be fully included as part of the backdrop to the ceremony.

As a celebrant, I often ask my clients what made them choose a particular ceremony site. Frequently their answer is that they have attended a ceremony at this particular site or it has been highly recommended to them. Either way, most couples invest carefully in researching the ceremony location and setting. Once the bride and groom's choices are narrowed down, they need to get a number of referrals.

The Ceremony Location

When choosing your ceremony location, think clearly about all the practicalities as well as the romantic atmosphere and beauty of the location. Be creative but be realistic: the two need not be mutually exclusive. Ceremony venues can be odd or even down-right outrageous, but with careful and intelligent forethought, many sites can work perfectly. Some of the less typical sites at which I have personally officiated ceremonies include:

- A surprise home wedding announced as a "Halloween party," at which I arrived dressed as a "minister"

- A fifties-style diner

- A beach

- A zoo (the reception dining tables were arranged around the indoor carousel)

- The end of a pier

You may want to search out and consider some of the following ceremony site locations:

- A banquet hall or wedding hall
- A party or entertainment boat
- A beach
- A church
- A corporate conference center
- A country club or private club
- A cruise ship
- A fairground
- A golf club
- A hilltop
- A home garden
- A home orchard
- A home
- A hotel or resort
- A mansion or manor house
- A mountaintop
- A municipal park or garden
- A museum or gallery
- A pier
- A restaurant boat
- A restaurant
- A riverfront or dock
- A riverboat
- A state park or garden
- A temple
- A university chapel
- A zoo

- An independent nondenominational or interfaith chapel (they are often difficult to locate, though I know of three)

The Restaurant Ceremony

A restaurant is often a perfect choice for a small, less formal wedding ceremony and reception. However, be aware of the limitations. A restaurant will not generally employ a banquet manager or bridal assistant to cater to the occasional small wedding. My solution to this problem is to ask the bride to provide the celebrant with a bridal assistant, as described in Chapter 4. This assistant will help with the processional rehearsal. She will line up the wedding party once the celebrant is waiting at the altar or ceremony site. Taking cues from the celebrant, she will direct the attendants in the correct order. She will maintain eye contact with the celebrant and the musicians to cue them for processional and recessional music.

Another possible venue is a seasonal restaurant that serves a larger clientele in summer than it does in the off-season months. The summer expansion of this type of location is generally accomplished by the construction of a temporary or semi-permanent tent-like addition to the restaurant. Some of these are freestanding types. Some are fitted with heavy plastic wall-like enclosures to protect guests during inclement weather. Whatever type of expansion the restaurant has devised, it is always wise to check the structure first, and then to make sure there are adequate bathroom facilities.

The Indoor Ceremony at Home

A home setting can make a wonderfully intimate ceremony location. Planning is vital and maintaining a sense of reality about the home as a wedding venue also is necessary. Ask yourself the following questions:

- If the ceremony is to take place in the house, are there adequate bathroom facilities?

- Where will the actual altar site be?

- Will there be adequate seating for the ceremony (especially for those guests who cannot stand for long periods)?

- Is there enough room for an aisle?

- Is there enough room for a wedding party to process or stand?

- If a space is designated for two uses—for example, if a living room is to be set up for the ceremony and then rearranged to accommodate the reception dinner, where will you put the guests during the process of rearranging?

- Is there enough room for musicians to set up and play at the ceremony or the reception?

- Is there adequate parking?

The Outdoor Ceremony at Home

When the decision is reached to plan for a home garden or home outdoor ceremony, the temptation often is to extend the guest list based on the potential size of the outdoor space. Some of the reality considerations are the same as those listed for the indoor ceremony at home. However, since more guests can be accommodated outdoors, the issue of bathroom facilities becomes a primary concern. One solution is the rental of portable toilets.

I officiated a wedding ceremony at a lovely country home in the Catskill Mountains in upstate New York. There were two port-a-potties set up at the back of the property. Fortunately, they were far enough away from the ceremony and reception site to go somewhat unnoticed. The mother of the bride was thoughtful and creative enough to place flowers, designer hand towelettes, and sweetly scented soaps inside them.

Though a home outdoor ceremony will generally be planned for the summer months, consider the ramifications of a serious rainstorm. More than once, when I officiated outdoor home ceremonies, unseasonably cold and windy weather wreaked havoc. On one such occasion, a storm gained quick and fierce momentum, threatening the underpinnings of the structure of all three tents. Fortunately, the tents did survive the storm, but the guests were miserable—particularly the women, as their stiletto heels sank into the mud and their silk gowns became splattered with filth. The musicians' expensive instruments were in serious jeopardy and the caterers struggled in their cooking tent. The party folded early when table and chair legs slowly began sinking. Unfortunately, this large gathering could not be accommodated inside the house. Most of the guests stuck it out as long as possible, but overall, the ceremony was close to, if not entirely, a disaster.

Ask yourself the following questions:

- If portable toilets are set up outside, where will they be located and are there adequate facilities?

- Is there adequate room for an aisle?

- Is there enough room for a wedding party to process or stand?

- If a space is designated for two uses, where will you put the guests during the process of rearranging—particularly in the case of rain?

- Is there enough room for musicians to set up and play at the ceremony or the reception?

- Is there adequate cover for the guests and musicians in case of rain, intense heat, or broiling sun?

- Is there adequate parking?

- If there is adequate parking, is it far enough from the ceremony site and dining tent to avoid noise and exhaust fumes caused by late-arriving guests?

The Outdoor Location Ceremony

When the ceremony is to be held at an outdoor location other than the home, particularly in one of the following venues, careful and detailed planning is vital:

- A beach

- A hilltop

- A mountaintop

- A municipal park or garden

- A pier

- A riverfront or dock

- A state park or garden

I officiated a wedding some years ago at a state botanical garden. There was a threat of rain but the bride and groom forged ahead, undeterred, with their plans. Fortunately, a full-force downpour never actually occurred, but sporadic sprinkles kept the guests on the edge of their seats. More upsetting was the musicians' refusal to risk damaging their precious and valuable instruments. They understandably abdicated their responsibilities by packing up and leaving. This could have been avoided if some shelter had been provided. In addition, bathrooms were a ten- to fifteen-minute walk from the ceremony site; parking was also a ten- to fifteen-minute walk, in the opposite direction from the bathrooms; and the ground was quite uneven and posed a threat to seating stability.

As you plan your own outdoor ceremony, ask yourself the following questions:

- Are bathroom facilities available?

- If so, where? Are the bathroom facilities easily accessible?

- Is there adequate room for an aisle?

- Is there adequate room for a wedding party to process or stand?

- If you have hired musicians for the ceremony, is there adequate room for them to set up and play at the ceremony or the reception?

- Is there a tent, structure, or other cover, in case of rain, intense heat, or broiling sun?

- Is there adequate parking?

- If so, where? Is the parking area easily accessible?

Seating

Carefully consider the issue of seating, even if you are planning a small, short, and informal ceremony. Standing is often uncomfortable for most guests. Research the cost of renting chairs and set them up carefully. Try to think in terms of what the guests will see from their seats. Most seating arrangements work well if they are staggered in a way that ensures that the person seated in front does not block the view of the wedding party and ceremony site. Set up the rows in a slightly curved formation to give each guest as much visual access as possible.

In addition to providing your guests with the comfort of a seat, there is also the issue of children. If parents are seated, their children are more easily "corralled" and less likely to run around.

Once you have decided on the guest list and you have a head count, order the chairs accordingly. Please do not skimp on seating.

Draw an illustrated diagram of the seating configuration of your choice. Then, in the event that the chair rental company does not set up the chairs for you, you can select and assign some obliging helper who will set them up for you. Do a rehearsal with the person or people assigned to set up the seating.

At a banquet hall venue, with well-trained staff, the seating of guests is the responsibility of that wedding hall after all, that is what they are paid to do. For the informal, outdoor, home, or small-restaurant ceremony, the issue of seating is left up to the bride, groom and families, and it can be an important matter.

From my observations during more than twenty years of officiating weddings, this is the general protocol, though not every couple adheres to it:

Traditionally, the parents are seated in reverse order of precedence: the groom's grandparents, the bride's grandparents, the groom's parents, and the bride's mother. Generally, the mother of the groom defers to the mother of the bride in order for the bride's mother to be the last person seated before the procession begins (closest in time to the entrance of the bride). The rationale is that the bride's parents typically pay for the wedding, therefore they are given this subtle yet special honor.

Obviously if the father of the bride escorts the bride down the aisle, then the mother of the bride will need an escort or an usher to guide and seat her. Otherwise, she would have to enter alone and seat herself. From my experience and observations, when parent couples enter together, an usher is not necessary. During a Jewish ceremony, both parents escort the bride down the aisle and process to the chuppah, where they join the groom's parents and the wedding attendants who have already taken their places there.

If you are using ushers, you may want to ask relatives or friends to oblige. My daughter Penelope asked some guests from England to serve as ushers at her wedding. Unintentionally, this added a rather dignified touch as guests were greeted and ushered so ceremoniously by these young English gentlemen.

Guests and family of the bride are seated on the left as they enter the ceremony site or chapel and guests and family of the groom are seated on the right. If one side of the couple has substantially more guests than the other side, it may make sense to have all seats filled evenly and do away this with formality, except for the seating of family members. For Jewish ceremonies, the seating is in reverse order: Guests of the bride and family are seated on the right while guests of the groom and family are seated on the left.

Ushers need to be aware of where people should be seated. They may offer female guests their right arm, or simply lead the way for male or female guests, saying: "Please follow me, Madam (or Sir)." The level of formality is up to the bride and groom. Older people, especially those with walking difficulties or in wheelchairs, need careful attention and sensitive seating assignments. The aisle end of the seating row is appropriate for guests with special needs.

The first row on either side of the aisle needs to be reserved for the parents and immediate families of the bride and groom.

Depending on the size of these families, it may be necessary to reserve additional rows in the front for other close family members.

Finally, please be sensitive when seating divorced parents and their significant others. I have witnessed and overheard some unpleasantries.

A Sacred Space: Creating an Altar

The perfect altar sites for an indoor home wedding ceremony are a luxurious fireplace mantle, the bottom landing of a large staircase, or a large window—particularly a bay window—with an expansive view. If none of these options are available, then you may want to pay a little more attention to decorating and enhancing the altar sufficiently. You can create the perfect ambiance by adding extra flowers and accoutrements to your altar.

If you have chosen a home garden or an outdoor setting for your ceremony site, as previously discussed, creating the altar is now your responsibility. Think of the altar not only as a sacred place, but also as the focal point of your ceremony. Therefore, the adornments of your altar need to reflect the theme and spiritual ideals of your ceremony. Remember that you and your wedding attendants are standing at the altar and all eyes are on you. Therefore, keep in mind the color scheme you have so carefully chosen for wedding bouquets, boutonnières, and attire, and choose altar objects and embellishments that compliment these choices.

Also, consider the surroundings of this natural setting. It may be by the ocean or a pine-covered forest. It is important to choose decorations that not only blend with the setting, but that enhance the natural ambience of the setting. For example; if you choose a beach location, use seashells; by a forest, create a pine-needle wreath. Imagine the beauty of an altar set in an apple orchard in the springtime, decorated with apple blossoms.

Be creative.

I often use candles on outdoor altars and am rarely deterred by a heavy breeze. If they become extinguished, I remind the guests that unpredictable weather can never "snuff out" the inextinguishable light of true love. Candles add light and beauty to the altar. The effect is quite moving, particularly when the candles are incorporated into the ceremony as unity candles. The unity candle set is an especially significant and a lovely altar decoration. A hurricane lamp may also be used to protect the candle flame. The Unity Sand Ceremony and the Universal Wine Ceremony are perfect alternatives to the Unity Candle Lighting Ceremony. The ritual objects used in these ceremonies visually enhance the beauty of the altar.

Depending on the proximity to the reception site, you may want to incorporate a podium into your decorating plan. Additional decorative enhancements may include the draping of tulle, a sheer, stiffened silk, rayon, or nylon material that is commonly used in wedding decorations. Bows and swags are often made from tulle and attached to the seats along the aisle. If you are planning to place bowls or baskets of flowers on each side of the altar, be sure to secure them well.

When constructing the outdoor ceremonial altar, be especially careful to find an area where the ground is even. If you are planning to include a floral hoop, make sure that it is firmly and well secured.

Review Checklist

❏ Decide on the location of your ceremony.

❏ For the restaurant ceremony, note and review the checklist on page 43.

❏ For the indoor ceremony at home, note and review the checklist on page 44.

❏ For the outdoor ceremony at home, note and review the checklist on page 45.

❏ For the outdoor location ceremony, note and review the checklist on page 47.

❏ Review the section entitled "A Sacred Space: Creating an Altar" and make your altar choices.

❏ Create a diagram depicting your choice and location of altar décor. Assign a trustworthy person to help construct this altar for you based on your diagram.

❏ Make sure you have chairs or other seating for each adult guest.

❏ Create a diagram of the seating configuration of your choice. If the chair rental company does not set up the chairs for you, select someone who will set them up based on your diagram.

❏ Do a rehearsal with the person or persons assigned to set up the seating, to make sure that they understand and can carry out your intentions.

Chapter Four

From Procession to Program

The pageantry of the processing
Is not solely to show the fine dressing
Of attendants that day
Nor just for their display
But to honor each one with a blessing.

The Pageantry of Procession

The pageantry of processing adds magic and anticipation to the ceremony as it helps to set the mood for the entire wedding event. Traditionally, this is a serious—even somber—yet magnificent moment when the guests are seated, and the chatter settles first into quiet whispers and then a hushed silence, pulsing with expectation. What I love about the procession is that it allows each of the participants to be honored and recognized individually. As a minister, I see each participant receiving an acknowledgement and a blessing as they enter the aisle and process to the altar. Regardless of whether the ceremony is formal or informal, a procession adds a certain splendor and dignity. The procession is a ceremony in and of itself, and in addition, it pays tribute to the overall ceremony of which it is a part.

The Wedding Procession

The general rule at a wedding is that the order of procession is the responsibility of the banquet manager or the bridal assistant. In most cases, the procession follows a standard outline, although since each ceremony varies in size, style, and religious affiliation, there is some flexibility to this order. In addition, wedding locations may differ in their processional format. Some banquet hall locations will routinely have the groom, best man, and groomsmen unobtrusively enter the indoor chapel via a parallel side aisle and wait at the altar. Or, they may enter in single file through a side door by the altar and wait. The bridesmaids, the maid of honor, and the bride, along with her escort, then enter from the back of the chapel and process down the aisle. The rationale for this arrangement is simply to avoid the convergence of the bride and groom in the hallway before the actual ceremony begins. At a location where there are serious space constraints, the bride is hidden behind an ornate screen before processing down the aisle. The varieties of processional orders are often constructed because of the wedding location's unique configurations and space availability.

Although most wedding location facilities generally handle the processional order, some facilities may welcome the celebrant's participation in this part of the pre-ceremony. There are, however, many exceptions. I was once officiating at a small manor-house location. The bride was under the impression that there was no available processional assistant, so I began setting up and directing the processional order myself. I was quickly put in my place by an irate in-house female assistant; She told me that *she* was in charge and that I should "butt out and mind my own beeswax."

In the case of a wedding location where no bridal assistant is available, the celebrant's help is appreciated. At a less formal restaurant location, home, or outdoor ceremony, the help of the celebrant is necessary. When I officiate under these circumstances,

I often request that the bride provide me with an assistant. Generally, an aunt or friend will be thrilled to assist.

The function of this helper is to work with the celebrant during all aspects of the procession. She assists in the processional rehearsal. Once the rehearsal is complete, the next step is to direct the wedding party into the ceremony site in the correct formation as practiced at the rehearsal. At this point the celebrant is waiting at the altar site for the wedding party to enter. As the assistant keeps close eye contact with the celebrant, she directs the members of the wedding party down the aisle. Maintaining eye contact, she may have to cue the musicians at the appropriate time to begin processional and recessional anthems and musical interludes during the ceremony. Once the ceremony begins, the assistant quietly slips into her seat until the conclusion of the service. She then resumes her duties guiding the recessing bridal party out of the ceremony site.

My personal experience has been that whenever I request an assistant, the bride and groom almost always choose a female. However, the assistant can be male or female.

Important Tips on Processing

The general rule for the male escort is to offer the female his left arm.

For a natural and balanced look, his elbow should be bent softly, his gently closed hand resting slightly below his navel. The position of his hand should allow his left shoulder to drop comfortably.

The female partner should slip her right arm through his as she holds her bouquet in her left hand at her navel.

Adequate space is required between the pair to enable them to walk naturally and comfortably.

In the event that there is a great height differential in favor of the male escort, this scenario will not work. In this case, I suggest that the female hold her bouquet with both hands at navel height. The male escort can then gently support her right elbow with his left hand, allowing his left elbow to drop in and slightly back as he guides her down the aisle.

I have become aware, throughout the years of my ministry, that males and females react to the performance anxiety of wedding party participation in completely different ways. Males, when stressed, tend to rush or charge down the aisle. Conversely, females often freeze, slowing down to a snail's pace. In order to achieve processional harmony, a brief rehearsal is all that is required. My recommendation is that this be done shortly before the actual ceremony, so that it remains fresh in the minds of the participants.

Many brides prefer not to be seen by the groom before the ceremony. An important fact to remember is that the bride is the only person in the wedding party who does not need a rehearsal. She is simply escorted down the aisle, met by the groom, and then escorted to the altar.

Creating Your Own Processional Tradition

The processional orders outlined above are the most typical and popular sequences. But why follow these protocols if they just don't appeal to you? Clients will often ask my opinion on the correct processional order. I always say that there is no correct order, only a common, general, or traditional order—one that by no means must be adhered to. You can certainly create your own procession and in doing so, create your own tradition.

At a recent wedding I officiated, the bride and groom entered the aisle together with their dog, a sweet-natured boxer, who strutted with them, proudly carrying the rings threaded in a ribbon that was tied around his neck. He insisted on laying at their feet, sprawled out on his back with his legs in the air. He sporadically yawned and snored through the ceremony. Since the ceremony took place at a restaurant owned by the couple, there was no permission required for the pet.

Occasionally, a bride will prefer to enter the ceremony alone; many brides—particularly older brides—take offense at the ancient tradition of being "given away," feeling that it tends to be demeaning to women. In this scenario, my suggestion is for the bride to stop at a designated halfway point along the aisle: the groom will walk up to meet her, and then escort her to the altar. I have also worked with brides who have had a child or children from a previous marriage escort them. In creating a procession, the main thing is that it feels comfortable and right to the bride and groom.

Sample Orders of Procession

Sample 1

- The celebrant waits at the center altar, facing front. She or he announces that the ceremony is about to begin and requests that cell phones be closed.

- The groom's parents are seated in the front row on the right, adjacent to the aisle.

- The bride's mother is seated in the front row on the left, adjacent to the aisle.

- The groom enters with the best man and waits on the right side of the altar, facing front.

- Groomsmen enter in single file and take their places next to the best man, standing shoulder to shoulder, facing front.

- Bridesmaids enter in single file and take their places at the left side of the altar, facing front. They allow enough room for the maid or matron of honor and the bride.

- The maid or matron of honor enters and takes her place at the left side, closest to mid-altar, facing front.

- The flower girls and ring bearers enter. They divide at the point closest to the altar; flower girls step to the left of the altar and ring bearers step to the right of the altar. They take their places at the outside of the line of attendants or are brought by parents or family members to seats.

- The celebrant asks the guests to stand.

- The bride enters, alone, or with her father, escort, or both parents. The celebrant or clergy may address the bride's father or escort, asking, "Who gives this bride to be married?"

- The groom walks forward to greet the bride's father or escort. He may greet the bride's mother, who will be standing close to the left side of the bride.

- The bride's father or escort offers the hand of the bride to the groom.

- The groom escorts the bride forward to the altar.

- The groom and bride face each other.

- The celebrant requests that the guests be seated.

Sample 2

- The celebrant waits at the center altar, facing front. She or he announces that the ceremony is about to begin and requests that cell phones be closed.

- The groom enters with his parents. He seats them in the front row on the right, adjacent to the aisle. He then proceeds to the altar and waits on the right side, facing front.

- The bride's mother is seated in the front row on the left, adjacent to the aisle.

- The best man enters and joins the groom who stands at the right side, closest to mid-altar.

- The bridesmaids enter, each escorted by a groomsman on their right. Each stops in turn before the altar. Each groomsman waits until his escort has taken her place at the left side of the altar. The groomsmen then proceed, in turn, to take their place at the right side with the groom and the best man. Groomsmen stand shoulder to shoulder, facing front.

- The maid or matron of honor enters and takes her place at the left side, closest to mid-altar, facing front.

- The flower girls and ring bearers enter. They divide at the point closest to the altar; flower girls step to the left of the altar and ring bearers step to the right of the altar. They take their places at the outside of the line of attendants, or are brought by parents or family members to seats.

- The celebrant asks the guests to stand.

- The bride enters, alone, or with her father, escort, or both parents. The celebrant or clergy may address the bride's father or escort, asking, "Who gives this bride to be married?"

- The groom walks forward to greet the bride's father or escort. He may greet the bride's mother, who will be standing close to the left side of the bride.

- The bride's father or escort offers the hand of the bride to the groom.

- The groom escorts the bride forward to the altar.

- The groom and bride face each other.

- The celebrant requests that the guests be seated.

The Wedding Party Attendants

When deciding on the members of the wedding party, try not to be driven by sudden impulse. Carefully choose friends and family members with whom you have deep and lasting relationships. Also, try not to act out of a sense of obligation. Think clearly about the choices you make. Remember that you will have a lasting photographic record and permanent memory of the choices you have made.

Frequently, for a variety of reasons, many couples have to choose one friend over another, or overlook or omit someone that they really wanted to include. If this occurs, you might want to think of alternative ways of honoring those who are omitted, unintentionally or out of necessity, from wedding party participation. Consider the following possibilities:

- Reading a poem, blessing, or Bible passage

- Blessing the wine or passing the chalice (see "The Wine Ceremony" on page 248)

- Lighting the altar candle

- Assisting in the hand-joining ritual

- Holding and passing the rings

Do not necessarily be driven—or limited—by tradition. Sometimes a bride or groom will choose a member of the opposite sex to serve as their witness. Reversing wedding party attendant roles can be fun and unique. For example, at the wedding of my son Joseph and daughter-in-law Kerri, Joseph requested that his (very pregnant) sister Penelope be his "best woman." He then asked his other sister, Penelope's twin, Rosalisa, to be his "grooms-woman." Kerri also broke with tradition by including in her attendants her brother as a "brides-man." Although we created opposite-sex titles for some of these attendants, their position and importance in the ceremony was not in the least diminished.

The following is a list of titles of bridal party attendants and their opposite-sex equivalents:

- Best Man = Best Woman

- Maid of Honor = Man of Honor

- Bridesmaid = Brides-Man

- Junior Bridesmaid = Junior Brides-Man (or Brides-Boy)

- Junior Groomsman (or Grooms-Boy) = Junior Grooms-Maid (or Grooms-Girl)

- Ring Bearer (Male or Female)
- Flower Girl = Flower Boy
- Pageboys = Pagegirls

The Rehearsal

Who is responsible for conducting the rehearsal? This is an interesting question with more than one answer. Much is made of the rehearsal when, in fact, many rehearsals require and consist mainly of a rehearsal of the processional. Many couples incur unnecessary expense organizing a rehearsal dinner, which is often given at a restaurant with little room for setting up a procession. In addition, couples often confuse the dinner and the rehearsal. The rehearsal dinner, generally given a night or two before the wedding, is a time for the families to meet and discuss the last-minute details of the impending event. I have been privy to these rehearsal dinners, where most of the rehearsal instructions and configurations are long forgotten by the day of the wedding.

The Church or Temple Ceremony Rehearsal

If the ceremony is to take place at a church or temple, the obvious person responsible for the rehearsal is the clergyperson. She or he will guide the wedding party, parents, close relatives, readers, and any other people participating in the ceremony through a processional rehearsal and a ceremony rehearsal.

The Wedding Hall or Banquet Hall Ceremony Rehearsal

Wedding halls and banquet halls are the quintessential experts on the subject of the wedding rehearsal. These venues are catering both daytime and evening weddings from Friday evening to Sunday evening, every weekend. They conduct a "procession rehearsal" only. This they do approximately one hour before the actual ceremony, depending upon the time the bridal party arrives. If the ceremony is to be held outside, they may conduct an early rehearsal, timed to occur before guest arrival. They often conduct the rehearsal in the actual ceremony site, out of sight of the guests; at other times, they may use a simulated ceremony site in another area of the facility. In some cases, they may even accommodate a separate rehearsal for the bride, if she opts not to have the groom see her before the ceremony. When officiating at a wedding hall or banquet hall, the role of the celebrant at the ceremony rehearsal is simple and straightforward. For example, all I need to do is a reading rehearsal for the designated reader offering a ceremony reading, a candle lighting ceremony rehearsal, or a wine ceremony rehearsal, when applicable. These are essentially just reminders of what to do, since I will be verbally guiding and instructing the participants during the ceremony anyway. During a standard rehearsal conducted at a wedding hall or banquet hall, I try to stay out of the way. As mentioned previously, before I understood the rehearsal policies of some of these venues, I would begin conducting the rehearsal myself. I was quickly put in my place. They really don't need the input of a "pushy" celebrant.

The Small, Informal Restaurant Ceremony Rehearsal

Most likely, but not always, a small restaurant location will value the help of the celebrant, since very few of these wedding venues have an on-staff coordinator. In fact, they may even make the request that the celebrant take it upon herself to conduct the entire rehearsal. An exception would be made in the event that the couple has hired a private wedding planner.

The Indoor or Outdoor Home Ceremony Rehearsal

In a home wedding ceremony, whether indoors or outdoors, it is almost exclusively the responsibility of the celebrant to conduct the ceremony rehearsal. Situations like these often provide perfect examples of the need for a celebrant's assistant. Such an assistant can prove invaluable in helping the celebrant with the details of both the rehearsal and the processional order.

The Outdoor Location Ceremony Rehearsal

There are many variables that affect an outdoor location ceremony. Assuming the venue is large and is being catered by an upscale company that primarily caters at wedding halls, there *may* be a staff member who will do double duty as a wedding coordinator. Generally, though, this duty is delegated to the celebrant. Once again, this is a perfect situation for an assigned rehearsal and processional assistant for the celebrant.

Music

Without a doubt, the role of music in your ceremony is very important. Music can add so much. Music—especially the timeless classical pieces—speaks to the soul. Music sets a mood and generates an emotional response. Music can soothe and calm the mind or uplift and inspire the spirit. A wedding ceremony *is* an emotional experience and is the perfect setting for musical accompaniment.

Before selecting the ceremony music, think of what you want the music to convey during the ceremony. Select your pieces accordingly. Generally, musical accompaniment works best during the following segments of the ceremony:

- The seating of guests

- The processional anthem (for the wedding party entrance)

- The processional anthem (for the bride's entrance)

- The recessional anthem (for the departure of the entire wedding party)

Ongoing, continuous accompaniment throughout the entire ceremony can be distracting, and at times downright irritating. Sometimes a very short musical selection in mid-ceremony may work—though not always.

Let us begin with the seating music selection. The tone needs to be softly celebratory, melodic, and welcoming—not obtrusive and certainly not raucous. Guests will be chatting as they are seated. They don't want to have to compete with the background music.

When selecting the processional music, my suggestion is to have the wedding attendants enter to one musical selection, while the bride enters to a separate air. When they all enter to the same song or melody, the bride is barely noticed. She is more or less *tagged on,* almost as an afterthought. In my opinion, the bride needs to be honored separately and appropriately. Once the wedding attendants have entered and taken their places at the altar, there needs to be a musical pause. It is during this pause that the celebrant will request of the guests, "Please stand." It is at this moment that the bride enters, to her own special anthem.

When selecting the recessional anthem, one could deviate from traditional classical recessional music. After the couple has finally been pronounced husband and wife (or wife and husband) and sealed the deal with a final kiss, and the guests are applauding, that is the time to celebrate. So why not choose something upbeat, funny, or even outrageous? I have witnessed some of the most creative recessional anthems imaginable. At least three couples whose ceremonies I have officiated have chosen the "Charlie Brown Theme." Some other very creative recessionals have been "Celebration" by Kool and the Gang, "The Hallelujah Chorus" from Handel's *Messiah*, "Can't Help Falling in Love" by Elvis Presley, and "You Send Me" by Sam Cooke. A couple who had been engaged for twelve years chose Etta James's "At Last."

For the remainder of the ceremony, traditional classical selections are a better choice.

Consider how quickly a popular song becomes outdated and untrendy. I suggest that you keep your own special, romantic love song for the first dance at the reception rather than using it for the processional anthem. Even so, I have included ideas and selections for the bride who prefers a contemporary, rather than classical processional anthem.

At this point, I would like to offer a little advice on avoiding a musical disaster. If you are considering having a friend who is an untrained singer perform at the ceremony, please proceed with caution. Have this person rehearse in front of someone with a musical ear. Determine whether she or he is comfortable performing in front of an audience or is prone to performance anxiety or panic attacks. Most importantly, make sure this person *can actually sing!* I have been present at some rather atrocious performances by ceremony singers. At one very large ceremony, the bride had requested that a personal friend offer a performance. It was so incredibly dreadful that a few guests stifled giggles. Most guests were so obviously embarrassed that they lowered their heads during the performance. The mortified groom visibly blushed. After the ceremony ended, no one mentioned the performance, which prompted the bride to solicit comments on how wonderful it had been. It turned out that the bride was clearly quite tone deaf (as apparently was the singer). What a sad, embarrassing, and unfortunate disaster!

Though you may want to consult your musician for advice, my suggestion is that you do your homework first. Most wedding party processional music is suitable for seating music. Bear in mind, however, that any musical piece that serves solely as a bridal anthem will usually not work for seating music; the piece will be way too upbeat.

As William Shakespeare said, "If music be the food of love, play on..." On that note, here is my list of possible music selections.

Processional music for the wedding party attendants (also suitable for seating music):

Bach, "Air on a G String" from Suite no. 3 in D Major
Bach, Arioso from Cantata no. 156
Bach, Largo from Concerto for Two Violins in D Minor
Bach, "Jesu, Joy of Man's Desiring" from Cantata no. 147
Bach, March in D Major
    from the *Notebook for Anna Magdalene Bach*
Bach, "Sheep May Safely Graze" from Cantata no. 208
Bach, Wachet auf, ruft uns die Stimme!" (Sleepers, Awake!)

Franck, Panis Angelicus, no. 5 from *Messe Solonelle*, op. 12
Handel, "Largo" from Xerxes
Handel, "Air" from *Water Music Suite*
Mozart, *Ave verum corpus*, K. 618
Mozart, "Andante" from Divertimento no. 1, K. 136,
    Salzburg Symphony
Pachelbel, Canon in D Major
Mozart, "Wedding March" from The Marriage of Figaro

Processional anthem for the bride:

Clarke, "The Prince of Denmark's March" (this is my personal
    favorite bridal anthem)
Bach, "Jesu, Joy of Man's Desiring" from Cantata no. 147
Bach, "Air on a G String" from Suite no. 3 in D Major
Beethoven, "Ode to Joy" from Ninth Symphony
Delibes, "Flower Duet" from *Lakmé*
Pachelbel, Canon in D Major
Mendelssohn, "Wedding March" from *Midsummer Night's
    Dream* (this is not one of my personal favorites)
Vivaldi, "Spring" from *The Four Seasons*
Wagner, "Bridal Chorus" from Lohengrin, also known as "Here
    Comes the Bride" (this is my least favorite)

Recessional music for the entire wedding party:

Vivaldi, "Spring" from The Four Seasons
Bach, Gigue from Orchestral Suite no. 3 in D Major
Beethoven, "Ode to Joy" from Ninth Symphony
Clarke, "The Prince of Denmark's March"
Handel, "La Réjouissance" from Royal Fireworks Music

Handel, Hornpipe (D) from Water Music Suite
   (this is one of my favorite recessional choices)
Mendelssohn, "Wedding March" from
   Midsummer Night's Dream
Purcell, Trumpet Tune and Air
Verdi, "March" from Aida
Mascagni, "Intermezzo" from Cavalleria Rusticana
Campra, "Rigaudon"
Charpentier, Prelude from "Te Deum"
Tchaikovsky, Coronation March for Czar Alexander III
Handel, "Overture" from Royal Fireworks Music
Mussorgsky, "Promenade" from Pictures at an Exhibition
Bach, "Sinfonia" from Cantata no. 156
Bach, Cantata no. 29
Bach, Prelude and Fugue in C Major
Monteverdi, "Toccata" from L'Orfeo
Mozart, "Romance" from String Quartet
Mozart, Piano Concerto no. 21 in C Major
Johnson, Trumpet Tune in A Major
Mendelssohn, incidental music, "Wedding March"
   from op. 61, *A Midsummer Night's Dream*

Contemporary processional anthems for the bride:

As previously noted, my preference tends toward more traditional processional anthems, particularly for a formal ceremony. For a smaller, informal or more casual ceremony a contemporary anthem may be fitting. My suggestion is to choose the more classic of the contemporary musical pieces, songs, or ballads. The following is a partial list of the favorites and preferences of many of my clients:

"Always and Forever," Heatwave, Kenny Rogers, and Luther
   Vandross. Written by Rod Temperton.
"Appalachia Waltz," Mark O'Connor, Yo-Yo Ma, and Edgar
   Meyer. Written by Mark O'Connor.

"At Last," Etta James.

    Lyrics and song by Mack Gordon and Harry Warren.

"Can You Feel the Love Tonight?" Elton John.

    Written by Elton John and Tim Rice.

"Can't Help Falling in Love," Elvis Presley.

    Written by George Weiss, Hugo Peretti and Luigi Creatore.

"Come Away with Me," Norah Jones.

"Have I Told You Lately," Rod Stewart. Written by Van Morrison.

"It's Only Time," Magnetic Fields.

"Only Time," Enya.

"The Greatest Love of All," Whitney Houston.

    Lyrics and song by Michael Masser and Linda Creed.

"The Look of Love," Dionne Warwick. Music by Burt Bacharach.

"The Rose," Bette Midler. Lyrics and song by Amanda McBroom.

"The Vow," Jeremy Lubbock.

"Unforgettable," Nat King Cole. Written by Irving Gordon.

"Wedding Processional" from *The Sound of Music*.

    Written by Richard Rodgers and Oscar Hammerstein.

"What a Wonderful World," Louis Armstrong.

    Written by Bob Thiele and George David Weiss.

"When I'm Sixty-Four," The Beatles.

    Written by Lennon and McCartney.

"Wind beneath My Wings," Bette Midler.

    Written by Larry Henley and Jeff Silbar.

"Your Song," Elton John. Lyrics by Bernie Taupin.

Theme Weddings

In general, I am not a fan of "theme" weddings. There's always the possibility that the significance and inherent beauty of a marriage ceremony will get swallowed up and absorbed in the theatricality of the theme. To me, a more serious risk is the possibility of a poorly concocted, amateurish theatrical production, setting oneself up for a serious flop. Unless you have an uncle who is a Broadway producer, I would steer clear of the risk. Still, I have officiated some unusual and creative ceremonies, including a "Renaissance wedding" which is described later in this book. This outdoor ceremony took place in the couple's charming English garden, which worked beautifully. Thankfully, no one tried to speak Elizabethan English nor were there any Henry VIII impersonations. The costumes were lovely, and though I am not a musical expert, the madrigal-style music and Old English folk songs fit the period beautifully.

The issue of music is important here, For couples planning on a theme wedding, my suggestion is to take the time to research authentic and appropriate music.

The Program

There are many ways to create a program and almost as many ways to distribute one. When my son Joseph and daughter-in-law Kerri decided to print a program for their ceremony, they opted for a simple outline. Their method of distribution was memorable and personal. They created a new category for a child attendant, a "program pagegirl." Their choice for the honored position was the groom's niece, my granddaughter, Rachel. The English traditional wedding ceremony includes pageboys who either precede or follow the bride in the processional order and carry her train. Also, child bridesmaids or the maid of honor may be assigned to hold the train. Rachel's job as a program pagegirl was to walk along the aisles, handing programs from a decorated basket to each guest individually. This lovely, personal touch served as a special greeting to each person present.

An alternative to this method of program distribution is to

position pageboys or pagegirls at the entrance to the chapel to hand out the programs. I feel the former method offers a more personal touch.

You may wish to consider making your own program, thereby avoiding printing expenses. Programs can be generated from your own computer. A photo of the two of you or a piece of clip art and a short poem or appropriate quote, followed by the necessary information about the wedding ceremony, is all that is required. For those whose computer knowledge is rather limited, it may be worthwhile to research the process. A number of my clients have created their own marvelous, professional-looking programs. Do remember to use card paper. A sample program might look something like this:

Cover:

The Celebration of Marriage Uniting

Kerri Lynne Cranston

and

Joseph Orfino

Saturday the thirty-first of May

? o'clock

at

The Hammond Museum and Japanese Stroll Garden

North Salem, New York

Sample Program - Page Two:

The Order of Procession
and the Wedding Party Attendants

Entrance of celebrant .... Named

Entrance and seating of groom's parents .... Named

Entrance and seating of bride's mother and escort . Named

Entrance of groom .... Named

Entrance of best man .... Named

Entrance of bridesmaids and groomsmen .... Named

Entrance of junior bridesmaid .... Named

   and junior groomsman .... Named

Entrance of flower girl .... Named

   and ring bearer .... Named

Entrance of maid of honor .... Named

Entrance of bride escorted by her father .... Named

Seating Music:

Antonio Vivaldi,
  "Winter," "Spring" Allegro from *The Four Seasons*

Wolfgang Amadeus Mozart,
  Piano Concerto no. 21 in C major

Processional Music:

Wedding party attendants:
  Johann Pachelbel, Canon in D Major

Bridal entrance processional music:
  Classic Bagpipes Anthem

Sample Program - Page Three:

The Order of Ceremony

Lighting of memory candle and dedication

Opening benediction

Opening welcome

Marriage foundation address

First reading..........Named

Read by.........Named

The unity candle-lighting ceremony

(or)

The sand ceremony

(or)

The wine sharing ceremony

The blessing of the rings

The celebrant's pre-vows statement or charge

Wedding vows and exchange of rings

The celebrant's final benediction or charge

The pronouncement

The first nuptial kiss

The presentation

The recession

Bride and groom recessional music:
Classic Bagpipes Anthem

Review Checklist

After the wedding location has been chosen and secured and the bridal party attendants have been chosen, review the following:

❑ What type of procession would you prefer: large or small, formal or informal?

❑ Review the processional formations and make a decision on your preference.

❑ Draw an outline or chart of the processional formation of your choice.

❑ Bring the outline or chart to the banquet hall to inform the banquet manager or bridal assistant of your preferences.

❑ If you are planning a small, informal or home ceremony, decide whether a processional assistant will be needed.

❑ Decide who to assign as processional assistant, making sure that she or he is reliable and will arrive at the ceremony early.

❑ Read the information on wedding party attendants, page 62.

❑ Choose the attendants (wisely).

❑ Review the section on music, page 66.

❑ Listen to samples of wedding music.

❑ Carefully make your musical choices.

❑ Inform your musicians or DJ of your choices.

❑ Decide whether you want to include printed programs at your ceremony.

❑ Review samples of program outlines.

❑ Decide whether or not you want to create your own printed programs. If so, make one or two test versions, then review and make choices. If you decide on professional printed programs, be sure to review them before finalizing the transaction with your printer.

Part Two

Ceremony Advice – From Hot Tips to Cool Traditions

Chapter Five:
Avoiding a Wedding Disaster

In avoiding a wedding disaster
Please, heed the advice of this chapter
If these tips you attend
You'll save tears in the end
Forging memories of joy ever after.

Keep It Simple, Plan It Well

I am deeply invested in avoiding a near or, heaven forbid, an actual disaster. I tend to take ceremony disasters personally, even when I have had no control over the circumstances that led to the unfortunate event. I almost obsess as to whether and how disasters can be avoided. Over the years, this personal preoccupation on ceremony disaster-proofing has served its purpose by building and reinforcing my knowledge of how to help prevent catastrophes.

The intense care and planning that a couple invests in their ceremony requires time and careful thought to the minutiae of every detail. A wedding day is one of the most significant and memorable days of one's life. If a wedding disaster occurs, it is magnified a thousand fold, not only in the memory of the couple, but also in the memory of each guest. Wedding disasters have become the subject of a number of television reality shows. Couples willing to showcase their personal disaster stories on national television are indeed courageous. It leaves one wondering whether they are driven by the need to heal their disappointment over the ill-fated situation by laughing at themselves. They are certainly being good sports by sharing their stories.

Without a doubt, it is worth making an effort to disaster-proof your ceremony. All that is required is a little time and information.

One basic rule for the creation of a disaster-free ceremony is: *Keep it simple*. Over the years, I have become increasingly aware of the reasons ceremonies spiral into disasters. The major problems occur when a ceremony is particularly complicated and overloaded, involving many components and many people who flit about doing many things. The more complex things are, the more baffled the guests become. The overall theme is swallowed up in a mystifying and insincere mishmash of a disjointed production; thus, a ceremony of this type at its best still falls flat. In extreme cases, it can become silly; in the worst cases, it can become funny. An unintentionally funny ceremony is the ultimate wedding disaster. In addition, a complicated ceremony sets you up for a disaster simply because there is so much more to go wrong.

The second basic rule is: *Plan carefully*. A major reason for a failed ceremony is very simple: poor planning. Be particularly careful to check with everyone involved in the production or overseeing of the ceremony to make sure that all of your needs have been addressed.

The following description of a wedding disaster shows what can happen with a difficult and complicated ceremony.

The Duck Walk Disaster

When constructing a ceremony, the advice of the celebrant can be very helpful in avoiding unnecessary problems, especially if she or he has had plenty of experience. An unfortunate example that comes to mind is a ceremony I officiated some years ago. This couple was planning an extravagant and complicated ceremony. It was the third marriage for each of them. They were determined to "get it right" this time and they appeared to be driven by a "we'll show 'em all" attitude. I realized later that, had I refused to officiate the ceremony or had I at least negotiated some format changes, this disaster could have been avoided. They rigidly refused advice. Each was in their mid-fifties and each had a number of grown children whom they insisted should participate in the ceremony. These adult children were quite obstinate and particularly uncooperative. None of them got along with one other—not even with their own siblings. Though I tried to advise the couple regarding their joint vision for the ceremony, they absolutely would not listen. Their outdoor ceremony took place directly behind the catering restaurant by a golf course and stream. The ceremony included a complex production involving the passing of a wooden box from adult child to adult child, the symbolic meaning of this I cannot clearly recall—although I do remember thinking at the time that it made no sense. Though the box was empty, it may have somehow represented a bonding of families. Each child would say something as the box was passed. Since the children disliked each other intensely, they more or less plopped the box to one another while uttering something unintelligible. This did not go unnoticed by the guests, who snickered and giggled. Once the box had been passed, the couple participated in a ceremonial stroll, walking across a bridge over a stream and then back again. The bride's very full and ornate gown kept catching and tearing on the rustic wooden bridge slats as a golf ball flew dangerously close. In this ritual walk—again, the symbolism of which I cannot quite recall—the children followed in single file. I do remember overhearing a guest whisper, "Mommy duck, daddy duck, and baby ducklings." Another guest whispered in agreement. As if the tearing gown, the flying golf ball, and the plopping box were not enough, one of the grown children took it upon himself to begin a Charlie Chaplin-esque duck waddle across the bridge, as though he had just read the guests' minds (or actually overheard their comments). He then, very theatrically, repeated the duck walk on the return journey as one of his siblings joined in and mimicked his waddling. At this point, one of the restaurant staff inadvertently turned on a very loud generator, which groaned into action, drowning out the final words of the ceremony. The guests laughed, the bride cried, and I felt utterly helpless, ineffectual, and quite embarrassed for them all!

Both couples and celebrants can learn valuable lessons from this story. When constructing the ceremony, it is essential to keep it simple, meaningful, and authentic. The couple should find an experienced celebrant and listen to her or his advice. Then, try to envision the ceremony from the perspective of the guests as well as from your own perspective as the wedding couple. Though a ceremony is ultimately for and about the couple, remember that the guests are also participating as witnesses. The marriage ceremony is, after all, not only private but also shared. Otherwise, why have a public ceremony in the first place?

This ceremony was officiated in the early years of my ministry, at a time when I was still relatively inexperienced. Nevertheless, I was remiss regarding my compliance with this couple. Under the circumstances, I could have been less docile. The celebrant needs to be effectual in conveying advice to the couple that might steer them away from a potential wedding disaster. When you consider the number of ceremonies a celebrant officiates in the course of a lifetime, you can then grasp the depth of that celebrant's experience and expertise.

The Behind-the-Scenes Disaster

First of all, do you *need* an event planner? For today's couples whose daily obligations consume and overwhelm them, finding the time to plan a wedding is no easy task—in fact, it can be almost impossible. This is generally where parents step up to the plate to organize the event. Typically, the bride's mother opts for the role of wedding planner, though parents of both families can join forces and work together—providing they all get along.

In circumstances where family help is not an option, a wedding event planner can be a godsend. If an event planner is on your agenda, it's worth remembering that they are quite diverse in their approach and their personalities. This profession is definitely not for the faint-hearted but it is ideal for a multi-talented multi-tasker with an inborn gift for organization, a sense of artistic style, and the ability to think and respond immediately, in the face of logistical difficulties. This person needs to be sharp, alert, energetic, responsive, and a good psychologist and mediator if family conflicts flare up. Moreover, these attributes need to co-exist with a caring disposition and softer characteristics—quite a tall order! If you find the right person, she or he can be extremely helpful in planning every detail of the ceremony from start to finish, including ordering the flowers, the cake, and the bridal party attire; preparing the invitations; hiring the photographer, musicians, and vendors; and getting the best possible rates for the client. Typically, the wedding event planner oversees every detail of the wedding from the rehearsal to the napkins and place settings.

When searching out an event planner, get personal recommendations and be sure you conduct an interview before making a commitment.

I remember an occasion when a wedding couple brought their event planner to the consultation appointment. As we proceeded to write the ceremony, this planner began advising me on the wording of the ceremony. She had no idea of the legal requirements regarding the exchange of wedding vows. It became necessary for me to kindly, though reluctantly, enlighten her, but it grew a bit embarrassing as the bride and groom were witnesses to the conversation.

Hold in mind that there are some extremely well-organized wedding hall locations that are so expertly staffed that a personal, "out-of-house" planner is unnecessary on the day of the actual ceremony. That may not necessarily preclude the helpful services of someone during the initial stages of the wedding planning. In terms of both overall cost and convenience, it is worthwhile considering the quality of services offered by the location hall before negotiating with a wedding planner.

I officiated a wedding recently at one of those expertly organized and staffed wedding locations, exquisitely situated in New Rochelle, New York, overlooking the Long Island Sound. The bride hired her own wedding event planner. At this particular wedding hall, not one but several banquet managers coordinate and oversee each wedding party. In addition, each bride is assigned her own female personal bridal assistant. As it happened, at this particular ceremony, the bride's own unnecessarily hired event planner decided that she wanted all of the two hundred and sixty guests to remain in their seats in the in-house chapel after the conclusion of the ceremony. It was the preference of this planner that all the guests be present as onlookers for a post-ceremony photo shoot of the wedding party. The managers and the in-house bridal assistant politely informed this event planner that the cocktail hour directly follows the ceremony and by that point in time, the guests—many of whom might have traveled a great distance—would most likely be ready to eat. They also warned her that the guests might simply take it upon themselves to leave the chapel of their own accord. Of course, predictably, and in spite of the request of the planner, all the guests piled out of the chapel and headed for the cocktail hour.

As mentioned, the staff members at this location are particularly polite. They were also right.

Here is another true story. It is included primarily for the benefit of couples that are considering hiring a wedding event planner; in addition, it may be helpful to celebrants. I preface the account with the fact that while on the surface this ceremony appeared to be perfect, unfortunate incidents took place out of earshot of the guests. For the bride and groom and their immediate families, the undercurrent of unpleasantness may forever overshadow their memories of the ceremony—all because of the unfortunate behavior of an event planner named Sharon. In fairness to Sharon, her training was in coordinating large corporate functions, not weddings. A wedding ceremony, unlike a corporate event, generates feelings of deep emotions, love, and romance, and is generally a religious or sacred ritual. Therefore, everyone involved in the production of a wedding ceremony needs to be sensitive and mindful that they are assisting in a sacred and spiritual marriage rite.

At any wedding, regardless of the careful planning, the unexpected can—and in this case did—occur. Jessica and Zev, the wedding couple, were both kind and wonderful people, expressing a beautiful spirituality in their soft-spoken demeanors. A friend of theirs, whose ceremony I had previously officiated, had recommended me to them. They had traveled from out of state for their ceremony, which took place at an enormous, multi-level hotel complex in Jersey City, New Jersey, by the Hudson River, with a spectacular view of the Manhattan skyline and the Statue of Liberty. They were expecting two hundred guests. The ceremony site was situated on the large, ground floor, outdoor balcony, which also served as the cocktail-hour location and the "waiting area" for the guests to gather before the ceremony. One of the logistical problems this hotel location presented was the complex assignment of ceremony components and guests, who were scattered hither, thither, and yon throughout this vast, incomprehensible, multi-level maze. Since I had never officiated at this location, I planned to arrive one-and-one-half hours early. I requested and received the name and phone number of the in-house event planner. I phoned her several weeks before the wedding to check ceremony particulars and directions; she never responded, so I downloaded directions from the Internet. Problems began when I reached Jersey City and encountered major urban redevelopment and reconstruction. Many streets were closed, and many alternate routes were also closed and barricaded. Immensely stressed, I phoned Sharon's office number but she could not be reached. After leaving her a voicemail message, I phoned the hotel's main number. They could not locate Sharon. Fortunately, in spite of the delay, I arrived twenty minutes before the scheduled ceremony time (after resorting to driving the wrong way down a one-way street). After a search, I found Sharon—who greeted me with a very unpleasant comment regarding the time of my arrival. When I explained that I had phoned her, she waved her cell phone at me! I was stunned. I rattled off her office number that I had called. Her response was to march off!

I followed to ask her for the location of the wedding party, so that I could make contact and check last-minute details. She informed me that I could not see them! Nor would she tell me where they were. Unfortunately and sadly, the tone of our interaction had been established. I tried reaching the couple by their cell phones, but they had turned them off. I then observed Sharon's unpleasant interactions with some of the vendors, one of whom looked at me, rolled his eyes in her direction, and silently mouthed an expletive. It was no consolation that her behavior was not exclusively directed at me!

It took immense focus to be fully present for Jessica and Zev. (The fact that I had phoned home to learn that I had a slight ceiling leak and my husband was away, added to my distress.) I needed the marriage license and naively thought that requesting it from Sharon would help me gain access to the bridal suite. No such luck! I then informed her that *by law,* I *must* have access to the marriage license. Still no luck!

Thankfully, the ceremony itself flowed beautifully, *but I needed the license and the witnesses.* Sharon still had possession of the license.

Directly after the ceremony, the bride asked if I could bless the food during dinner. Concerned about the ceiling leak, I agree to do so providing that the dinner directly followed the cocktail hour. Sharon assured me that the food blessing at dinner would take place fifteen minutes after the cocktail hour ended. No problem! I could bless the food, then drive home and deal with the leak.

After my unrelenting demands, Sharon finally produced the marriage license and the witnesses. She then insisted she take possession of the license. I again explained that a marriage license is a *legal document* and *by law,* once signed, it remains in the possession of the celebrant, who then mails it to the appropriate registrar of marriages. I had received another call regarding the ceiling leak and I needed to leave. The fifteen-minute waiting period promised by Sharon had now dragged into almost two hours. I needed to find Jessica and Zev to explain. But—of course—Sharon would not inform me of their whereabouts. I prefer not to repeat Sharon's comments to me, upon my explaining my predicament to her. In the end, though, I did decide to stay and bless the food. This I did for Jessica and Zev. Sharon had said some rather unpleasant things about me to their respective families, particularly to the bride's father, who became angry. The bride and the groom defended me. They trusted in me without fully knowing the extent of what had transpired. My initial instincts about this wonderful couple had been accurate from the moment I had met them.

What can we take away from this experience? First, there is the issue of the event planner. After all, she was rallying for the wedding party—but unfortunately she insulted me, the workers, and the vendors. My advice to a couple when planning a large wedding is to be sure to check the wedding hall location to establish whether or not an out-of-house event planner is even necessary. Then, if you require or prefer to hire one, do your homework. In this particular case, Sharon was actually a member of the banquet hall staff and functioned as their primary "in-house" event planner. Still, the situation warrants the identical advice: Ask whether she or he is used to working with wedding parties rather than, or in addition to, business functions. Ask whether she or he is courteous. Find out to whom this event planner reports and answers, and check with the event planner's superior. Whether the event planner is privately hired or is part of the banquet hall staff, directly or indirectly, you are paying for the event planner's services.

What is my advice to any celebrant who may find herself or himself in a similar situation? Insist on speaking with the event planner before the ceremony, if possible. Inform her or him of what you require in terms of access to the wedding party and of your other ceremony needs, particularly concerning the legalities of the license. Be fair, yet firm. Do not allow yourself to be bullied. As a celebrant, you need to check with the event planner's superior if you are ignored. My own unfortunate experience with Sharon could have been avoided if I had have taken my own advice about insisting on a pre-ceremony conversation. In my own experience with Sharon, when my requests were ignored, I should have obtained the name of her superior on the spot, and then informed that superior of the problem. I simply had never encountered or imagined a situation like this one.

When it comes to the issue of the blessing of the food, understanding the role of the celebrant is important. What Sharon did not know (and because of her unfortunate interactions with the bride's father, neither did he) is that the role of the celebrant is to officiate the ceremony, thereby legally solemnizing the marriage. The blessing of the food is optional and is offered by the celebrant when that celebrant is invited to be a dinner guest at the ceremony. I tried to explain this to Sharon, but she didn't listen. Jessica and Zev graciously did, in fact, invite me to the reception as a guest. I declined the invitation, however. In the early years of my ministry, I did accept the occasional invitation as a dinner guest at weddings I officiated, but now, unless the bride and groom are personal friends or family members, my policy is generally to decline. I have found that the presence of a minister at a table can inhibit the behavior of the tablemates. I have observed guests hiding their cigarettes and trying to curb their language in front of me. On one occasion, a group of tablemates moved to the ladies' room to engage in conversation they considered inappropriate for a minister to hear. Unfortunately, they didn't notice me as I walked *into* the bathroom, but they all noticed me as I exited the stall. Quite embarrassing!

I have to own up to my own culpability in this behind-the-scenes disaster. I simply should never have agreed to bless the food. Had I declined, most of the problems would have been averted. So I am also in part responsible. Even before I knew about my ceiling leak emergency, I should have stuck to my general policy and not wavered. It would have saved a lot of trouble. My advice to a celebrant can also serve as a metaphor for life: define and be clear about your role (in this case as a celebrant)—and then stick to it!

The postlude to this narrative is worth sharing. When the hotel management learned of what had transpired, they were apologetic, and as courteous and gracious as Sharon was not. Not only did Sharon's direct supervisor phone me, but in addition, I received a personal call from the hotel manager himself. The response, concern, and overall decency of the managerial staff were exemplary. They also expressed great concern about whether Sharon's interactions had been directed towards any of the guests, and I assured them that from my own observations, they had not. I told them the truth as I had observed it.

In the end, I learned that Sharon had been removed from her position as a wedding planner and returned to a corporate position. The bride and groom apologized for Sharon's unfortunate behavior. In addition, the bride explained that her father has "unresolved anger issues" that resulted in his getting in lockstep with Sharon and playing into her negative behavior. I received a wonderful card from the bride in which she thanked me and again apologized for the unpleasant events and for, in her words, "any disrespect you may have undeservingly experienced." The consolation, other than the lesson I learned, is that I still think fondly of Jessica and Zev.

The Inebriated Groom

The last thing I expected to encounter when I arrived at an elegant location in New Jersey to officiate an afternoon ceremony was an *inebriated groom!* When I presented myself to the bridal suite, I was shocked to discover the distraught bride pacing back and forth. I was informed that she could not locate the groom! In fact, she had not heard from him all day. We discovered later that the groomsmen had spirited him away (no pun intended) in an attempt to sober him up for the ceremony. When news arrived that he had turned up, just seconds before ceremony time, we all breathed a collective sigh of relief. None of the bridal party or family members had any idea of his condition until the ceremony was underway. The stench of whiskey permeated the altar. He looked rather sickly as he wavered slightly. The situation demanded a rapid—and creative—solution. In a whisper, I requested that the best man position himself close to the side of the groom, as a kind of "leaning post." The groomsman stood closely behind the groom.

To justify their close proximity to the groom, I then announced that these two men were required to hold and pass the rings to the bride and groom at the appropriate time. Not too subtle, but the best I could do under the circumstances! The next problem was the candle lighting ceremony. I did not think it wise to allow the groom to walk to the altar, let alone light a candle. Since the unity candle set was centered on the altar, in plain view of everyone, it seemed that to cancel the candle ceremony might draw more attention to the groom's condition. I made a quick decision to light the candles myself. I then carried them to the bride and groom to hold very briefly. This also necessitated omitting parts of the ceremony and rewording others. We were all quite nervous about the groom holding a candle for even a few seconds. However, he managed it well. I think we pulled it off—but I will never know what the guests really thought.

The only advice I can offer to a celebrant in a situation like this one is to think quickly, be creative, set the attendants close enough to the afflicted one to serve as prop columns, and try to the best of your ability to eliminate candles and matches, or at least re-work them to avoid mishaps.

The Clumsy Father and the Flimsy Floral Hoop

Floral altar decorations add visual beauty and ceremonial ambiance to a wedding ritual. A freestanding floral hoop is a wonderful addition to the ceremony site, but careful attention must be paid to the security of a structure of this type.

Coincidentally, this "disaster" occurred at the same elegant New Jersey location where I encountered the inebriated groom. The floral structure had been rented from a florist who artistically and painstakingly wove flowers and vines throughout the body of the structure. The framework looked as if it might be constructed of wrought iron, but on close scrutiny, I realized that it was made of very lightweight plastic, obviously for the sake of portability. The hoop was placed at the entrance of the altar as is customary. The father of the bride was to offer a reading during the ceremony. Not only was this man exceptionally tall, he was vastly robust. When I noticed his size, I tactfully suggested to the bride that he enter the altar from the side. He could still gain access to the centrally placed podium by walking from behind it. Agreeing, she cautiously broached him with this suggestion. He looked rather insulted and adamantly refused. Predictably, as he entered through the front of the floral hoop, it collapsed sideways. Fortunately, it was immediately rescued as it began toppling—primarily because everyone was anxiously expecting it to fall.

Words and Double Meanings

During the exchange of vows at a wedding ceremony I officiated recently, the groom mispronounced a certain word. Unfortunately, the mispronunciation bore a very suggestive and sexually crude connotation. Giggles and whispers rippled through the banquet hall. Had the groom left it at that, all might have been half-forgotten. However, once the groom realized his faux pas, he began reveling in the attention, particularly from the knowing laughter of his many groomsmen. He continued quietly to elaborate on the crude comment, most likely for the sake and the appreciation of "the guys"—not realizing that his half-whisper was being broadcast loudly and clearly through the very effective PA system.

What can we take away from this disaster? One important word of caution: please do not make uncouth remarks during the ceremony. Though any off-color remarks can easily be edited out of your wedding video, there will be a permanent and indelible record of those words etched in the memories of the guests.

The Jittery Mother and the Candle Lighting Ceremony

The last thing you need is an accident—particularly a flammable accident—during a ceremony.

Some years ago, during a candle lighting ceremony, the mother of the bride—a rather jittery and emotional woman—decided to wipe her tear-stained cheek with a tissue that she had previously tucked into her sleeve. This lady fumbled unsuccessfully for the tissue; thereby losing her focus on the candle flame. Her ruffled sleeve began to smolder. Fortunately, an astute and fast-acting bridesmaid immediately snuffed it out with a hanky she was discreetly holding beneath her bouquet. A potential disaster was averted!

If mothers are to be involved in the candle lighting ceremony, please do not have them walking around with candles in hand—to do so is definitely to be inviting a flammable disaster. In addition, try inconspicuously to check the clothing that the mothers are wearing to determine whether or not they are walking fire hazards. Candle lighting ceremonies can be restructured to avoid having participants walk around with candles. In addition, there are alternatives to candle ceremonies that essentially convey the same symbolic meaning.

The Cell Phone Scenario

Sometimes the unpredictable will wreak havoc on the best-laid plans. However, some situations are avoidable. Nowadays it's a given that most guests will be carrying cell phones. So, who is to address the guests before the ceremony requesting that cell phones be shut off? Good question!

Since cell phones are a relatively new phenomenon, there is really no fixed protocol. From my own observations when officiating, most (but not all) upscale wedding halls generally have their own banquet manager make this request. If they do not attend to this potential disaster-proofing detail, then it needs to be the responsibility of the celebrant. The celebrant should ask the banquet manager whether she or he wishes to make this request of the guests, or prefers that the celebrant do so.

As usual in these situations, we generally learn from our previous mistakes, as did I during a ceremony I officiated a few years ago at an exquisite wedding hall location in New Rochelle, New York. The probability that the irritating electronic jingle of a cell phone would unexpectedly inflict itself into a ceremony never occurred to me until it happened during the romantic pause between the "exchanges of vows" segments of the ceremony. It could not have come at a worse moment. The culprit was the bride's uncle, who sat only a few short rows from the altar at mid-front. I was informed later that this uncle was partially deaf. Nevertheless, not only did he actually answer the phone, he unbelievably began engaging in a prattling conversation! The best impromptu solution I could think of was to offer a silent blessing between the exchanges of vows. I then repeated my request for silence—obviously to no avail, this fellow could not hear me! Even so, he should have known better than to conduct a personal phone conversation during a ceremony.

Thankfully, the incident culminated in his furious and very wise wife elbowing him rather viciously and effectively to the end of the row and out of the chapel.

I will never be sure whether making a preliminary announcement regarding the shutting off of cell phones would have changed the outcome of this particular situation. My advice to wedding couples is to be sure that *someone* makes an announcement before the ceremony regarding the closing of cell phones. For celebrants, the solution is simple: Simply ask the management who should make the announcement regarding the shutting off of cell phones, the celebrant or the banquet manager.

Mazel Tov: The Breaking of the Foot

The marriage ceremony of Helene and Adolfo flowed beautifully. The plans for their ceremony had included participation by Helene's grown children from a previous marriage. In fact, when we met for the consultation, her children attended. Helene is Jewish. Adolfo, though half Jewish, was raised as a Catholic. Neither Helene nor Adolfo considered themselves observant or religious. Their joint vision and focus for the ceremony was a customized, lightly ecumenical, spiritual ceremony that would include some elements from Judaism. We set to work on ceremony construction and personalization. They had met one another while working together. Helene is a registered nurse and Adolfo is a physician at a Manhattan hospital. The ceremony was to be held at the same wedding location that my son Joseph and daughter-in-law Kerri had chosen. Situated in Northern Westchester County, New York, this picturesque museum setting is nestled amid a Japanese stroll garden, complete with a frog pond covered with floating water lilies. This small pond includes a minute island, linked to a stone footpath for access. The ceremony site is on this island. The most extraordinary and surprising feature of this setting is the frogs! As the musicians commence playing the processional anthem, throngs of bullfrogs, as though on cue, float up to the surface and expose their silly heads among and between the water lilies. These bug-eyed amphibious choristers kindly and comically accompany the musicians by croaking loudly and in *absolute and perfect disharmony!* The guests always find this croaking choral prelude quite hilarious.

This, then, presented a perfect setting on a perfect day for a perfect ceremony. As she processed, Helene looked utterly stunning—graceful and svelte-slender in her simple, elegant size two gown...or was it a size zero? The ceremony flowed wonderfully until the very end, at which point the groom raised his foot to break the glass. In retrospect, Helene is still not sure what came over her at that precise moment, but some devilish impulse from deep within prompted her to slip her foot under that of the groom's. At that instant, Adolfo's large, manly foot came crashing down on Helene's petite and dainty one. The crash was loud and the pain was immediate.

Her foot was badly broken. Helene relied on aspirin and vodka to get her through the reception. Though Adolfo administered makeshift first aid, it was not sufficient to avoid an inconvenient but necessary trip to the local hospital in the early hours—

an unplanned, and imperfect, conclusion to the perfectly planned reception.

Avoiding a Disorder of Ceremony

Do not ever allow a reader total freedom of speech during a ceremony; rowdy toasts are for the rehearsal dinner. I have witnessed ceremony horrors when a reading progresses into a long-winded speech. One reader droned on for twenty minutes or more while the guests yawned and squirmed, resulting in a stunted ceremony and a practically nonexistent cocktail hour. Speeches are appropriate for the reception, not the ceremony. It has become my general policy to advise the couple to choose readings that are short. Generally, couples choose a reading from the celebrant's samples or they choose one themselves. Be sure that the celebrant has a copy to bring along in the event that you forget your copy. Occasionally a couple will trust the reader to choose a reading. In this scenario, I will ask for a copy so that I am aware of the length of the actual reading. On more than one occasion, I have had to request that the reader shorten the reading. One reader produced a seven-page reading; when I asked her, she reluctantly shortened it to one page—and even that was far too long.

Do not double up readings back to back. This minimizes the impact of the individual reading. Simply put, it falls flat.

Do not include unnecessary words in the ceremony. Keep it simple and meaningful. Do not include extra readers and readings just to appease the hurt feelings of someone who may feel left out or bumped from the wedding party. When a bride complies with an angry, offended friend, she allows herself to be manipulated and coerced. It's perfectly fine to select and assign a reader as an alternative to a position in the wedding party. This request—though a compromise—is still sincere and heartfelt. Because of the couple's love for this friend, the request is offered out of caring and respect, not out of obligation.

Do not include passages or rituals that you dislike just to please others.

Do not coerce someone to participate in the ceremony who does not want to be involved. Coercion breeds resentment and resistance, conscious or unconscious. Do you really want that kind of energy spoiling your ceremony?

Do not create a long and complicated ceremony.

Do not be rigid or have unrealistic expectations regarding the participation of children in the ceremony. Children can add freshness and spontaneous humor. But be prepared. Give the ring bearer artificial rings and have a parent on alert to guide or carry an uncooperative flower girl down the aisle or even out of the chapel if necessary. Even with the unpredictability of children, I think it is definitely worth it to include them, providing you are prepared.

Do not be too perfectionist regarding the overall ceremony. The unpredictable can always occur even in the most well-planned wedding. My advice is to make lists and plan ahead to eliminate or minimize the possibility of a glitch. If glitches do occur, they will probably be infinitesimal or even sweet and memorable. For example, if the groom drops the ring or the flower girl runs instead of walks down the aisle, what is the general reaction? Most guests will find it very amusing.

Disaster-Proofing an Altar

In disaster-proofing the altar site, think clearly and practically. Altar objects need attention and forethought as to all conceivable scenarios *before* constructing the space. Those participating in the ceremony are generally excited or nervous and can become clumsy.

- Make sure that the altar table is secure.

- If the altar is set up outside, make sure that the ground is flat and even.

- Be sure that candles are securely held in the candlesticks and make doubly sure they do not wobble about.

- Check that the wick is long enough to ignite and sustain the flame. This can be remedied by scraping away some of the wax around the wick.

- Do not skimp on candles; rather, consider purchasing the commercially packaged sets. They are generally more reliable.

- Have a back-up box of matches in case the lighter does not work.

- In the case of a wine ceremony, unscrew the cap from the wine bottle before the ceremony begins.

- If the wine is to be set up in a glass from the start of the ceremony, only fill the glass one-third to one-half full, to minimize spills.

- Consider using white wine instead of red, in mindfulness of the white bridal gown.

- Make sure all standing structures are secure, whether the structure is an ornate chuppah or a single floral hoop.

- Do not allow parents or readers access to the altar through a structure that appears dubious or flimsy; have them walk around it and then proceed to enter from the back.

- Do not have wedding party attendants standing too close to a candle-lit altar.

- If there is a candle lighting ceremony, do not have participants walking around with candles in hand. There are many alternatives to candle ceremonies that do not require walking with the candles.

Review Checklist

- ❑ Be sure that someone makes the request for the shutting off of cell phones during the ceremony.

- ❑ Keep the ceremony simple, meaningful, and authentic.

- ❑ Listen to the advice of an experienced celebrant regarding the ceremony.

- ❑ Make sure you plan and organize each detail.

- ❑ Commit your plans to paper by making detailed lists.

- ❑ Always check with the services of the wedding hall before contracting with an out-of-house wedding planner.

- ❑ If a wedding planner is necessary, interview her or him and obtain references.

- ❑ Do not ever allow a reader total freedom during a ceremony speech.

- ❑ Do not double up readings back to back.

- ❑ Do not include unnecessary words in the ceremony.

- ❑ Do not include extra readers and readings just to appease the hurt feelings of someone who may feel left out.

- ❑ Do not include passages or rituals that you dislike just to please others.

- ❑ Do not coerce someone to participate in the ceremony who is reluctant to do so.

- ❑ Do not create a long and complicated ceremony.

- ❑ Do not be rigid or have unrealistic expectations regarding the participation of children in the ceremony.

- ❑ Be organized but not too perfectionist regarding the overall ceremony.

❑ Make sure that the altar table is secure.

❑ If the altar is set up outside, make sure the ground is flat.

❑ Be sure that candles are securely held in the candlesticks so that they do not wobble.

❑ Check that the wick is long enough to sustain the flame. This can be remedied by scraping away some of the wax around the wick.

❑ Do not skimp on candles. Preferably purchase the commercially packaged sets. They are generally more reliable.

❑ Have a back-up box of matches in case the lighter does not work.

❑ In the case of a wine ceremony, unscrew the cap from the wine bottle before the ceremony.

❑ If the wine is set up in a glass from the start of the ceremony, only fill the glass one-third to one-half full, to minimize spills.

❑ Consider using white wine instead of red, in order to avoid staining the white bridal gown.

❑ Make sure all standing structures are secure, whether that structure is a chuppah or a simple floral hoop.

❑ Do not allow parents or readers access to the altar through a dubious or flimsy structure. Have them walk around it instead and enter from the back.

❑ Do not have wedding party attendants standing too close to a candle-lit altar.

❑ If there is a candle lighting ceremony, please avoid having participants walk around with lit candles.

Chapter Six

All About Traditions:
Ancient Customs for Today's Weddings

Traditions are often concealing
Odd facts that are quite unappealing
From demon obstructions
To bridal abductions
This chapter may prove quite revealing.

The Origins of Traditions

My friend Rebecca tells a story of a young bride who carefully followed the family recipe for pork roast. She painstakingly reproduced this recipe in every detail, as had her mother, grandmother, and great-grandmother before her. Before placing the roast in the roasting pan, the final step was to cut off an inch of the roast and discard it. One day, while visiting her elderly great-grandmother, the originator of the recipe, the subject came up in conversation. The young bride asked her great-grandmother to explain the rationale for cutting off the end of the pork roast. "Isn't that rather obvious?" replied the great-grandmother. "I didn't have a large enough pan!"

What does a pork roast have to do with a wedding? Well, many accepted wedding traditions evolved from once-necessary actions and behaviors that have no relevance in the modern world. Like the women in this story, brides and grooms continue repeating these old traditions without knowing why. While researching this book, I sometimes encountered multiple explanations for the origins of some traditions, which, I must admit, leaves me questioning their authenticity. No one knows whether this information is true or simply folklore. Which traditions have authentic origins? Which do not? We can only speculate. It is difficult to substantiate their true origins, so the best I can do is to pass on as hearsay what I have learned. As a wedding celebrant minister, I have a fondness and sentimentality for some of these traditions, many of which I became aware of while I was living in England, and I am often amused, surprised, and even disappointed when I learn about their origins.

Still, I find it fascinating that these ancient customs survive, even in a modern or nontraditional ceremony. These old rituals have linked generation to generation from century to century. I have to surmise that most of us, especially brides and grooms, are deeply touched by continuing the same rituals that their own ancestors included in their nuptials generations ago. There is a certain mystery and magic when linking in this way to those unknown beloveds whose clan and bloodline we share. A wedding ceremony is the perfect opportunity to reach back in history and bring these ancient traditions to life. In the freshness of the present, we can honor the customs of two people in love, their families, and their histories.

The White Wedding Gown

In some eastern cultures, white is the standard color worn at funerals. Conversely, in most western cultures, white is considered a symbol of purity. The white wedding gown, therefore, represents innocence and maidenhood.

During the early 1800s, a bride would simply choose her favorite, most ornate dress to wear to her wedding ceremony. In 1840, Queen Victoria wore an elegant all-white gown to her wedding, instead of the typical silver dress (the traditional color worn by royal brides). This led to a new fashion trend, which continues to this day. Once popularized by Queen Victoria, the white gown came to be seen as a sign of affluence.

The following is a traditional rhyme offering advice on wedding dress colors:

Married in white, you have chosen right.
Married in blue, your love will always be true.
Married in pearl, you will live in a whirl.
Married in brown, you will live in town.
Married in red, you will wish yourself dead.
Married in yellow, ashamed of your fellow.
Married in green, ashamed to be seen.
Married in pink, your spirit will sink.
Married in grey, you will go far away.
Married in black, you will wish yourself back.

Tying the Knot

This tradition appears to be multicultural. Currently, in Great Britain, some celebrant ministers tie the ministerial stole around the right hands of the couple and then offer the final pronouncement. The actual wording of this ritual may vary, from the standard pronouncement of religious wedding rites to phrasing reminiscent of the Celtic tradition known as "hand fasting."

The actual tying of the hands symbolically represents the tying, or joining, of two separate lives into one life. This ritual is similar to the Mexican tradition of wrapping the couple in a shawl.

Another explanation of "tying the knot" comes from the days of wearing corsets. This tradition may be particularly ancient, since it seems to precede the invention of buttons, zippers, and hooks and eyes. According to the tradition, the bride's corset was tied together with dozens upon dozens of tiny ribbons. These ribbons were tied in tight knots, rather than bows, making them much more difficult to untie. The bridesmaids were given the task of tying these ribbons. The groom had to undo the knots if he had any hope of consummating his marriage.

The Bridal Bouquet and Flowers

Traditionally the bride's bouquet was composed not only of flowers, but also of aromatic herbs. Most of us are aware of the medicinal benefits of herbs. In recent years this branch of traditional medicine has re-emerged and is practiced as aromatherapy. In ancient times, aromatic herbs were also attributed the power of warding off evil spirits. Thus, the bride carried a "posy" of flowers and herbs to protect her from demonic spirits, bad luck, and jealous curses, as well as from ill health.

Another, entirely different, explanation for the carrying of a bouquet of flowers is that the flowers symbolize a woman in bloom and her wish for a fertile union. Bouquets once incorporated dill, an herb that allegedly promotes lust.

A third explanation for this tradition of the bridal bouquet was the popularization of the sending of flowers. During the Victorian era, flowers took on great significance. Lovers would send covert messages to one another, often unbeknownst to their parents, by way of the particular flowers selected and sent. A specific hidden meaning was ascribed to each species of flowers, thus creating a secret code for lovers. These associations were soon adopted for the bride's bouquet and are still used today by many brides.

The Renaissance Bouquet

I have observed some interesting and unusual bouquet and boutonnière creations. At a recent ceremony I officiated, the couple had chosen a Renaissance wedding theme. Their color palette combined deep rich green, purple, plum red, and gold. I am unsure of the seasonal and period authenticity of the combined flowers and herbs, nor do I know whether they were grown locally or flown in from far afield. Each bouquet, secured by velvet ribbons, was woven into a rich bed of ivy with tendrils of unidentifiable twisting greenery which cascaded downward almost to the floor. Cupped within the ivy nests were wildflowers, deep red and plum-colored berries and pods, and herbs, including sage, thyme, and many others. Tips of goldenrod added a subtle splash of sunny lightness. The men's boutonnières combined ivy, a sprig of berries, pods, and a tiny piece of goldenrod. The effect was spectacular. As the celebrant, I was not required to wear a costume, but I own a robe of rich brown brocade with wide flowing sleeves. As I entered the ceremony site, an ivy-and-berry garland was placed on my head by someone apparently unaware that I was the minister. It was perfect.

My Own Personal Favorite Bouquets:

The Locally Grown Bouquet

Three years ago, my services were requested to officiate a wedding for a vegan couple. The reception dinner was entirely vegan fare. The ceremony setting was atop a cliff, within a semi-open structure that was a five-minute walk from the reception hall, down a path between pine trees. When I arrived at the ceremony site, friends of the bride and groom were filling large red clay tubs with mixed seasonal flowers. Each tub was asymmetrical. I was informed that the bride, a potter, had made each one. I assisted in the flower arranging and learned that some of the flowers, particularly the multi-colored dahlias and roses, were actually from the bride's own garden, while the others had been purchased from the local farmers market the previous afternoon. The effect was stunning for this setting. I was not surprised to learn that the bride and maid-of -honor were carrying bouquets

drawn from the same floral sources. A florist and close friend of the family had made the two bouquets and boutonnières the previous evening. These bouquet arrangements were uncomplicated, consisting of closely woven posies in various shades from pale pink to deep rosy red, without greenery. As the ceremony commenced, a wild turkey confidently wandered into the ceremony space, looked around for a while, and then slowly sauntered back out! We'll never know whether it was just a random action or if the atmosphere of harmless veganism had drawn the lovely creature inside.

The Green on Green Bouquet

For me, the most unusual and surprising floral combination I have observed was at a lavish wedding ceremony where all the numerous floral arrangements, bouquets, and boutonnières were varying shades of green, from light green to emerald. Perhaps the flowers were picked at the point where the buds had not yet fully matured. I remember scrutinizing the pale green hydrangeas and the whitish-green delphinium blossoms. It was probably at this ceremony that I was introduced to and fell in love with Bells of Ireland. These highly fragrant, emerald-green plants remind me of foxglove.

My research assures me of their availability all year, including during the winter months. Alas, here in New York, I have not had the luck to locate any so far. Add a little holly to these stately beauties, and they are all dressed up for Christmas.

Boutonnières

Traditionally, the groom's boutonnière, which he wears on his left lapel, closest to his heart, is made of the same flowers as those in the bridal bouquet.

Occasionally a single flower within a bouquet or an arrangement may be the recipient of a little damage during the transportation process. This is rarely noticed, but if a boutonnière made up of one single floral stem is broken, there is nothing left but a miniscule bit of greenery. On a few occasions I have been present at the unfortunate beheading of a boutonnière and it is a sad sight indeed

My advice is to always order at least one extra boutonnière.

Tossing the Bridal Bouquet

Tossing the bridal bouquet is a custom rooted in English folklore. Becoming a bride was ranked the greatest and most admired position any woman could ever hope to attain. It was a common belief that the bride could pass along her good fortune to others. In order to attain the same good luck as that of the bride, female guests would try to tear away pieces of her clothing and flowers. In an attempt to escape from these women, the bride would toss her bouquet into the crowd. The belief was that the single woman who caught the bouquet would be the recipient of good luck and would be the next to marry.

The following are alternatives to the tossing of the bridal bouquet:

Though I'm from England, I had never witnessed this English tradition until I arrived here in New York. I recall being a guest at a ceremony many years ago where two young women fought over a tossed bridal bouquet. As each claimed their right to it, they both slipped to the floor, still clinging unrelentingly to the pathetic tattered remnants of what had once been an exquisite bouquet. I have to wonder if this custom is worth a potential disaster and the personal humiliation as women wrestle for the bridal bouquet.

A gentler alternative to tossing the bouquet could be for the bride to wear a blindfold and—with an escort—walk before a line or circle of single young ladies. The bride could then 'place' the bouquet in front of the woman she feels will be the next one to be married.

The following departure from tradition is definitely the closest to my heart:

Directly following the wedding ceremony of my parents: John Edmund and Violet Burwell, my mother placed her bouquet—a large cascade of white trumpet lilies—at the foot of The Cenotaph, located in front of the Henry Moore Institute in the center of Leeds, England. As my mother solemnly laid down her bouquet, my father—dressed in the uniform of the Royal Artillery—stood to the salute. On the top of this imposing war memorial stands a statue of an angel carrying roses, and at the base is the statue of St. George conquering the dragon.

When my mother passed away recently, we placed her funeral flowers—an arrangement of trumpet lilies and violas—at The Cenotaph; the violas were woven into the arrangement in honor of her name, Violet. What a fitting tribute to a life fulfilled. As we placed the flowers at the foot of the monument, we knew this gesture was the perfect completion and conclusion of her life of service to us, her family and to a loving marriage that spanned more than sixty years.

Throwing Confetti or Rice

In England, the showering of paper confetti over the newlyweds occurs at the end of the ceremony, as the couple exits the church. The honor of confetti throwing was often assigned to the children—a duty they always loved. Pre-dating throwing paper confetti was a pagan ritual using petals, grains, seeds, rice, and small flowers. These items were showered over the bride and groom as symbols of prosperity and a fruitful (or fertile) union.

The Italian word *confetto* translates as "a sweet." The plural of *confetto* is *confetti*. Traditionally, this *confetti* consisted of nuts and raisins, which were thrown over the couple as they exited the church, in the same manner that paper confetti is traditionally used in England.

I have witnessed the giving of confetti to guests, rather than the bride and groom, at an Italian wedding; confetti confections were offered as mementos and were individually placed next to each guest's place setting.

The Giving Away of the Bride by Her Father

This tradition originally dates back to the custom of arranged marriages where the bride was considered the property of her parents. This was a symbol of the father's *giving over* of his property to the groom. In addition, it was seen as an endorsement by the father, before witnesses, that the groom was an acceptable choice as a husband for his daughter.

In general, this ritual has survived the centuries, even though western society has progressed beyond the practice of arranging the marriage of a daughter. In addition, few modern cultures consider women the property of their fathers. It's understandable that as a celebrant, I encounter brides who dislike the thought of being "given away," particularly those independent, self-assured brides, who view this custom as sexist and even repugnant. I am often given other valid reasons that brides may not wish to walk down the aisle with their father. Perhaps it is a second marriage or the father is deceased. I have witnessed occasions where the bride requests that her mother escort her down the aisle since mother has raised the bride alone and the estranged father has had little or no involvement in her life. Whatever the reason, there are plenty of alternatives to the giving away of the bride by her father.

In the situation of a second marriage, the bride's teenage or grown children can escort her down the aisle. Another alternative is to have the children walk their mother halfway down the aisle. At that point, the groom meets them, escorts the children to their seats, and then continues escorting the bride to the altar.

For brides who wish to enter the aisle alone, an alternative to being fully escorted is to proceed to the halfway point, where a parent, or the groom, or a chosen escort waits. When the bride arrives at the midpoint, the escort walks her to the altar.

Of course, even when given the most creative of alternatives, some brides still insist on walking alone. If this is their heartfelt and well considered choice, they have my complete respect and blessing.

The most extraordinary alternative bridal procession I have witnessed took place at the ceremony of a couple who had a beautiful infant daughter. First, the groom took his place at the altar. He then slowly proceeded down the aisle to the halfway point to meet the bride. She surprised all of the guests by slowly entering the aisle drawing behind her an antique Victorian perambulator. The carriage had been decorated with flowers and vines. The baby slept silently though the ancient wheels wobbled and squeaked. When the bride reached the waiting groom at the mid-point, he kissed her, blew a silent kiss to their sleeping infant, and then assisted in drawing the carriage down the aisle to the altar. The carriage remained at the altar where the cooperative baby continued to slumber deeply through the entire ceremony.

Something Old, Something New

The traditions described in the familiar rhyme, "Something old, something new, something borrowed, something blue, and a silver sixpence in your shoe," date back to Victorian England. "Something old" refers to the wearing of something that represents a link with the bride's family. Typically, the bride wears a piece of family jewelry or a family dress or article of clothing. "Something new" represents good fortune in the bride's new life. "Something borrowed"—an item that has already been worn by another bride at her wedding—is meant to bring good luck to the marriage, and could be an item of clothing or jewelry. "Something blue" dates back to biblical times, when the color blue symbolized purity. In recent years, this has changed from the wearing of blue clothing to the wearing of a garter, piece of jewelry, or an undergarment of blue. In England, finding a silver sixpence meant good fortune. Placing a silver sixpence in the bride's shoe is not only a symbol of financial wealth; it also represents abundance, and is a prediction of future joy throughout the marriage.

Child Attendants

Children were originally included in the ceremony to add a touch of innocence.

The White Aisle Runner

The white aisle runner symbolized the presence of God in a marriage and walking on pure and holy ground in honor of God's presence.

Taking Each Other's Right Hand

In many cultures, the right hand is a symbol of strength, character, and morality. The joining of both right hands symbolizes the joining of those characteristics and qualities, in order to strengthen and merge them together.

Breaking the Glass

This Jewish tradition represents the destruction of the temple in Jerusalem. Often couples save the shards of broken glass from this ceremonial ritual, and place them in a symbolic box. More recently, other newlyweds have the shards reconstructed into a design and affixed in a frame, as a memento of the wedding.

The First Kiss

In early Roman times, the kiss represented a legal bond that sealed the marital contract.

The Arch of Swords

Walking through the arch of swords following the ceremony ensured the couple's safe passage into their new life together.

The Wedding Cake

Cakes have been associated with weddings throughout history. The Romans shared a cake during the wedding ceremony itself. This was not the rich, traditional English fruitcake or the multi-flavored, filled sponge cake that most Americans prefer. These ancient Roman cakes were rather simple, unadorned, and unsweetened confections made from salt, water, and grains—generally wheat or barley, which were symbols of fertility. Fijians and some Native American tribes also incorporate cakes in their wedding ceremonies.

Early British cakes were flat and round, and contained fruit and nuts, which symbolize fertility. This fruit-filled flatbread is probably a forerunner to the wonderfully rich, moist, flavorful fruitcake. An ancient custom was to throw many small cakes over the bride, in a manner similar to that of throwing confetti. A modification of this custom was to crumble the cake over the bride's head, and in some versions, to actually break the cake over the bride's head. Ouch! In Scotland, oatcakes were traditionally used in this tradition.

In Yorkshire, a plate holding a wedding cake was thrown out of the window as the bride returned to her parental home after the completion of the wedding ceremony. According to this tradition, if the plate broke, she would enjoy a happy future with her husband; if the plate remained intact, her future was considered rather grim.

Another old English custom was to place a ring in the wedding cake. The guest who found the ring in her or his piece of cake would be ensured happiness for the next year.

A traditional belief was that a spinster who placed a piece of wedding cake under her pillow before sleeping would greatly increase her prospects of finding a husband.

Some couples keep the top tier of their cake, which they share at their first wedding anniversary.

It is a common belief that the spire of St. Bride's Church, Fleet Street, London, inspired the shape of the modern three-tiered iced wedding cake. St. Bride's Church, named after St. Bridget (Bride) of Kildare, is the eighth church to stand on that site. As a place of worship, it may date back as far as the sixth century, but the present church was rebuilt by Sir Christopher Wren in 1671–78, after the Great Fire of London. The layered spire of St. Bride's Church rises 226 feet and was added in 1701. Originally, it stood eight feet higher but the top was lost in a thunderstorm in 1764. A short finial spire tops its four octagonal arcades of diminishing size. It is believed that this magnificent structure is the inspiration for the modern wedding cake. A local baker, William Rich, created a replica of the church spire for a wedding cake. Other bakers, inspired by his creative design, copied this model and the spire has been known as the "wedding-cake steeple" ever since. That the church is called St. Bride's happens to be a perfect coincidence.

Signing the Guest Book

The signing of the marriage certificate is a public record of the marriage. Similarly, the guest book serves as a record of all of the people who witnessed the marriage. For that reason, the guest book is supposed to be signed following the official wedding ceremony.

Throwing the Garter

It is not clear where this fifteenth-century tradition actually originated. It was believed that the single man who caught the garter when it was thrown would be the next to marry.

Sprinkling Rose Petals

Rose petals were sprinkled before the bride as she processed down the aisle to ward off evil spirits who were lurking, hidden, below the ground.

Tying Shoes to the Bumper

Traditionally, old shoes were tied to the back of the exiting carriage to represent the transfer of ownership of property from the bride's father to her new husband—in this case, the property was the bride herself. Tying shoes to the bumper of the car represents the symbolism and power of shoes in ancient times. Egyptians would exchange sandals when they exchanged goods. When the father of the bride gave his daughter to the groom, he would also give him the bride's sandals to show that she was now the groom's property. In ancient Anglo-Saxon times, the groom would tap the heel of the bride's shoe to show his authority over her.

The Honeymoon

The term "honeymoon" is believed to have originated from the era when the groom abducted his bride. The couple would hide from the bride's parents before marrying. After the wedding, they would remain in hiding for a cycle of the moon. During this period, they toasted their union by drinking honey wine.

More Traditions and Superstitions

In Scotland and some parts of Britain, the bride would never wear her entire outfit before the wedding day. Some brides would leave a final stitch on the dress undone until it was time to leave for the ceremony, when the outfit would be hurriedly and finally completed.

The following traditions also originate in Scotland: Summer as a whole was considered an optimal and advantageous time to marry. This is partly related to the sun's association with health and fertility. A popular custom was for the bride to "walk with the sun," thereby bringing good health upon herself. She would walk from east to west on the south side of the church, and then continue walking around the church three times. Another custom was for a woman with milk in her breasts to prepare the marital bed to encourage fertility in the life of the newlywed.

In Armenia, two white doves were set free to symbolize love and happiness.

A typical Bermudan wedding cake was a multi-level fruitcake that included a small cedar tree on top. After the wedding ceremony, the couple then planted this tree. The belief was that the more deeply the bride and groom loved one another, the more likely the tree would be to thrive, flourish, and grow.

In England, it was considered unlucky to be married on a Saturday, or on Friday the thirteenth. A famous old rhyme advises that a wedding take place during the first half of the week rather than the last:

> *Monday for wealth*
> *Tuesday for health*
> *Wednesday the best day of all*
> *Thursday for losses*
> *Friday for crosses*
> *Saturday for no luck at all*

Advice on the month in which to marry is offered by the following rhyme:

> *Married when the year is new,*
> *   he'll be loving, kind, and true.*
> *When February birds do mate,*
> *   you wed nor dread your fate.*
> *If you wed when March winds blow,*
> *   joy and sorrow both you'll know.*
> *Marry in April when you can,*
> *   joy for maiden and for man.*
> *Marry in the month of May,*
> *   and you'll surely rue the day.*
> *Marry when June roses grow,*
> *   over land and sea you'll go.*
> *Those who in July do wed,*
> *   must labor for their daily bread.*
> *Whoever wed in August be,*
> *   many a change is sure to see*
> *Marry in September's shrine,*
> *   your living will be rich and fine.*
> *If in October you do marry,*
> *   love will come but riches tarry.*
> *If you wed in bleak November,*
> *   only joys will come, remember.*

> *When December snows fall fast,*
> *marry and true love will last.*

Historically, May has been considered an unlucky month to marry for a number of reasons. During Roman times, the Feast of the Dead and the festival of the goddess of chastity both occurred in May. In the Victorian era, the end of April and the beginning of May were busy times for most churches. Queen Victoria is thought to have forbidden her children from marrying in May. The following rhyme advises:

> *Marry in Lent, live to repent*
> *Marry in May and you'll live to rue the day*

Lent was thought an inappropriate time for a wedding, since it was a time of abstinence. June was considered a lucky month in which to marry; it is named after Juno, the Roman goddess of love and marriage.

These following superstitious traditions also originated in Britain:

- Just as the bride left the house for the wedding ceremony, one last look in the mirror would bring her good luck. However, if she returned to the mirror again after she had begun her journey to the church, she could expect ill luck.

- Seeing a chimney sweep on route to a wedding was considered good luck. Some English brides still hire a chimney sweep to attend their wedding as a good luck omen. Other good luck omens when observed on the way to the ceremony include lambs, toads, spiders, black cats, and rainbows.

- Seeing an open grave, a pig, a lizard, a monk, a nun, or hearing a cockerel crow after dawn are all thought to be omens of bad luck.

- Bad weather while en route to the wedding is thought to be a sign of an unhappy marriage, although in some cultures rain is considered a good omen. Cloudy skies and wind are believed to cause stormy marriages. Snow, on the other hand, is associated with fertility and wealth.

In Ireland, a laying hen was tied to the bed on the first honeymoon night in the hope that the fertility of that hen would somehow be passed on to the couple. Eating a double-yoked egg was also thought to predict fertility.

The following traditions originated in Africa:

- The tradition of jumping the broom is a custom that symbolizes jumping the doorway or threshold from a carefree single life into married life and all the responsibilities that marriage necessitates.

- Some African brides will hide their face behind a veil of braided hair as a symbol of modesty.

- In order to encourage fertility, the bride will wear a necklace made of cowrie shells.

- During the ceremony, the African wedding couple is bound together at the wrists as a symbolic way of joining them together. In addition, wine is poured onto the ground as an offering to the gods, as a way of inviting them to join and bless the celebration.

The Native American ceremony begins with the washing of the hands by the bride and groom. This symbolizes the washing away of evil and of their past loves. Traditional colors which symbolize the four corners of the earth are woven into the bride's ceremonial dress: white for east, blue for south, yellow for west, and black for north. To symbolize the joining of the two, during their ceremony the couple share a dish of corn meal made of both white and yellow corn. White represents male and yellow represents female.

The wedding ceremony of the Amish is uncomplicated and rather basic. The bride and groom personally deliver to each guest an invitation. The wedding is celebrated after the harvesting season, often midweek, so all guests can attend. The ceremony is simple, as is the bride's dress, which, though new, can be worn again, perhaps to church on Sunday.

For Chinese wedding ceremonies, it is customary to send the invitations wrapped in red paper, since the traditional colors of happiness and wealth are red and gold. Gifts of money to the newlyweds are also presented in red envelopes for the same reason. Gold purses filled with jewelry are presented to the bride by female relatives and close friends. The ceremony is followed by a reception. Firecrackers are lit for the purpose of chasing away evil spirits.

Traditionally, the religious ceremony of a Japanese wedding was held in a Shinto shrine. These days, a shrine may be recreated inside the hotel or banquet hall where the festivities take place. A Shinto priest conducts the ceremony, which is attended only by close family members. The bride and groom each dress in the traditional kimono. During the wedding ceremony, the couple participates in a ritualistic purification. They each drink sake, Japanese rice wine, and the groom reads the words of commitment. Both bride and groom pay homage to their parents and elders for the guidance and wisdom they have bestowed upon them. The reception banquet is generally quite large, often including one to two hundred guests and sometimes even more. These reception festivities begin with the introduction of the bride and groom. During the reception, several guests make contributions such as speeches. The reception menu could include kai fish, which symbolizes happiness, red rice, kelp, and sake. During the celebrations, the groom and especially the bride may change clothing several times. At the very end of the party, the couple addresses all the guests, offering them their heartfelt thanks.

In recent decades, many Japanese couples have introduced Western elements to their weddings. Many brides choose to wear white, Christian-style wedding gowns; some ceremonies are officiated at a Christian church, even though the couple may not be Christian. The rituals of cake cutting and the exchange of rings are now commonly adopted elements.

Before a Czech ceremony, the couple's wedding bed is "blessed" by laying an infant on the bed to enhance fertility. On the steps of the church, the couple receives a stern lecture on their duties as husband and wife from their *starosta*, the male sponsor of the couple. After the ceremony, the bride's veil is removed and is replaced by a traditional matron's bonnet while the guests sing a traditional wedding song.

After a Dutch wedding ceremony, the couple plants lily-of-the-valley in their garden so that every year when the plant blooms, they are reminded to renew their love for one another.

In France, as the bride and groom exit the church, laurel leaves are scattered outside the doorway. During the reception, the newlyweds toast one another using a special two-handled cup, the *coupe de marriage*, which has been passed down through the generations.

In Haiti, it is customary for guests to offer the couple wedding gifts, but not gifts of money. The wedding cake is not cut and served at the reception party; rather, it is saved to be served at the home of the couple later.

A wedding celebration in India often lasts for three days. The house of the bride's parents is considered an "open house" where uninvited guests drop by to participate in the celebrations. The Indian bride, after a ceremonial cleansing, is painted with henna designs on her hands and feet. After the wedding ceremony, the brothers of the groom toss flower petals to ward off evil and negativity.

A Korean bride is welcomed into the groom's family by participating in a Korean introduction ceremony. The bride's makeup includes a large red dot on each cheek for the purpose of warding off evil spirits. Her silk gown is made of brightly colored material, with the exception of the sleeves, which are white. The groom formally introduces his parents to the bride, and his father collects a handful of red dates that he tosses towards the bride, as a symbol of fertility.

In Lithuania, during their reception, the bride and groom are given bread and salt, the "elements of life," symbolically ensuring that they will never be hungry. They are then given wine and honey, which symbolizes that their marriage will be filled with sweetness.

The Moravian wedding ceremony is simple, yet elegant. The bridal couple lights one large candle. The flame is passed along to each guest, each of whom has been given a handmade candle. Each guest lights their candle from the candle of the person in the next seat, until the entire church is aglow with candlelight.

In a traditional Polish ceremony, the bride's braided hair is unbraided by her bridesmaids in a custom called *rospleciny*. In addition, during the couple's walk to the church, children block the couple's path. In order to continue past these children, the best man must pay "toll" to them. Guests offer the bride gifts of money, and she offers them small gifts in return.

Clergy is not included in the Quaker marriage ceremony, so the wedding certificate is not only signed by the bride, groom, and witnesses, but by all the guests. This document is hung in a prominent place in the new household as a memento for the couple to treasure. The Quaker bride is not escorted to the groom; rather, she presents herself to him, for it is believed that she belongs to no one but herself.

The origin of the traditional Claddagh wedding ring of Ireland is described in a tale about a man in ancient Galway. He was about to be married when he was taken prisoner by sailors and forced into a labor camp in a foreign land. During his time in labor, he taught himself the art of jewelry making. When he returned to his homeland, he discovered to his surprise, joy, and relief that his maiden had never married. He presented her with a ring that he had designed in captivity, featuring a heart held by two hands with a crown over it.

One of the more notable dances at an Irish wedding reception celebration is the "janting char," where the groom is carried overhead in a chair (similar to the Jewish tradition of lifting the bride and groom in chairs). The Irish shamrock is often used in the flower arrangements, as decoration on the cake, and sometimes as a motif on the wedding stationary. It is also traditional and customary to serve Guinness for the toasts at the reception.

In the small villages of Italy, the bride and her family members walk to the church through the village streets, followed by neighbors, particularly children. After the wedding ceremony mass, the newly married couple processes through the town plaza, greeting their friends, relatives, and neighbors. The bride carries *la busta*, a white drawstring gift bag, to hold gifts of money, generally the most common gift at an Italian wedding. Food is an extremely important part of an Italian wedding; in fact, it is the focal point of the festivities. Certain foods, such as twists of fried dough, symbolize good luck. Sweet liquors are served to the women and strong liquors to the men. At an Italian reception, guests are offered *bombonniere*—almonds covered with hardened icing—representing the bitter and sweet things in life. Today, these Italian wedding traditions are becoming less fashionable. Sometimes *bombonniere,* the original *confetti*, are still thrown over the bride and groom by the guests. It is believed that they ward off infertility.

In Scandinavia, en route to the church, the wedding procession includes violinists and trumpeters. The bride wears a jeweled crown as a symbol of purity.

In a Vietnamese ceremony, the groom leads a procession to the bride's house, accompanied by family and friends who join along the way. When they arrive, they present the bride with gifts of clothes, jewelry, and money.

Some Final Thoughts about Traditions

A wedding is still one of life's surprisingly unchanged rites and to this day couples continue to include many of these ancient traditions in their ceremony. Linking to one's ancestry in this ritualistic way honors and connects us with past and current generations. It also offers a way for the couple to acknowledge and join with the family and history of their new in-laws. Over the passage of centuries, the meanings of some traditions may have been diluted, forgotten, or misinterpreted, and our understanding of their purpose may be completely inaccurate. Even so, they continue to thrive as we remain awed and moved by these ancient customs. Rather than analyze a tradition, my suggestion is to feel whether it stirs the heart. Try to find a ritual that speaks of the message you wish to convey, yet don't shy from taking poetic license to put your own fresh new spin on it. Many of the traditions we observe today are mere echoes of a long-gone era. By rewording them, we can convey a more authentic message. My experience has also shown me that the most deeply moving traditional rituals tend to be less wordy, and carry a more visual message.

Review Checklist

❑ Are there any specific traditions you would like to include in the ceremony?

❑ If the answer is yes, think clearly and realistically as to whether or not it is feasible to incorporate them into your own ceremony. You may wish to check with your celebrant to determine whether it is possible.

❑ Are there any species of flowers you would now consider using for:

    ❑ The bridal bouquet

    ❑ Bouquets for bridal attendants

    ❑ Corsages

    ❑ Boutonnières

    ❑ The chapel or church floral arrangements

    ❑ The wedding ceremony site altar floral arrangements

    ❑ The reception photo or card table floral arrangements

    ❑ The guests' dining tables floral arrangements

    ❑ The bride and groom's head table floral arrangements

    ❑ Any other reception area floral arrangements

Part Three

Wedding Words–
The Ceremony Text Handbook

Chapter Seven:

Timelines and Creative Ceremonies

Ceremony Timelines

When planning a wedding ceremony, we rarely think in terms of the time and length of the actual ceremony. Whether the ceremony is an informal, at-home affair or a large banquet-managed extravaganza, timing is not only important, it is essential. Each segment of a wedding event should be carefully planned and timed, particularly at the more formal venues. There is an entire workforce to consider, including caterers, cooks, chefs, and wait staff. They must meticulously adhere to a carefully orchestrated schedule. Sometimes even a slight delay can cause the spoiling of carefully prepared food. Therefore, thoughtful attention given to the ceremony timeline is key to a harmonious wedding experience.

Generally, the optimum length of a ceremony should be within thirty minutes. However, a thirty-five minute ceremony can work, providing the overall schedule permits. A ceremony lasting longer than thirty-five minutes may become tedious for the guests. In addition, consider the bride, groom, and attendants who, besides feeling rather nervous, are required to stand for the entire ceremony! I'm sure that some of those embarrassing—and dangerous—fainting spells experienced by wedding party attendants are caused by standing during an overly long ceremony.

The following timelines are estimates. Bear in mind that the length of the procession and recession may alter the overall estimated ceremony time.

The Thirty- to Thirty-five-Minute Ceremony

- Lighting of the altar candle

- Remembrance and dedication

- Opening benediction

- Opening welcome

- Marriage foundation address (including personalization)

- First reading

- Bride and groom unity candle ceremony or unity sand ceremony

- Honoring of mothers and giving of roses

- Bride and groom sharing of wine ceremony (Jewish, Celtic or universal)

- The ring blessing

- Celebrant's pre-vows charge

- Wedding vows and exchange of rings

- Second reading

- Celebrant's short wedding charge

- Silent blessing

- Celebrant's final benediction

- Celtic or universal hand-joining

- Final pronouncement

- The kiss
- The presentation

The Fifteen- to Twenty-five-Minute Ceremony

- Opening benediction
- Combination opening welcome and foundation address (including short personalization)
- Unity candle ceremony, including the honoring of parents
- The ring blessing
- Short version of parental permission and family vows
- Wedding vows and exchange of rings
- A reading
- Silent benediction
- Celebrant's final wedding blessing and charge
- Final pronouncement
- The kiss
- The presentation

The Ten- to Fifteen-Minute Ceremony

The following simple ceremony is the shortest I would personally recommend:

- Combination opening benediction and welcome
- Foundation address (minimal personalization)
- The ring blessing
- Wedding vows and exchange of rings

- A short reading or short charge by celebrant
- Combination silent blessing and celebrant's benediction
- Final pronouncement
- The kiss
- The presentation

The following outlines and excerpts illustrate the unique qualities of each ceremony and how the individual needs and preferences of each couple vary immensely. Yet, if you look a little deeper into the basic outline, you will see the overall similarities.

Timelines for Creative and Unusual Ceremonies

When a couple opts to write a large part of their ceremony, the celebrant needs to be aware of, and responsible for, the timing of the service. The bride and groom also need to be informed and guided on the sequence, flow, and required questions that must legally be asked by the celebrant. Generally, most couples who are considering writing their own ceremony tend to create only the exchange of vows. Some couples also include the marriage foundation address and the opening welcome. In order to ensure that the couple does not wax too long, we really need to sit down together at a consultation appointment and go over the plans. I recall couples that have given me a handwritten ceremony that would have required over an hour, without even including the procession and recession.

The following samples are quite beautiful examples of what a couple can create when they tap their creativity and stay aware of the timeline.

Elise and John: A Twenty-Minute Multicultural and Ecumenical Ceremony

Following are selections from the marriage ceremony of Elise and John. John describes himself as ethically spiritual. He is quietly spoken and has a wonderful sense of humor. He is a caring veterinarian and an obvious animal lover. His maternal Asian grandparents practice Buddhism. To assimilate into American society, his Asian mother converted to Presbyterianism. John's American father is a non-practicing Episcopalian. Elise is a bright, quick-witted attorney in a busy New York law practice. Her Catholic mother raised Elise. Her father is Jewish. Though she describes herself as universally spiritual, she is drawn to the traditions of Judaism.

This ceremony offered quite a challenge. It required honoring many traditions while avoiding sounding too serious or austerely religious. The bride and groom's joint concerns were that no one be offended at any specific religious reference. In addition, we wanted the overall tone to be heartfelt and light, while reflecting the bride and groom's open-minded approach to universal and ethical spirituality. You may notice that the word "amen" was replaced with the phrase "and so it is." This was fully intentional and designed to convey a more universal, Buddhist-like conclusion to the benedictions.

Lighting of the Memory Candle

Celebrant: "The candle is lit in loving memory of the bride's grandmother, Gina. The bride requested that she herself light the candle in honor of Gina's life so that her presence is felt here with us today. Let us open our hearts as we take a moment to remember Gina and all of those beloveds who no longer share our lives in this world. Our memories we hold of them are precious and sacred to us, and live on eternally in our hearts. And so it is. The bride, groom, and their families dedicate this ceremony to the memory of Gina."

Opening Benediction

Celebrant: "Welcome. A sincere wish offered in love is a prayerful benediction. May each gathered here hold precious the following wishes: that this is the beginning of a joyful new life for the bride and groom, that is filled with special moments within a full lifetime together. That this day is the beginning of a lifetime of sharing, of trust, of mutual respect, of growing together in ever-deepening gratitude and love for one another. We give thanks for the miracle of love. We call upon all that is sacred and divine in all time-honored traditions to bestow blessings upon this union. May their love and devotion for one another be an anchor that holds them together throughout this shared life. May they treat this love between them with reverence, as they walk forward together in the sacred union of marriage. We ask that this union be truly and perpetually blessed. We ask also for a blessing upon each gathered here as witness to this union. Because of the love we witness, we may be inspired in our own lives."

Opening Welcome

Celebrant: "Welcome to the wedding celebration of Elise and John. We gather here today in joy and in celebration. In their love and devotion for one another, Elise and John wish to unite in the sacred commitment and bond of marriage. Welcome all who gather here. Eventually, we begin to realize that love is more than romance. As we grow in wisdom, we experience true love as a guiding force in our lives. Love is the creator of our deepest dreams and highest aspirations.

Love gives us the courage to forge ahead in times of difficulties. Love restores and revives us when life becomes discouraging. Love impels us to share our joys and celebrations with those we love. Love is an extension of all that is good. Love is Divine. As we embark upon this ceremony, I ask each of you gathered here, as witnesses, to hold in your hearts the very best of wishes and highest good for the bride and groom in the creation and continuation of a marriage based on love."

At this point in the ceremony, the bride and groom shared in a very simple and universal version of the Jewish wine ceremony.

Foundation Address Personalized

Celebrant: "Marriage is the joining of two lives, in the presence of all that is Divine, before whom the secrets of all hearts are revealed. This outward ceremony is but a symbol of that which is inner and real; a union of love, which religions may bless, but can never create. A true marriage partakes of the mystery of love and creation. It grows through the joy of life fully shared and grows again through understanding and forgiveness. While it can be the font of the greatest happiness, it is not meant for happiness alone, but also for the birth and growth of greater qualities and character development through the many life lessons and challenges inherent in each and every marriage. As two separate beings join together, each with his or her own separate ways, each becomes stronger and more self assured because of the loving support of the other. To this end, there must be a dedication of each to the other, and of both to the noblest purposes of life. Marriage is a mystery embarked upon by those who wish to join together their hearts, lives, and individual destinies. Marriage offers the opportunity in which each of you can be challenged to discover the very best, not only within each other as a unit, but within yourselves. This ceremony is the gateway into the marriage. Only the two of you, in the love you share, can create your marriage.

"Elise and John, when I asked you to tell me how a marriage is created, you both offered me the following words, which I will quote: 'Through love and patience and through respect, which is so essential. We always try to keep the lines of communication open, although we both agree that we need to try a little harder in that area. Through being able to let go of unimportant things and focus on the important issues; for example, remembering what brought us together in the first place. We also need to be willing to forgive.'

"John, also, you shared these very beautiful insights about Elise and what she contributes to your union, and again I will quote: 'Elise has a sweet and trusting nature—actually, she is sometimes too trusting. She is so caring and sensitive. She always surprises me with her kindness. I love the way she is committed to me and to our relationship. She is also tireless and so energetic. I often wonder where she gets her energy. Actually, she helps me to laugh and lighten up a bit. Without her, life would be a little boring.'

"And Elise, you added the following words of the heart regarding John: 'John is the most stable person I know. I think he is probably one of the most intelligent persons I have ever met. Yet below his serious external persona, he is hilariously funny.

He is so kind and caring, yet private. He is supportive regarding my interests. He is also absolutely committed to our relationship. John has the ability to calm me when I am a bit frazzled—and I am often frazzled.'

"Elise and John, you are the authors of this life and this union you are about to embark upon. May all that you have and all that you are, be joined, and woven into a true marriage of love, with the vows you are about to share today."

Exchange of Vows and Rings

Celebrant: "Elise and John, it is now time to state your vows to one another. These promises are not lightly and frivolously made. In true love, and from the depths of your hearts, these words declare publicly the love, trust, and respect that you already hold for one another. These words reflect the deep and abiding commitment that you are about to make. Let your love, trust, and respect build an even stronger bond between you as the years go by. Therefore, John, will you accept Elise as your wife?"

John: "I will."

Celebrant: "Therefore, Elise, will you accept John as your husband?"

Elise: "I will."

John then offered his personal vows to Elise.

John: "Elise, I am honored and awed that you have chosen me as your husband and life partner. Today in the presence of those we love, I promise that I will do my best to be a source of comfort to you when you feel overwhelmed and sad, to be a source of strength to you when you feel weak and ineffectual, to listen to you when you feel ignored and dismissed, to make you laugh and lighten you up when you become too serious. I promise to make you my famous Italian espresso when you bake those delicious lemon bars. Elise, you are the light of my life."

Elise then offered her personal vows to John.

Elise: "John, I am honored that you are awed at my acceptance of marriage. If you had not proposed to me, I would have
popped the question to you myself. You are my strength. You add
zest and meaning to my life. You are a constant reminder of what
is important in life. I am always overjoyed to return to you at the
end of a busy day in court. You provide a safe haven for me. I
promise to do my best to listen to your needs, even though listening is difficult for me—I promise to work on that. I will hold you
and comfort you when you need a soft stroke. I will remind you of
your strength and your gentleness. I promise to make those lemon
bars—mostly only on weekends—and I insist that you continue
making that wonderful Italian espresso with one clause: that you
serve it to me in bed. John, you are the love of my life."

After a simple exchange of rings, a very short Chinese saying
was offered, read by a friend of the bride and groom. This was followed by the final benediction and the pronouncement.

Joseph and Kerri: A Thirty-Five-Minute Elegant and Formal Nondenominational Christian Ceremony Accompanied by Thunder and Bagpipes

As a clergyperson, it is always an honor to officiate the wedding
of one's own child. So, there was no hesitation when my husband
and I were invited to officiate the ceremony of my son, Joseph,
and our daughter–in–law, Kerri.

They planned a rather formal affair at a delightfully picturesque museum setting in northern Westchester County, New York.
They were both particularly impressed with the ceremony site,
situated on a small, natural stone island. This island, linked by a

stone footpath, is nestled within a frog pond fringed with flowering shrubbery and so liberally covered with floating water lilies that the water is barely visible.

Joseph and Kerri hired a bagpiper to "lead in" the bride. The long and winding walkway from the museum to the frog pond offered the processing wedding party a dramatic, pageant-like bridal path.

Alas, after one of the most glorious weeks of May, the morning of the wedding began with a torrential hurricane-like rainstorm that continued throughout the day and long into the evening. Cousins who flew in from England were shocked at the unrelenting, thunderous downpour; it reminded them—a little too much—of the damp, overcast Yorkshire moors. So, within a tent appended to the museum's main building, the ceremony commenced. To the monotonous white-noise hum of rain, punctuated with the crackle of thunder, the ceremony began with the haunting wail of bagpipes. It was truly dramatic.

The ceremony, reflecting both Joseph and Kerri's primarily Celtic roots, combined English, Irish, and Scottish traditional elements. A surprising addition, to honor Joseph's Italian ancestry, was the offering of an Italian reading by Joseph's Aunt Nietta, who is originally from Italy.

When we met for the wedding consultation, Joseph strongly insisted that I reword the "declarations and promises" portion of the vows, so that I could read these declarations and promises as questions *to* him, rather than have him follow a prompt-and-response format. He, in turn, would answer "Yes," "I do," or "I will." His concern was that he might "freeze" during the exchange of vows segment. Because of his concern, of course I agreed. I do encounter couples from time to time who make this request to me. (See Chapter 8, on the exchange of vows and rings.)

There are four parts to the exchange of vows: the questions and agreements, the statement of acceptance, declarations and promises (optional), and the exchange of rings (also optional). All that is legally required is that the questions and agreements are answered; therefore, we were free to reformulate the declarations and promises and tack them onto the questions-and-agreements section.

The choice of wedding party attendants was clearly unique and creative—as were their titles. Joseph asked his sister to be his "best woman." He asked his other sister to be his "groom's woman." Though she included her two sisters as maid of honor and bridesmaid, Kerri requested also that her brother be her "brides-man." (See Chapter 4, on creating your own processional tradition.)

The ceremony began with an opening benediction, followed by an opening welcome and a Celtic prayer. The bride and groom, predictably, decided to do away with tradition, once again, by asking their fathers to assist during the unity candle-lighting ceremony. They were appointed on-the-spot as "candle ceremony assistants" and "keepers of the flame." The pre-vows charge used is outlined in Chapter 9. The format we agreed upon for the vows and ring exchange was perfect: it necessitated nothing more than an affirmative response from the bride and groom, allaying any performance anxiety, particularly on the part of Joseph.

Exchange of Vows

Celebrant: "As you join with one another today in marriage before Almighty God and before these witnesses, I ask you, Joseph/ Kerri: 'Do you take Kerri/Joseph to be your wife/husband?'"

Groom/Bride: "I do."

Celebrant: "Do you promise to respect and support her/him, to be patient with her/him, to work together with her/him to achieve your individual and your mutual goals, to accept and respect his/her unique and special gifts, to communicate openly, to listen carefully, to inspire and to uphold one another, to celebrate your similarities, to respect your differences, to express your love for one another, to always be full of gratitude for the gift of the love that you both share? Do you, before God and this company, offer these fervent and heartfelt vows and promises this day and all the days of your life?"

Groom/Bride: "I do."

Exchange of Rings

Celebrant: "Place this ring upon your bride's/groom's finger. As you place this ring upon the hand of your bride/groom, I ask you before almighty God, do you give your promise that from this day forward, your hearts are joined and your lives are united as a pledge of your constant faith and abiding devotion?"

Groom/Bride: "I do."

After the Celtic hand-fasting ceremony, the final pronouncement, the first nuptial kiss, and the presentation, the wedding party recessed to the sound of rain and howling wind, which competed unsuccessfully with the ancient Celtic jig-like recessional anthem played by the bagpiper. With his kilt flipping and swinging rhythmically, his shoulders squared, his chin tucked, he ceremoniously—and very seriously—marched them out. It was truly and breathtakingly dramatic!

Lisa and Kip:
A Twenty-Minute, Lightly Humorous, Spiritual Ceremony

When I met Kip and Lisa for the ceremony consultation, our bond was instantaneous. They were articulate in their ideas and overall joint vision for the ceremony. Their overriding criterion was that the ceremony wording and content be authentic to the two of them. On this, they were unequivocal! It was settled, then: no soppy clichés and platitudes for these two.

These two great people are dynamic, ethical, intellectual, and nonreligious yet spiritually idealistic. Both are extremely creative and so much fun to be with. Kip, a musician, is smart, sharp, bright, and funny. Lisa is a teacher; she is a witty and brilliant writer. They make a perfect team for a joint collaboration in ceremony writing. They are also a wonderful and caring couple. In addition to writing their foundation address (see Chapter 8 for more information about the foundation address), they also wrote their own vows, which I have included. They combined the statement of acceptance and the declaration and promises, directly following the legally required questions and answers.

The Marriage Foundation Address *(written by Lisa and Kip)*

Celebrant: "Marriage is the opportunity to grow in love and friendship. We all seek someone to share the life we choose, someone to help us through the never-ending attempt to understand ourselves. In the end, we seek someone to comfort us along the way. Marriages do not fail; people fail when they enter into marriage expecting another person to make them whole.

"Love does not consist of gazing at each other, but rather in looking outward together in the same direction. Let your individuality be your strength. Treat yourselves and each other with respect. Remind yourselves often of what brought you together. Give the highest priority to the tenderness, gentleness, and kindness that your connection deserves. When frustration, difficulties, and fear assail your relationship, remember to focus on what is right between you, not only on what seems wrong. In this way, you can ride out the storms. Remember even if you lose sight of it for the moment, the sun is still there. If each of you takes responsibility for the quality of your life together, your marriage will continue to grow in depth and understanding that will foster a true partnership. The words you speak today are just a first step in the lifelong journey that you will accompany each other on, as you walk side by side into the future."

Kip: "What I love about Lisa is that she will stick with me through just about anything.

"She is an excellent listener, even when I am talking in circles and making little sense. She doesn't mind when I ask her random questions about anything, she pretty much always has an answer for me, too. She is very intelligent and knowledgeable about so very many things. She fully supports my musical instrument habit. She introduced me to the wonderful world of Harry Potter. She is strong and independent, even feisty. She has a calming influence on me. We balance each other like a scale—yin and yang, if you will."

Lisa: "What I love about Kip is that he is passionate about so many things—his interests, his music. When he takes something on, he is absolutely absorbed in it. He is always in search of something new. He is always growing and surprising me. He never bores me. He is so very funny—sometimes childlike, sometimes clever. He has a really warm heart, so caring and generous. He never holds back."

The Exchange of Wedding Vows *(written by Lisa and Kip)*

Celebrant: "Kip, do you take Lisa as your wife?"

Kip: "I do."

Celebrant: "Kip, do you promise to love Lisa, with all her strengths and faults? To make her laugh at life's absurdities? To trust her judgment as well as your own? To offer a cup of tea and a back rub when she has had a rough day? To give her space when needed? To always speak your mind? To listen when she speaks hers? To celebrate your similarities and respect your differences? And to always vote Democrat? Do you choose Lisa as the person with whom you will spend your life?"

Kip: "I do."

Celebrant: "Lisa, do you take Kip as your husband?"

Lisa: "I do."

Celebrant: "Lisa, do you promise to love Kip with all his strengths and faults? To make him laugh at life's absurdities? To trust his judgment as well as your own? To flatter his music profusely? To give him space when needed? To always speak your mind? To listen when he speaks his? To celebrate your similarities and respect your differences? To always vote Democrat? Do you choose Kip as the person with whom you will spend your life?"

Lisa: "I do."

Ginny and Alan: A Thirty-Minute, Come-as-You-Are, Universally Spiritual Garden Ceremony

When I officiated the home wedding ceremony of my friends Ginny and Alan, I anticipated a ceremony that would be like no other in terms of content, style, and uniqueness. The fact that they are an interfaith couple is not an issue in their lives nor was it reflected in their ceremony. Neither of them practices their respective religions of birth. They are both very spiritual and opted for a universally spiritual ceremony, which included Native American and earth-honoring traditions. A unity candle-lighting ceremony, in which all of the guests participated, and the Jewish wine ceremony were also included. The groom himself offered the wine blessing in Hebrew. In addition, Buddhist and Hindu prayers were recited. The ceremony setting was an outdoor altar constructed in their backyard under a great sprawling oak tree. In the early dusk shadows, the guests formed a circle around the bride and groom. Ginny's son Noah read a poem by Rumi. What I found most remarkable was the intentional lack of preparation. The couple opted to speak extemporaneously as the spirit moved them. Since a celebrant is legally bound to ask the specific questions of acceptance, Alan agreed to the questions providing they could be reworded. Rather than asking, "Alan, do you take Ginny to be your wife?" Alan's suggestion was "Alan, will you receive Ginny as your wife, your life partner, and your deepest love?" I have since asked their permission to use their version of the questions of acceptance in some of my other ceremonies, to which they graciously assented.

The mostly extemporaneous wording precluded a written record of the ceremony. During the ceremony, dusk crept into evening, which necessitated the holding of a candle by each guest. After the ceremony, we all gathered indoors, where we were treated to an informal buffet-style dinner of the most scrumptious Thai food, while Ginny's teenage son Noah serenaded us with Beatles songs while strumming his guitar. Because of the nature of the ceremony, my own outline was rather scant and, alas, the dripping candle wax pretty much obscured what was left of it. Miraculously—and thankfully—Alan wrote and saved a few notes of his personal wedding vows to Ginny; the rest we reconstructed from memory.

The following vows to Ginny from Alan are excerpts from one of the most unique and deeply soulful wedding vows exchange I have had the pleasure to witness. Each time I re-read them, they leave me breathless. My own contribution to this ceremony, in terms of wording, was practically nonexistent.

The Vows

Alan: "Ginny, I promise, I vow, I make a commitment, I choose: to open and reopen my heart, my mind, my body to you; to your beauty inside and out; to your wisdom, spoken and unspoken; to your passion for life and for me; to your love that heals and comforts everyone you touch, and of which you have chosen to give so much to me (for which I am so grateful). I promise, vow, commit, and choose to open and reopen inwardly to access the love, the beauty, the wisdom, the will, the passion that is inside me, and to share it with you abundantly. I promise to open to your needs and sometimes pull away, to contract, to be afraid or sad or angry, even though that might scare me. I promise to continue to stay with my love for you and with *our* love and to trust our journey. I promise to share with you making the coffee in the morning, washing the dishes, cleaning the house, the laundry, the gardening, the shopping, the cooking, making the bed and supporting Noah *(Ginny's teen-age son)* in becoming the creative, strong, wise man that he is."

Though Ginny and I racked our brains trying to remember and reconstruct her vows to Alan, all that Ginny can recall is the following:

Ginny: "Alan, from the depth of my heart, I faithfully promise that whenever I get mad at you and peal out of the driveway, I will always return."

Speaking for myself, I believe that I was so awestruck and deeply moved by Alan's vows to Ginny that they may still have been echoing in my heart and mind, thereby obliterating my recall of Ginny's words.

Carolyn and James: **An Informal, Thirty-Minute Poolside Remarriage Ceremony to a Former Spouse**

When I received a call from Carolyn and James requesting my services, they informed me that Helene and Adolfo had kindly recommended me to them. (Helene and Adolfo are the lovely couple featured in Chapter 5, in the section "Mazel Tov: The Breaking of the Foot.") The ceremony of Carolyn and James was to take place at the home of Helene and Adolfo, in a garden setting by their pool. They live in the picturesque town of Cold Spring, New York, nestled on the shore of the Hudson River, offering a spectacular view of West Point Military Academy situated on the opposite shore.

When we met for the consultation, I was surprised to discover that Carolyn and James had been married and divorced—to and from each other. This was the first time in my ministry that I have officiated a remarriage to the same person. What a remarkable honor!

Carolyn and James met when they were children and lived in the same neighborhood. They continued their friendship throughout young adulthood and they predictably fell in love. They eloped and were married for twenty-six years. Once divorced, they discovered to their surprise that what they missed most about each other was the deep and intimate friendship that had grown and flourished throughout the years of their marriage. As a result, they began to feel bereft of that deep comradeship. The solution to the void they now experienced in their separated lives was to remain friends. They realized that their friendship had never for a moment faltered. They counted on one another for support and counsel, they relied upon each other when issues arose regarding their children, and they celebrated together the birth of their many grandchildren. What I find most significant (and most extraordinary) is that they actually double-dated when they were each dating other people!

After an eleven-year "sabbatical," they decided it was now time to reconnect. When I asked them for the defining moment and reason as to why they felt it was time to rejoin in marriage, they both said: "We are connected to one another at the level of the soul. We are soul-mates; soul-friends." Being privy to such tender moments is an enormous honor. I realized that I could not have been as articulate in expressing these sentiments as were they.

Admittedly, I listen very carefully to the way my clients express their feelings and to the words they choose. After this consultation, my mind rewound and replayed their mutual use of the terms soul-mate and soul-friend, and I began researching ceremonies that incorporated those terms. We were in luck! The Celtic *"Anam Cara"* or "Loving Cup" ceremony not only incorporates the identical wording we were looking for, but in addition, James is of Celtic origin. We knew this ceremonial expression of love and union was perfect for these two. Following are excerpts from their remarriage ceremony, which I carefully and thoughtfully reworded:

Opening Benediction

Celebrant: "Dear God, we offer thanks to You for the great miracle of love. We thank you also for the great depth and power of this love, which You in Your great wisdom and generosity have bestowed upon Carolyn and James. Theirs is a love that will not diminish and that will not let them go. This love with which they have been blessed by You is of such magnitude that they stand here before You once again and ask You to place your Divine Hand upon their lives and sanctify this union of hearts, of lives and of families. Amen."

Opening Welcome and Marriage Foundation

Celebrant: Carolyn and James, today is your wedding day, a day of reconnection, and yet this day is a day you will always remember, one of the greatest and most important in anyone's life. Once again, you begin this day as two people in love, and once again, end it as husband and wife. This is the beginning of a new journey, a new chapter in your lives. Yet, it is familiar. All of your individual hopes and dreams will now be joined and rejoined. Some are different and some are the same. Yet, they become woven together for the greater good of your union. Once again, you now become a team who together build a marriage, requiring the very best that you each can be. As the marriage begins to take form, so do your individual characters. You two are the authors of this life that you share and build. Yet, the very process of doing so, of committing to the creating of this marriage, will in fact build *you*...will build your inner strength and character. Most importantly, this will deepen and open your hearts. For the greatest characteristic in this union is love. Love is what will support and sustain you over the years. The depth of the love you have shared is what never allowed you to wander far away from one another. Marriage is like a mirror of your own heart, reflecting back to you in your life together all that you are. As each one of you now can attest, a union is unbroken when the strength of love is unbreakable. For the love that brought you together is the love that brought you back to one another. This love is the love that will hold you together as God has ordained. For a love of this magnitude is divine and sacred."

The Celtic *Anam Cara*, or Loving Cup Ceremony

Celebrant: "Wine is the symbol of life. This Loving Cup in which it is contained symbolizes both of your lives, which are to be joined together today, as will your fates and your futures be so joined. Carolyn and James, as you each share wine from this Loving Cup, you are symbolically sharing a life together. Please face your beloved and repeat."

Celebrant, with pauses, repeated aloud by Carolyn and James: "Today I accept you as my Anam Cara, my soul friend. I invite you to become a part of my life in the sacred kinship of marriage. I will share with you my thoughts and deepest longings. I will share with you my heart, my love, and my life. In times of fear and uncertainty, I offer you my courage to help strengthen you and my compassion to help to comfort you. In times of abundance and plentitude, we will joyfully celebrate our gratitude together. We each have once again found one another our *Anam Cara*. And a new beginning has dawned in our lives. You have awakened in me a rebirth, a new beginning.

"We are now home again within each other's hearts, for we two have become one."

Exchange of Vows

Celebrant: "Therefore I ask you, James, after the passing of these years, will you once again receive Carolyn as your beloved wife?"

James: "I will."

Celebrant: "Will you continue to love, honor, respect, and cherish her? Will you give thanks to and for her, not only in your words but also in your actions? Will you continue to honor and support her growth and aspirations?"

James: "I will."

Celebrant: "Therefore I ask you, Carolyn, after the passing of these years, will you once again receive James as your beloved husband?"

Carolyn: "I will."

Celebrant: "Will you continue to love, honor, respect, and cherish him? Will you give thanks to and for him, not only in your words but also in your actions? Will you continue to honor and support his growth and aspirations?"

Carolyn: "I will."

Ed and Natasja: A Thirty-Five Minute Ecumenical, Come-As-You-Are Outdoor Ceremony (as featured in *The New York Times*)

Mutual friends referred Ed and Natasja to me. They are both unbelievably relaxed and easygoing, to the extent that the night before their July outdoor wedding, the bride calmly stated that she wasn't sure what kind of food they would serve, how many guests would show up, or what they would do if it rained. "We'll know by tomorrow," she said. "The only thing we're sure of is that we're getting married."

Natasja is a dancer who studied and performed with the Dance Theater of Harlem in New York, and now teaches ballet and tap. She had met Ed ten months earlier at a street fair in Nyack, New York. They got along so well that a few months after they met, Ed drove down to the bride's apartment in Riverdale, New York, to move her to his home in Nyack.

The way they planned their wedding was downright, nail-bitingly terrifying, even to the most carefree and casual of couples. They relied on fortune, helpful friends, and happenstance. No one—not even the bride and groom—knew exactly how things would turn out.

Eighty or so guests began arriving at the wedding site, a picnic area on Hook Mountain in Nyack, New York, and then everything began to flow. A few of the guests set up chairs in rows at the bottom of a rock cliff. Some decorated the trees by tying sunflowers and ribbons to the branches, and others brought trays of food and laid them out on the buffet table. A musician friend arrived, just in case they needed musical accompaniment.

The bride and groom had requested that guests "come as you are." The particularly good-looking groom arrived wearing a baggy white linen outfit, sandals, and sunglasses, and even though he carried a single, slightly wilted, sunflower, he still managed to look elegant as he gracefully entered. The bride, in a white sleeveless linen dress, put together her wedding party on the spot, inviting children from the crowd to walk down the aisle with her.

As hawks circled overhead, the ceremony took place at a site the couple had spontaneously chosen, under a magnificent shade tree.

Ed and Natasja wrote their own vows. In honor of the natural setting by the Hudson River, the Apache wedding blessing was read, and friends gave from-the-heart extemporaneous speeches. Afterward, guests sat or perched for a picnic, and although it was a surprise to the couple, there was even a wedding cake, brought by the groom's mother.

When interviewed by the journalist covering the ceremony for *The New York Times,* I offered the following insights: "They trusted their friends were going to bring enough food, and they did. They trusted the weather was going to be perfect, and it was. Beforehand, I said: 'Let's be realistic, what happens if it rains?' and their joint answer was a casual, 'We'll do it the next day.' That is their style. They just went with the flow. Natasja is a dancer, and her work is all about flow, and that's how they see things."

Scottie Mirviss and Paul Carvajal: Fifteen-Minute, Simple Ecumenical Ceremony Following a Forty-Minute Quaker Ritual Silence (as featured in *The New York Times*)

Though Scottie is Jewish and Paul is Christian, they opted for this unusual blending of traditions. They both have a love for the Quaker wedding ritual. Their wedding ceremony was held at a Friends Meeting House in Manhattan, which featured pro-environment and pacifist pamphlets in the lobby. Had someone entered during the first half-hour of the ceremony, they might have been rather puzzled and not even recognized it as a wedding ceremony at all. The guests sat quietly and contemplatively. Quaker weddings, like Quaker meetings, follow no scheduled agenda or written text; participants wait quietly in respectful silence until someone is moved to speak. Each person prompted to speak, according to Quakerism, is inspired by God to do so. Though the ceremony itself is conducted in silence, during this period of silence anyone gathered is free to speak up and offer words or blessings as the spirit moves them. Some may express their love for the couple, others may offer up prayers. Since these words arise out of mutual stillness and prayerfulness, these spoken expressions are highly respected and are considered inspired by the presence of God.

A traditional Quaker wedding ritual is conducted *without* a celebrant. Since a celebrant is legally required to officiate and solemnize a marriage, the couple usually becomes legally married before the Quaker ceremony.

This unusual ceremony included a combination of both a celebrant-officiated ceremony and a Quaker-style ceremony. I was slightly concerned that the guests would be restless and bored. I need not have worried; the guests were receptive and extraordinarily peaceful. I suspect that many of those attending may have been practicing Quakers. As the minutes ticked by, the gentle flow of silence was punctuated by the inspired comments of the guests, some of whom offered touching anecdotes about how the bride and groom met, others of whom quietly recited extemporaneous prayers.

At the close of the period of "silence," the simple ceremony began. The universally spiritual opening benediction and opening welcome were followed by a short and simple marriage foundation address. The highlight of the ceremony was the exchange of vows that Scottie and Paul wrote themselves, which included promises to share "equal financial responsibilities." The following final pronouncement was declared: "I now pronounce you wife and husband."

Review Checklist

❑ Check with your wedding hall location to determine the time span allotted for the ceremony.

❑ If you have not already done so, construct a hypothetical ceremony outline, including your favorite ceremony components.

❑ Review the section on ceremony timelines and determine, logistically and realistically, whether the length you are planning on is realistic and feasible.

❑ Review the information on creative and unusual ceremonies to determine whether there are ideas and components that inspire you. Is it possible to incorporate some of these ideas without compromising your own unique vision for a customized ceremony?

❑ If so, you have now begun the creation of your wedding ceremony outline.

Chapter Eight:
The Text: Words for Your Ceremony

The Power and Poetry, Wisdom and Wonder of Words

Writing a ceremony is all about the selection of the words you use. Remember the three rules of ceremony construction? They are: *meaning, authenticity,* and *flow*. In these final stages of ceremony construction, consider these rules as you think about the wording. Though some of the following points have been covered in previous chapters, they bear repeating.

At the very core of the ceremony lies the fact that this is a public declaration. Though this ceremony is all about the two of you, others also witness it. Therefore, while selecting ceremony wording, bear in mind that your guests will be witnesses to every word you choose.

Do not include words that could potentially embarrass your partner or your guests.

Do not suddenly decide to speak extemporaneously without pre-thought of what you will say. Though there are some exceptions, this generally does not work.

Do not decide to crack jokes during the ceremony. Unless you are a professional comedian, it rarely works.

Do not use unnecessary words or long-winded speeches. Waxing too long will bore your guests to tears. They will simply "zone out." Keep it short.

Remember that the words you choose have a profound effect on all who attend your ceremony and can remain in their memories for the rest of their lives. In addition, if you hire a videographer, there will be a permanent aural record of the ceremony.

Do not give guest readers/speakers freedom to say whatever they wish during the ceremony. Most readers have no idea about ceremony time constraints. They often drone on and digress. Speeches are appropriate for the reception, not the ceremony. *You* choose the reading and the length of time it will occupy in the ceremony, and make it clear it is to be adhered to.

Do not be unclear about the tone you want your ceremony wording to take. Talk it over with your fiancé and then decide.

Finally, keep your words meaningful and authentic. Words expressed from the heart have a natural, organic rhythm and flow.

Words of Promise

To respect each other's uniqueness

To respect each other's individuality

To share the good times and the bad times

To share times of joy and times of adversity

To share times of joy and times of sorrow

To share the ups and downs of life

To love and honor one another

To love and respect one another

To love and cherish one another

To listen to one another

To honor each other's life journey and growth

To grow together

To be open to one another

To be honest and trusting

To be honest and understanding

To be a good friend

To be a true companion

To be a loving life partner

To bring joy into the marriage

To bring joy and laughter into the marriage

Descriptive Words

Absolute	Charming	Endearing
Admiring	Compassionate	Enduring
Adorable	Concerned	Engaging
Adoring	Confident	Enlivening
Alert	Considerate	Enthusiastic
Alive	Constant	Exhilarating
Amazing	Contented	Exquisite
Appealing	Courageous	Exultant
Ardent	Dedicated	Faithful
Astonishing	Delighted	Fascinating
Authentic	Delightful	Fulfilling
Beauteous	Dependable	Gallant
Beautiful	Devoted	Gentle
Blissful	Ecstatic	Glorious
Captivating	Effervescent	Glowing
Celebrated	Elated	Helpful
Certain	Enchanting	Honorable

Important	Romantic	**Verbs**
Inspired	Safe	Acknowledge
Intriguing	Secure	Affirm
Invigorating	Sensitive	Appreciate
Joyful	Serene	Aspire
Joyous	Significant	Assert
Jubilant	Splendid	Assure
Kind	Steadfast	Avow
Loving	Sure	Commit
Loyal	Tender	Confide
Magnificent	Thoughtful	Confirm
Momentous	Thrilled	Declare
Ongoing	Total	Defend
Optimistic	Touched	Embrace
Overjoyed	Tranquil	Empathize
Peaceful	True	Encourage
Perceptive	Trustworthy	Endeavor
Permanent	Truthful	Entrust
Positive	Unchanging	Establish
Predestined	Undying	Help
Preordained	Unfailing	Honor
Protected	Unswerving	Inspire
Radiant	Unwavering	Listen
Rapturous	Warm	Love
Receptive	Wonderful	Pledge
Reliable	Wondrous	Proclaim
Responsive	Worthy	Promise

Pronounce	Safeguard	Understand
Protect	Seek	Validate
Realize	State	Value
Reassure	Strive	Verify
Respect	Support	Welcome
Reveal	Swear	

Word combinations (phrases)

The depth of my love

A measure of my love

A symbol of my love

A marriage built on love

A marriage built on mutual respect

A relationship built on love and respect

A bond of eternal love

All the days of our life together

All of our days together

All of our tomorrows

May all love surround us

May we stand together in a circle of love

Cherish and love

Cherish, love, and respect

Companion in life

Companion in love

For each moment together

For eternity together

For all of eternity

For all of our tomorrows

For an eternity of tomorrows

From this day forward

From the core of my heart

From the depth of my heart

From my heart of hearts

To stand together in a circle of love

To support and uphold one another

To join my heart with your heart

To join our hearts

To join my life with your life

To join our lives

To walk together hand in hand

To offer myself to you in love

To share my life with your life

To share my heart with your heart

To honor your growth as well as my own

To share our dreams together

To support your dreams

To support your aspirations

In sickness and in health

In joy and in sorrow

Throughout the ebb and flow of life

In the presence of God

In the presence of Almighty God

In the presence of all that is Divine

In the presence of all that is Holy

In the presence of all that is Holy and Sacred

In the presence of all that is Sacred and Divine

In the presence of friends and family as witnesses

Before all who are gathered here

Before all who gather here as witnesses

Words of personal endearment

Adored	Friend	Playfellow
Ally	Honey	Precious
Angel	Life companion	Soul friend
Beloved	Life mate	Soul mate
Companion	Life partner	Sweet
Darling	Love	Sweetest one
Dear	Lover	Sweetheart
Dearest	Mate	Treasure
Dearest one	Partner	

Words Describing Personal Attributes

Absorbing	Beguiling	Charitable
Alluring	Brave	Charming
Amusing	Bubbly	Cheerful
Animated	Candid	Chivalrous
Appealing	Candor	Clarity
Attractive	Captivating	Clear
Beauteous	Caring	Committed
Beautiful	Charisma	Compassionate
Beauty	Charismatic	Constant

Consistent	Humility	Reliable
Courage	Humor	Significance
Courageous	Humorous	Significant
Decent	Important	Simplicity
Dependability	Incorruptible	Sincere
Dependable	Independent	Sparkling
Determination	Innocence	Spirited
Devoted	Innocent	Splendid
Effervescent	Integrity	Splendor
Effortlessness	Interesting	Steadfast
Elegance	Intriguing	Steady
Enthralling	Joyful	Straightforward
Enticing	Kind	Tender
Faithful	Kindness	Transparent
Fascinating	Lively	Trustworthy
Fidelity	Loveliness	Truthful
Fond	Lovely	Unassuming
Frank	Loyal	Virtuous
Funny	Magnificent	Wholesome
Generous	Meaningful	Wit
Generosity	Mesmerizing	Witty
Gentle	Modest	Worth
Gorgeous	Open	
Grace	Plucky	
Graceful	Positive	
Gracious	Pure	
Honest	Purity	

Negative Words

The following list includes words that need to be carefully considered before use, although in the right context, some of these words may work. For example, you might say "I will stand by you in times of abundance and in times of *scarcity*." Or, "I will faithfully support and stand by you in times of hope and in times of *despair*." My suggestion is that you choose these words consciously and carefully.

Anger	Envy	Poverty
Annoyance	Failing	Powerless
Apprehension	Failure	Pressures
Bereft	Fear	Problems
Deficient	Forsaken	Sadness
Depressed	Frailty	Scarcity
Deprived	Grief	Sorrow
Devoid	Grieving	Suffering
Difficulty	Ignore	Suspicion
Disadvantage	Jealousy	Trials
Disregard	Lack	Tribulations
Disrespect	Limitations	Trouble
Distress	Misfortune	Unhappiness
Distrust	Neediness	Weakness
Emptiness	Neglect	

Twenty-Nine Words Never to Include in a Ceremony

Abandonment	Excruciating
Abhorrent	Gloom
Abominable	Hopelessness
Agonizing	Loathsome
Anguish	Misery
Besmirched	Rage
Contemptible	Resentment
Degraded	Ruination
Dejected	Tainted
Desolation	Torment
Despicable	Torturous
Despondency	Unbearable
Detestable	Vile
Disgraceful	Wretched
Disreputable	

The Opening Benediction and Invocation

First, a little clarification about the terms invocation and benediction. Though both are similar and often used interchangeably, there are subtle differences. An invocation is generally an appeal to a higher power, acknowledging or naming a higher power, or a short prayer calling upon God for help. The word benediction is less of an appeal and more of a request, a hope or affirmation of approval and blessings.

My personal feeling is that the invocation can sometimes be slightly more urgent or fervent a petition to God, whereas the benediction is a more relaxed joining with God in the expression of approval and good wishes.

When deciding on the invocation and benediction for a particular ceremony, this is the rule of thumb: For a more religious ceremony, the invocation should be emphasized by referring to God personally and directly. For example, "Dear Lord, we ask that you shower forth Your holy and sacred blessings today upon the bride and groom." For a lighter, less religious ceremony, the invocation needs less emphasis. Instead of calling upon God directly, we can refer to God indirectly, in the third person. For example: "We call upon the Divine Essence of Infinite Love to bless this union."

I generally like to weave the two together, beginning with the invocation and ending with the benediction. By the way, including an opening benediction does not preclude the use of a final benediction at the close of the ceremony.

The invocation, benediction, or prayer marks the beginning of the ceremony. It is at this point in time that we call upon and acknowledge the name and presence of God. This is the precise moment that the ritual becomes a sacred rite. The reciting of the invocation and benediction is what differentiates a civil ceremony from a spiritual ceremony. Once the name of God is invoked, the spiritual theme of the ceremony has been set, whether or not the overall wording remains similar in content and tone to the initial benediction or invocation.

In invoking the Divine Presence, the ceremony space is sanctified: God is present. The bridal couple and all who are gathered are "held" in a space made sacred and divinely blessed. Thus, they too are blessed.

For those whose preference is to have less emphasis on God, or whose concept of God is more universally spiritual than it is religious, there are many alternative invocations.

To begin, decide on the tone of the benediction in terms of the reference to God. Let us assume you have worked with the spirituality questionnaire in Chapter 2. You may now have a clear (or clearer) idea of where you fit in terms of your own personal spirituality and your perception of God. Ask yourself what your preferences are in terms of invoking God in the ceremony. Some couples would rather omit the word "God" altogether. There are many beautiful ways of invoking or calling forth benedictions. The following list offers forty-nine ways of invoking the Divine Presence. In twenty-six of them, the words God, Lord, Father, Holy, and Divine have been omitted entirely, and other terms have been carefully and respectfully substituted.

The following invocations include the words God, Lord, Father, Holy and Divine:

All that is Divine

All that is Holy and Divine

All that is Sacred and Holy

Beloved God

Dear Lord

Dearest Lord

Divine Presence

Divine Spirit

Essence of Divine Love

Eternal and Divine Presence

Eternal and Ever Living God

Eternal and Holy Presence

Eternal God

Father

Father God

Father-Mother God

God of Love and Light

Holy Power of Infinite Love

Holy Presence

Holy Spirit

Infinite Presence of Divinity

Sacred and Divine Power of Love

Sacred and Holy Presence

The following twenty-six invocations offer immense possibilities to those wishing to substitute a religious invocation with a universally spiritual yet nonreligious equivalent.

All that is sacred

Blessed and eternal spirit of love

Essence of infinite love

Essence of love

Eternal power of love

Eternal and infinite spirit

Eternal and infinite spirit of love

Eternal and universal Presence

Font of all blessings

Spirit of all that is sacred

Eternal essence of infinite love and light

Eternal power of love and light

Great and infinite power of love

Great Spirit of love

Higher power

Higher power of love

Higher power of love and light

Infinite love

Infinite Presence

Infinite Presence of love and light

Infinite Spirit of all that is sacred

Sacred power of love

Sacred power of love and light

Sacred spirit

Spirit of all that is sacred

Spirit of love and light

The Invocation

Invocation 1:
Celebrant: "Eternal God, as we join together today to witness the marriage of (name) and (name), we ask for Your blessings."

Invocation 2:
Celebrant: "As we gather here today, we call upon all that is Divine and Sacred to bless the marriage of (name) and (name)."

Invocation 3:
Celebrant: "Lord of Love and Light, we call upon Your infinite power of love and benedictions to bless and sanctify the coming together of (name) and (name) in marriage."

Invocation 4:
Celebrant: "We call upon the Power of Infinite Love to shower forth blessings upon the joining in marriage of (name) and (name)."

Invocation 5:
Celebrant: "Eternal and Infinite Spirit of Love and Light, we invoke Your Presence as we gather here today in joy to witness the joining in marriage of (name) and (name)."

Invocation 6:
Celebrant: "God of Love and Light: we call forth the power of the Holy Spirit to bless and sanctify the marriage of (name) and (name)."

Invocation 7:

Celebrant: "Sacred and Divine Power of Love: We call upon Your blessings and benedictions as we witness the joining together of the lives of (name) and (name) in the bond of marriage."

Invocation 8:

Celebrant: "Power of Infinite Love, we are gathered today in Your Presence to give thanks for the gift of love, and to witness the joining together of (name) and (name) in the sacred path of marriage."

The Combined Opening Benediction and Invocation

Opening Benediction and Invocation 1:

Celebrant: "Great and Infinite Power of Love: We join together our hearts and minds in the spirit of prayerfulness as we celebrate the union of (name) and (name) in the sacred and joyous bond of marriage.

"May the height and depth of their devotion be made fully known to one another, through their steadfast and unwavering commitment to this union of love. As the years stretch out before them, may their lives be filled with joy, deep peace, strength, courage, and perpetual blessings. And so it is. Amen."

Opening Benediction and Invocation 2:

Celebrant: "Divine Spirit, Font of All Blessings: We gather here today in joy and awe as we stand in Your Presence and enter into quiet prayerfulness. As family and friends of (name) and (name), we celebrate their joining in marriage. We offer up our deepest gratitude to You and we rejoice that these two have been blessed to have found this love that they share. We ask that the love between them grows broader and deeper with the passing years. May this union be filled with mutual trust and genuine affection. May these qualities of spirit stand them in good stead when difficulties and challenges assail them. May the sheer strength of their loving union forge a great shield of power and courage that they both can share. May this love that they share double their joy. May each of us here share this exquisite moment and as witnesses may we also be blessed. Amen."

Opening Benediction and Invocation 3:

Celebrant: "Sacred and Divine Power of Love, we invoke Your Sacred and holy Presence. We thank You for this miraculous day of celebration, for the fulfillment of love that we witness before us, and for the joy and honor of participating in this blessed occasion. As the bride and groom exchange their vows to one another that will unite them forever, may each gathered here unite in upholding and supporting their choice to marry.

"Lord, allow the words they share today to stand firm and true throughout the ups and downs of their lives together, so that they may call upon these words for comfort and inspiration. Let Your love and blessings shower forth upon them and upon each gathered here as witnesses. Amen."

Opening Benediction and Invocation 4:

Celebrant: "Dearly beloved, we come together in the presence of Almighty God the Father, Son, and Holy Spirit to witness and bless the joining together of (name) and (name) in holy matrimony. The bond and covenant of marriage was established by God in creation. It signifies to us the mystery of the union between Christ and His Church, and Holy Scripture commends it to be honored among all people. Therefore, marriage is not to be entered into unadvisedly or lightly, but reverently and in accordance with the purposes for which it was instituted by God. Amen."

Opening Benediction and Invocation 5:

Celebrant: "Holy Power of Infinite Love: we gather together before You as we witness, honor, and celebrate the joining together of (name) and (name) in marriage, which is a blessed and honorable estate, and from time immemorial considered the most intimate and noble of human relationships.

"As we stand firmly in the presence of all that is Holy and Divine, we ask that this union be blessed, protected, sanctified and guided by Your infinite love. May each one gathered as witnesses to this sacred covenant know in their hearts, that this ceremony is but an outward sign of something inner and deeper, a union of hearts that already exists, and which we now formalize and sanction before each person gathered. The role of each one gathered here as witnesses is to join and unify in their well wishes and blessings for the bride and groom. May all that is showered forth upon these two this day be returned and doubled as gifts and blessings to this community of loving family and friends. Amen."

Opening Benediction and Invocation 6:

Celebrant: "Divine and Eternal Spirit of Love: We ask for Your blessings today for (name) and (name) as they embark upon the path of marriage. May they enter this union fully blessed and guided by Your Sacred Presence. May each one gathered be loving witnesses to this union. May our lives be blessed and our hearts moved deeply by the words and the promises made today. May each gathered here support and empower (name) and (name) with their sincere and noble wishes for these two individual lives that momentarily will be joined as one, in a marriage based on true love and deep devotion. Amen."

Opening Benediction and Invocation 7:

Celebrant: "Divine Power of Love and Light: We call upon Your blessings as we gather together in the presence of Your eternal love to witness the joining of (name) and (name) in marriage. We pray that each of them find deep and profound gentleness, joy, and caring in this union that will provide a loving sanctuary as they journey through their shared life together. Through this union, may they each bring to the other positive, loving challenges, inspiration, wisdom, and joy. As the depth of their love expands and grows, may they come to know You more fully as the Loving Presence who resides within the purity and stillness of their own hearts. Inspired by their love, as witnesses may each of us gathered here offer up our own prayers of gratitude, not only for the privilege of being present at this union, but also for the blessings You bestow upon us as witnesses. Amen."

Opening Benediction and Invocation 8:

Celebrant: "Eternal Power of Love: We gather here in the spirit of love and support, as family and friends, to witness the joining and uniting in marriage of (name) and (name). We surround them with love, we ask for blessings and support as we offer our loving thoughts and our heartfelt encouragement as they make public their commitment to each other. We rejoice with them that they have found one another. We affirm that they will henceforth find the richness and fullness of both the human and spiritual life as they join and unite with each other in a union wholly blessed. Amen."

Opening Benediction and Invocation 9:

Celebrant: "Spirit of Eternal Love: We unite our hearts and minds as we come together to witness and celebrate the marriage of (name) and (name). May all that is noble, righteous, and lovely abide within each of them as they embark upon the path of marriage. May their lives be filled with blessings and may they gain strength, stamina, and the courage to overcome life's adversities and challenges as the years advance. Help them to keep their love alive and precious by their compassion for and their commitment to one another. These prayers and petitions we offer you that each gathered here will empower and uphold these benedictions by the mere depth of their prayerful intentions for the bride and groom. Let us remember that an unselfish wish is a prayer that will draw blessings back into our own lives as witnesses to this union. Amen."

Opening Benediction and Invocation 10:

Celebrant: "Father-Mother God: We gather here together in unity, blending our hearts and minds as we align with the One Divine Mind. We join and unify our prayers and genuine good intentions for the joining together in marriage of (name) and (name). May their individual dreams and aspirations be shared. May their love blossom. May their respect for one another grow fuller, deeper, and stronger with the passing of the years. Now and forever may they be united in a love that fortifies and lights the way for one another. May the mere strength of their love shower forth inspiration and blessings upon all who enter their home and their life. This we ask in Your name. Amen."

Opening Benediction and Invocation 11:

Celebrant: "Eternal and Ever Living God: As we join together today to witness the marriage union of (name) and (name), we give thanks to You for Your Holy Presence. There is no greater gift than for two in love who are blessed by You to feel that they are joined together to strengthen each other and to minister to each other, to share with each other in all gladness, to be one with each other even in the silent moments. Bless Oh Lord this union of hearts created by loving purpose and sustained by abiding will and spirit as they enter into the estate of Holy matrimony to be joined together. May all be blessed and hallowed. Amen."

The Opening Welcome

The opening welcome is more than a greeting to all who are gathered at the ceremony; it is a way of paying tribute to the marriage itself. When the celebrant begins these opening words, she or he is setting the tone for the ceremony by the style and wording chosen. Therefore, these beginning words need to reflect the overall tone of the unfolding ceremony as the celebrant offers a statement of intention on behalf of the bride and groom.

Opening Welcome 1:

Celebrant: "Welcome. We gather here today as witnesses to celebrate the joining in marriage of (name) and (name). This ceremony is but an outer ritual of that which is deeper and real; a union of body, mind, and spirit, which religion may sanctify and the state may authorize, but which neither can create. Marriage is a public recognition of the personal experience of two in love. It is the dedication of two, to one life fully shared. It is not intended for happiness alone, but for the personal inner growth of each one, who dedicate their life to a union of mutual support and respect, through the joining of a life fully shared, through life's tests and trials given and returned and forgiven.

"We, as witnesses, are asked to hold foremost in our minds and hearts the greatest and loftiest potential and possibilities for the bride and groom, so that they may fully know the wonder of a shared life of committed loving and caring.

"May they each, as a couple joined in love, come to know both the great power and the gentle tenderness of the love they share, as they walk together through the portal of this ceremony into a new life, a new beginning as husband and wife."

Opening Welcome 2:

Celebrant: "Welcome. We gather here today as witnesses to the wonder and joy of this marriage celebration.

"As they each journeyed through their individual lives, the bride and groom found one another and now embark on a new journey and life path—the noble and wondrous path of marriage. They will freely and generously give themselves into the lives of one another and in doing so, they will each receive the love, trust, and nurturance of the other as their most precious gift. When that gift is shared by two who are in love, it also radiates out like warm sunlight, blessing the lives of others.

"Each one gathered is honored as participants and as witnesses in this holy rite of passage. As the bride and groom join their hearts and their individual lives, let each of us here send back in full measure all of our greatest and highest hopes and wishes as our greatest gift to them."

Opening Welcome 3:

Celebrant: "Welcome. We are each gathered here today as witnesses to the joining in marriage of (name) and (name). From our hearts open with joy and from our minds softened with compassion may we each avow the following affirmations:

"That the creation of this new and joyful life for the bride and groom is filled with special moments within a full lifetime together.

"That this day is the beginning of a marriage of sharing, of trust, of mutual respect, of growing together in ever-deepening gratitude and devotion."

"That this union be abundant and overflowing with a love that grows ever wider, broader, and fuller as the years progress, for a lifetime of mutual growth and unending love."

Opening Welcome 4:

Celebrant: "We gather here today in joy to witness a celebration of marriage. The bride and groom, in their mutual respect, dedication, and devotion to one another, now wish to unite in the commitment and bond of marriage.

"For each of us gathered here, our most sincere hopes and wishes are that the bride and groom be always encouraged and motivated by that radiant power of mutual love that first brought them together. The power of love is stronger and greater than the conflicts they may face. It is bigger than life's unpredictability and challenges. It always invites each of them to learn, to blossom, to grow, and to evolve. It is always to love that we must return. May each gathered here send forth their wholehearted blessings and support for the bride and groom, for the fulfillment of a life committed to love and mutual married joy."

Opening Welcome 5:

Celebrant: "Welcome. The bride and groom have carefully chosen each one of you to create this gathering, for the loving presence you have offered to them, and for your support and friendship. You have celebrated with them, believed in them, upheld and encouraged them throughout the course of their individual lives. We now ask that you witness and support the joining of these two lives entwined in one blessed union. As you do so, please remember that what you witness is but a symbol of something deeper and greater. Marriage is a contract of hearts. It is the most intimate union and bonding of two souls in love. This is the dawn of a new life for these two. It is the creation of the lifelong unfolding of mutual kindness and growing love, and it is the most important relationship that two people can share.

"Today, it is my hope that those of you who have already taken the vows of marriage will witness the depth and breadth of the special love between the bride and groom. As you hear the sharing of their avowed intentions and promises, I ask that you offer up your own blessings, and they will be returned to you in full measure.

"Perhaps it will reinforce for you the meaning of the vows you yourselves once took and in doing so will fortify your own union so that all here will be fully blessed."

Opening Welcome 6:

Celebrant: "Welcome. Love is a miraculous gift that is treasured and hallowed and for which we offer sincere gratitude. We gather here today bathed in deep thankfulness as we witness the miracle of love by celebrating the marriage of (name) and (name). May this be a day of thanksgiving and new beginnings for this bride and groom.

"As witnesses may we shower forth our blessings upon these two as our greatest gift to them, and may this ceremony be an awe-filled inspiration for each of us to witness."

Opening Welcome 7:

Celebrant: "Family and friends: We welcome you today to witness the marriage of (name) and (name). You have shared and contributed to their lives in the past, by your love and support. You have joined with them and celebrated with them. Today, you will witness their marriage ceremony and in doing so, you will be sharing in their future.

"May each gathered here continue to love and support these two with your greatest hopes and deepest blessings for them."

Opening Welcome 8:

Celebrant: "Welcome all who gather here. As each of us evolves and grows through our own personal and unique life journey, we eventually come to the realization that love is much more than romance. We begin to fully know that true love is a guiding force and the most important thing in our lives.

"Love is the creator of our deepest dreams and highest aspirations. Love gives us the courage to forge ahead in times of difficulties. Love restores and revives us when life becomes discouraging.

"Love impels us to share our joys and celebrations with those we love. Love is an extension of all that is good and great. Love is Divine.

"As we witness this ceremony, I ask each of you to hold in your hearts the very best wishes and highest good for the bride and groom and for the creation and continuation of a marriage based on the power of Divine Love."

Opening Welcome 9:

Celebrant: "We are gathered here as loving friends and family to witness and support the joining in marriage of (name) and (name). They have opened their hearts and futures to one another, and today they will share their vows of marriage. We, as witnesses, are deeply thankful to them for opening their hearts to us also, and inviting us to share in these precious moments.

"To this union they bring the fullness of their being as a treasured gift to share with one another. They invite each other to share in a joined life, acknowledging this union is born of love.

"For what greater joy is there for two human souls than to unite and support one another in all their endeavors? Loving another person is the greatest and most precious gift we can ever wish for. The joining of two is not the diminishing of each individual, but the acknowledging and enhancing of the two in the creation of a marriage. Marriage is the joyful uniting of two unique and separate individuals who add their own special gifts and qualities to the union. It is into this state that bride and groom wish to enter, and each one of us gathered here has been chosen and honored to be witness to this union."

Opening Welcome 10:

Celebrant: "Each of us gathered is privileged to witness this union sanctioned by God. We are given the opportunity to be fully inspired by the commitment of (name) and (name) and by their shared love that has brought them to this moment. Today the bride and groom will declare their love for one another, before each of you as witnesses. As they make this covenant today before God, they do so fully knowing that He is the creator of this life that they share from this day forward, and He is the creator of the special and unique love that bonds and unifies their lives. May each of you gathered here hold them in your prayers, pour forth your blessings and special benedictions upon them and upon this union. Affirm in your hearts that this love that they share will continue to expand, intensify, and grow with the passing of the years. May God bless and sanctify this union and by His Love may all things be hallowed. Amen."

Opening Welcome 11:

Celebrant: "Welcome all who gather here today. (Name) and (name) have opened their hearts to each of us as they have opened their hearts and lives to one another. We are all deeply thankful to them for inviting us to witness and share in this precious and significant occasion. To this day they each bring the full measure of their being as a treasure to share with one another. They offer to one another their greatest strength as well as their deepest vulnerabilities. What greater joy is there for two beloveds than to join together to enhance, strengthen, and support each other in all their endeavors? As they have found each other, they have found the great joy that evolves from a connection of this magnitude. We each witness a moment in history as these two lives are joined together as one. As we listen to the promises they make today, let us each pray that the words and spirit of our gathering be filled with a truth that will deepen the reverence and joy of this union.

"May this ceremony build in each of us a sense of the vastness of that special love that the bride and groom share and the fulfillment of that love as this ceremony unfolds."

The Marriage Foundation Address

The marriage foundation address, in a traditionally religious ceremony, is the sermon or homily, which in a typical wedding format is central to creating the core religious theme. An independent celebrant, having more latitude in creative ceremony construction, is at liberty, when working with the couple, to decide on the level and focus of the religious content. Therefore, an independent minister will generally create a foundation address that speaks more of the purpose of marriage. The focus can be on the mutual ethics shared by the couple and the spirituality or the spiritual potential of the union, rather than on specific religious doctrine. Some couples prefer a more traditional religious theme. When this is their choice, the officiant will comply with their wishes. It is in the marriage foundation address that I include ceremony customization, adding the couple's own story and expressions of the love and values they share.

If you find a celebrant who will personalize your ceremony, it is key that she or he keep the marriage foundation address rather short, to allow time for these unique and special expressions.

Often, during the opening words of the marriage foundation address, I can sense the collective response of the guests as they prepare for what they think is "the sermon." Generally, within seconds, their bored, zombie-like expressions transform. They become attentive, alert, and even interested. This is the pivotal point in the ceremony where the light goes on, as it were. Truly, everyone loves a love story.

The beauty of marriage is that each couple forms a unique union. When two unique individuals join in marriage, the union is unlike any other marriage. Yet, most ceremonies consist of pre-composed formulae that each couple attempts to adapt to. Is it such a radical idea that the ceremony should be adapted to the couple, rather than the reverse? For this reason, I sometimes refer to the foundation address as the core, or underpinning, of the ceremony. A personalized address ensures that the words uttered in the ceremony are meaningful and relevant not only to the occasion and celebration but, most importantly, to the bride and groom and their unique partnership. This is their wedding ceremony, after all.

Since each couple's story is unique, I have opted to include the personalized commentary only to the first sample, "Marriage foundation address 1." As you peruse the following samples, bear in mind that each marriage foundation address allows for much latitude in its composition. It is also worth remembering that the versatility of the marriage foundation address is such that it can also serve, in full or in part, as:

- An opening benediction

- An opening welcome

- A pre-vows statement

- A wedding charge

- A final benediction

If you find it impossible to locate a celebrant who will personalize your ceremony, you might want to consider writing your own personal words and then asking your celebrant to incorporate them into the foundation address. Your answers to the following questions, part of the ceremony questionnaire from Chapter 2, should form the basis for the personalization of your marriage foundation address.

- What qualities do both of you require in order to create a strong and lasting marriage? (Answer jointly)

- (To the groom) Describe the bride's greatest characteristics and qualities that she will contribute to the marriage.

- (To the bride) Describe the groom's greatest characteristics and qualities that he will contribute to the marriage.

- How and when did you meet?

- Was there a defining moment when you realized you were in love?

- What made you decide to marry?

- Describe the proposal.

Marriage Foundation Address 1: *(Personalized Sample)*

Celebrant: "The bride and groom have known one another most of their lives. The bride readily admits that she would never have imagined, or predicted, that they would eventually fall in love and marry. The groom insists that he fell in love with her at the age of four, when she smiled at him and "twinkled her eyes" during a nursery school trip to the local post office. From that moment on, he imagined himself dressed in a postman's hat, carrying a mail bag full of valentines only for her, which he would deliver to her house around the corner from his.

"As the years progressed and they each grew and matured, he somehow never found the courage to confess to her how really he felt. Then, one summer, he returned from a vacation abroad to discover that her family had relocated to another state. He was bereft. As the years passed, he thought of her often.

"Eighteen months ago, on a particularly gloomy and overcast Monday morning, while at his office, working frenetically on a complex yet tedious assignment, he was asked to meet a new employee. His distracted response was: "I really don't have the time right now. Can it wait?" Unwittingly, he was postponing the beginning of the most momentous introduction of his life. So it was later that afternoon, while sipping the most appallingly bitter coffee, that the postponed introduction finally occurred. There she stood—his beloved of those past years. He was so taken aback that he dribbled the nasty brew down his pale blue tie while he searched for his voice. He found himself thinking back to the very first time she smiled at him all those years ago. He realized, at that moment, that her twinkling smile was still the same as that first lovely smile that had captured his heart. At that precise moment, they both burst out laughing.

"After the passage of many years, they stand here before us today, blessed by the miraculous power of love; a love that has stood the test of time. The greatest and most precious gift in life is the gift of love; a love that grows and matures. The discovery of another human being with whom this love is mutually shared is the greatest blessing anyone can wish for.

"As the bride and groom can attest, love creates a powerful union, a bond that grows with the passing of the years. Love is blessed by all that is good and divine. It is love that holds and sustains a marriage. Love grows in depth, beauty, and joy as the years increase. This progression of love from the deepest place within the heart, between two in love, is an expression, an out-flowing, of the love of God.

"Love is the most glorious gift of life. It must be remembered then, that a gift of this magnitude must be tended and nurtured, be given thanks for through expressions of love for the beloved. This is what creates a loving union that grows greater with the passing years."

Marriage Foundation Address 2:

Celebrant: "Today is your wedding day, a day you will always remember. This is one of the greatest and most important days in anyone's life. You begin this day as two people in love and end it as husband and wife—a team of two, united in one life. This is the beginning of a new journey, a new chapter in your lives. All of your individual hopes and dreams will now be now joined. Some are different and some are the same. But they become woven together for the greater good of your union. You now become a team who together build a marriage requiring the very best that you each can be. As the marriage begins to take form, so do your individual characters. You two are the authors of this life that you share and build. Yet the very process of doing so, of committing to the creating of this marriage, will in fact build *you,* will build your inner strength and character. Most importantly, this will deepen and open your hearts. For the greatest attribute in this union is love. Love is what will support and sustain you over the years."

Marriage Foundation Address 3:

Celebrant: "A true marriage is the deepest of all human relationships and bonds. It offers us the magnificent opportunity to open our heart to another in nurturance, comradeship, and understanding. It challenges us, offering us limitless opportunities to grow and expand our hearts to one another. It necessitates a commitment to selflessness, sensitivity, openness, honesty, and compassion.

"A marriage that is based on loving another fully and completely requires that we each tap the deepest place within, the very heart of compassion where God resides within us. Thus, a truly conscious and sacred marriage is an instrument and a vehicle for spiritual development and self-realization. Loving another and having that love reflected back is life's greatest, most cherished, and most sacred gift anyone could ever wish for.

"Let each of you, now and forever, always treasure—and be eternally thankful for—the gift of this special love that you share."

Marriage Foundation Address 4:

Celebrant: "On this, your wedding day, you are entering a new chapter in your lives. Your individual lives are over and you now give yourselves over to something entirely new—the creation of your unique marriage.

"The most precious gift that each of you brings to this marriage is *yourself*—all that you are at this moment, and all that you can be, all of those special and unique qualities, and all of your greatest possibilities.

"If you surrender your highest and deepest good into this union, you will build the strength and character to withstand all of the ups and downs of life. There will be times of agreement and disagreement. Times fraught with challenges and times blessed with joy. The future is now unknown to each of you. The unfolding of this marriage remains a mystery. But the secret of a joyful marriage lies deep within you. Marriage is like a mirror of your own heart, reflecting back to you both during your lives together all that you are, and all that you can be. A union is unbroken when the strength of love is unbreakable. The bond of love is indestructible, everlasting, endless, and eternal."

Marriage Foundation Address 5:

Celebrant: "Marriage is the greatest and most challenging of all relationships. It is based on love and deep respect that allows each individual to grow in his or her respective way. Marriage is the growing, the tending, and the maturing of love, freely given and willingly returned. It is unique yet universal, ordinary and yet extraordinary, because it is about living in love and respect, moment by moment, day by day, year by year, for a lifetime of mutual moments of love. For what greater gift exists than to love and be loved?"

Marriage Foundation Address 6:

Celebrant: "A marriage based on love is miraculous. The bride and groom have chosen the path of marriage together to experience this miracle as it unfolds in their lives, day by day. And the miracle of marriage is the commitment to making it work, every day, through the vicissitudes of everyday life.

"The willingness to dedicate themselves to this unique marriage is in itself a miracle of love, devotion, and deep commitment. Each marriage requires work and dedication, moment by moment, because a lifetime is created from many moments. The responsibility and ongoing commitment is made easier because of the love that is shared. Love that is joined builds upon itself. Every thought and act of love for the beloved is deepened and strengthened again and again. It is the power of this love that builds, strengthens, and enriches our integrity and character, enabling us to withstand and endure all of the disappointments and unpredictability in the life of a marriage."

Marriage Foundation Address 7:

Celebrant: "On this, your wedding day, you are entering a new chapter in your lives. Your individual lives are over and you are now to give yourselves over to something entirely new.

"What greater thing is there for two human souls than to feel that they are joined together to strengthen, support, and uphold each other, in joy and sorrow; to be friends, confidants, and lovers, and to be there for each other, both in words and in silence.

"Your union of love is an adventure you have embarked upon. The commitment to marriage builds, nourishes, and sustains this love. A public ceremony calls upon all who are gathered as witnesses to pledge to support this union by affirming and upholding in their prayers and well-wishes the intention each of you have made to be joined together this day in marriage.

"As you grow in this love that you share, all of those gathered here affirm the possibility that your days together will grow more joyous, more tender, and more devoted.

"Love has the capacity for the greatest magic. It is this special love you share that will nourish and sustain you in this union as the years unfold."

Marriage Foundation Address 8:

Celebrant: "A union based on love is the most holy and sacred of all loving relationships. Two people committed to one another who share this unique love are truly blessed. And the growth and development of this love does not begin with this ceremony. The wedding ceremony is the public affirmation and testimony to what already exists between you that you have already built together, through your love and respect for one another. This ceremony blesses and affirms the sacredness of this union. But it is the love you share that holds the two of you in this sacred bond. It is love itself that is truly sacred.

"As love grows greater, it becomes a great shield and stronghold that protects each of you from all of the distractions and difficulties that can erode the preciousness of this union. Always remember that your marriage is woven of the fabric of deep love, and it is this love that will hold, nurture, and sustain your union as the years go by."

Marriage Foundation Address 9:

Celebrant: "A ceremony is but a symbol of that which is inner and real; a committed union of hearts, which only two in love can truly create. Love grows through a life shared in love. It not only grows through the joy of this life fully shared; love grows through the pains and difficulties shared by two. It grows through supporting each other in times of turbulence and pain when each are most vulnerable and open. Love is the greatest teacher; while it can be the fount of joy and happiness, it impels us to examine the depths of our souls to offer up forgiveness and solace when our partner needs comfort.

"A marriage in love shapes us in ways that we never imagined were possible. It partakes of the mysterious process of inner-growth, of soul growth. A marriage built on love builds our characters, matures our souls, and expands our hearts."

Marriage Foundation Address 10:

Celebrant: "It is one of life's richest and greatest joys when the apparent accidental meeting of two lives leads them to join together in the union of marriage. Is such a meeting of two hearts coincidental? A multicultural legend states that for every man and for every woman, before each is born, a soulmate is chosen in heaven and is blessed by God and the highest archangels. According to this legend, it is predestined by God that they will meet on earth, fall in love, and join in marriage. For that which the Lord has preordained naturally must be fulfilled. Thus, the hand of God will forever bless them. Love is created in heaven; it is the divine outpouring of God's love.

"Love connects us to the inner space where the seed of divinity resides within the core of the human heart.

"A union fulfilled is a marriage based within a loving heart. It is a mutual remembering that the love that brought you together is an outpouring of God's love that created you and that will forever bless and sustain you."

Marriage Foundation Address 11:

Celebrant: "The decision to marry is one of the most profound and significant decisions the two of you will ever make. The giving over to one another in marriage is an awesome obligation of love and commitment that begins with the exchange of vows. The commitment to a lifelong partnership of love does not diminish either of you; rather, it strengthens both of you, through the character-building life lessons offered by a good marriage and through the miraculous healing power of love.

"As these words join you to one another in marriage, they also join you to the unknown. In making these promises, how can any one of us know how life will unfold day by day, moment by moment? Therefore, these promises are made in love. Only in love can we find the strength and trust to help us forge ahead unwaveringly, though all the unpredictable challenges we will encounter.

"As your love grows, so the bond of friendship between you will become stronger, building a marriage empowered by love and camaraderie. It will shape and transform you into the best you can be, building character and maturity and bringing joy to your union. May this marriage be empowered by the love that brought you together. The power of love will fortify and strengthen your union, throughout the ebb and flow of the life's unpredictable journey."

Marriage Foundation Address 12:

Celebrant: "(Name) and (name), you each hold a strong belief in God and his magnificent creations that so often go unnoticed and taken for granted. Remember, always, that God is the creator of this life that you share. He is a source of guidance and comfort, not only throughout every living moment of your lives, but during those special moments of celebration. The Divine presence and guidance is central to this wedding ceremony. We call upon God to guide you through both the joys and the disappointments of this life you will both share. May your faith in the Divine Presence help each of you to recognize how precious and unique your chosen partner is. Within each of us lie inherent gifts and qualities that can often be discovered and unveiled within ourselves by seeing them reflected in our partner. When we recognize the very best in our beloved partner, we also see the inner Divinity within ourselves. Each marriage then, is an opportunity to develop and achieve the highest and best we can ever hope to be.

"Each witness gathered here is a vital part of this ceremony and offers the bride and groom a powerful gift—the gift of encouraging thoughts, wishes, and prayers for their future lives together from this moment on."

Marriage Foundation Address 13:

Celebrant: "Marriage is the joining of these two lives before God and before these loving friends and family members as witnesses. The vows that you are about to take will bond together two apparent strangers through the miracle and magic of love. Each marriage is a mysterious path embarked upon by those whose ardent wish and full intention is to join together their hearts, lives, and individual destinies. Inherent in a good marriage are qualities contributed by each of you that can make it the very highest and most glorious expression of each of your greatest possibilities.

"Marriage is a tapestry woven of your special and unique qualities—those that now exist and those that are yet to be as each of you grow and develop over the years. The mystery of marriage is the daily unfolding of this union, in ways we cannot yet know. Marriage is as unpredictable as life itself. It is an opportunity in which each of you can be challenged to discover your innermost best, not only in each other, but in yourselves.

"This ceremony is the portal into the mystery of your marriage, but only the two of you can create a strong, sound, and lasting marriage through the power and the majesty of your love for one another. It is love that binds and holds you together for a lifetime."

Marriage Foundation Address 14:

Celebrant: "A strong and loving marriage is a spiritual journey of profound inner growth and selflessness. It requires the willingness to admit to being wrong, even when a stubborn mind tells you differently. It requires the ability to forgive the unimportant issues while having the conviction to steadfastly support and defend the important issues. The commitment to marriage is a noble path that impels us to develop selflessness and consideration. As love grows and expands deeper and fuller, we fully recognize how precious our chosen partner is. As we grow in our love for each other, we grow in wisdom. The glorious Presence of Divinity resides within the human heart. Here lies the inborn gift of deep wisdom; the wisdom to see ourselves reflected in our partner. We become mirrors for each other, helping one another to develop and grow. In wisdom we recognize that the difficulties and conflicts that arise in a marriage can serve to inspire and set in motion the necessary and required growth of character, which must be developed to ensure that a marriage will endure and remain whole.

"Working through these difficulties can be the perfect motivation for turning inward and tapping those inner reservoirs of love that lie deep in the heart. This is our most profound connection with one another, because it is here that we connect with the ever-loving God.

"With God all is possible."

Marriage Foundation Address 15:

Celebrant: "Marriage is the greatest and most cherished relationship two people can enter into. It is, indeed, the joyful uniting of two, whose friendship, caring, and respect for one another have blossomed into deep and profound love. This love is what holds together the marriage, as it builds the necessary qualities of hearts in those who are courageous enough to commit to it. For those who embark on this path; their lives are joined together as one.

"And yet, this bond and union does not in any way weaken or diminish either of them.

"On the contrary, a true marriage strengthens, enriches, and enhances each partner. In such a union, each one consciously and courageously gives themselves over to something deeply meaningful. They surrender themselves to something that, as yet, does not exist. This ceremony is the rite of passage into a mystery. It is a mystery because this day is the dawn and the birth of a new life which is still unknown to you. Your marriage at this moment is not yet created. Only the two of you can create your marriage.

"The deeper your love for one another grows, the stronger you build your individual integrity. It is the strength of your integrity that will build your marriage. Love also builds a strong foundation on which your marriage will prosper and thrive.

"Each one gathered today as a witness upholds and affirms the courageous choice that you both make today to begin this great journey into the future as loving life partners. We honor and bless you as you step through the portal of this ceremony into an entirely new life together."

Marriage Foundation Address 16:

Celebrant: "True committed marriage is a noble life path, offering us the greatest potential for spiritual growth and self-realization. Marriage is a commitment to life. It is a commitment to a lifetime of caring.

"The natural progression of love into marriage does not begin with the ceremony; the wedding ceremony is only a public declaration that gives testimony and witness to what already exists.

"Those who love are fully blessed because they can see with the eyes of compassion, understanding, and wisdom. They see the qualities—particularly in their beloved—that lie beneath the surface. When we see with loving eyes, we see with spiritual eyes. This is the gift that allows us to fully see and know another; to see our loved one's hidden sadness, fear, or loneliness, so that we may offer support and reassurance. Love has the power to overcome adversity and hardship.

"The beauty of knowing mutual wedded love is that we also are equal recipients of love. Being loved by our beloved is as great a gift as loving our beloved. Out of true love grows commitment, respect, and the ability to forgive. A love that is true grows deeper and fuller. Thus, love builds upon itself.

"Every loving and heartfelt wish directed towards another is a prayerful intention. As members of this community and as witnesses to this ceremony, I ask each one gathered here to take this precious opportunity to offer up your greatest and highest hopes for (name) and (name). As they enter an entirely new chapter, joining their lives and hearts, let each of us here be so inspired by their love that we graciously offer up thanks for all of the blessings in our own lives."

The Pre-Vows Charge/Statement

In the following outline, I have combined a pre-vows charge and a pre-vows statement. A charge, in the context of a wedding ceremony, is an instruction or advice-giving directive. A charge can be powerfully effective without sounding preachy. A pre-vows statement offers informative, pertinent information to the couple in a softer or more generalized way. Both a pre-vows charge and a pre-vows statement can be adapted from an appropriate reading.

The pre-vows charge or statement prefaces the beginning of the actual exchange of vows. Remember that the vows are verbal expressions of love and serve as the spoken contract of marriage. Since the ceremony has been leading to this pivotal moment of avowed declarations by the couple, the pre-vows charge or statement by the celebrant serves as a lead-in, with the same effect as a drum-roll preceding the highlight of a great performance. This statement can range from traditional to personal and is generally the decision of the celebrant, although the celebrant may ask the couple what their preferences are.

Nondenominational Pre-Vows Charge/Statement

I offered the following combined pre-vows charge/statement at the wedding ceremony of my son Joseph and daughter-in-law Kerri Lynne.

Celebrant: "Kerri Lynne and Joseph, it is now time to state your wedding vows to each other. These promises are solemnly and truthfully made before God and this company who witness the choice you have made to enter the portal of marriage today, to walk forward together hand in hand, joining together your hearts, your destinies, and your lives. As you embark upon the sacred and noble path of marriage, remember to cherish and honor the love that brought you together. In true love, you are about to formally affirm the love and respect that you already hold for one another. Therefore, Joseph and Kerri Lynne, before you repeat your vows to one another, I offer you this charge:

"May you always remain friends. May you laugh together and be joyful. Be a source of strength and comfort. Support each other's hopes and dreams. Listen to one another. Be there for one another, both in your words and in your silences. Share your thoughts, yet don't inflict. Support and comfort, yet don't constrict. But most of all, beyond all other, love and honor one another."

Traditional Pre-Vows Statement

The following Episcopal pre-vows statement is adapted from *The Book of Common Prayer*.

Celebrant: "Dearly beloved, we have come together in the presence of God to witness and bless the joining together of this man and this woman in holy matrimony. The bond and covenant of marriage was established by God in creation and our Lord Jesus Christ adorned this manner of life by His presence and first miracle at a wedding in Cana of Galilee. Marriage is not to be entered into unadvisedly or lightly but reverently, deliberately, and in accordance with the purposes for which it was instituted by God."

Nondenominational and Ecumenical Pre-Vows Charge/ Statement

The following nondenominational, ecumenical pre-vows statement is written in the style of a marriage foundation address.

Celebrant: "(Name) and (name), in presenting yourselves today to be joined in marriage, you perform an act of trust and faith; trust and faith in yourselves, in each other, and in this marriage.

"Remember, marriage is an awesome obligation of love and commitment that is about to be birthed with the vows you will momentarily exchange. As these words join you to one another in marriage, they also join you to the unknown; therein lies the trust and faith that is essential in a good marriage.

"In making these promises, how can any one of us know how life will unfold day by day? Therefore, these promises you are about to make, be sure to make them in love. Only in love can you find the strength, trust, and faith to help keep this union strong and enduring throughout the unpredictability of life."

Nondenominational and Jewish Pre-Vows Statement

Some of the following pre-vows charges/statements include quotes that I have adapted from a number of sources. When offering a pre–vows charge/statement that I have drawn from an outside source, I prefer to name the source of my quote, otherwise it would be inferred that I wrote it myself.

Celebrant: "From the Book of Ruth, I quote: 'For where thou goest I will go, and where thou lodgest I will lodge. Thy people will be my people and thy God, my God.'"

Ecumenical-Universal Pre-Vows Charge/Statement

Celebrant: " I offer you this charge: 'From this day forward walk together fearlessly upon the path of marriage. Respect one another's dreams and aspirations. Laugh together, play together, celebrate your similarities yet respect your differences. Offer your hands to support and encourage, offer your love to enfold and to comfort, and be gentle and kind. But most of all, love and honor one another.'"

Ecumenical-Universal Pre-Vows Statement

Celebrant: "I offer you these timeless sentiments, which I quote from the *I Ching:* 'When two people are at one in their inmost hearts, they shatter even the strength of iron.'"

Ecumenical-Universal Pre-Vows Statement

Celebrant: "From the ageless wisdom of the Brahma Sutras, I offer you this quote: 'When the one man loves the one woman and the one woman loves the one man, the very angels desert heaven and sit in that house and sing for joy.'"

The Vows and Exchange of Rings_

Regardless of the type of ceremony you have chosen (see Chapter 2, "The spirituality questionnaire"), the following samples may help as a guide to your ceremony creation. The wedding vows are comprised of four parts. The first two parts are legally required, part three is optional and involves personalization of vows, and part four is also optional.

- Part One consists of the questions and agreements.

- Part Two is the statement of acceptance.

- Part Three consists of the declarations and promises.

- Part Four is the ring blessing and the exchange of rings

Regardless of your final choice, remember that by law, wedding vows must include the questions by the celebrant and the agreement or statement of acceptance by the couple. For example:

Celebrant: (directed to the groom) "Do you, Joseph, take Kerri Lynne to be your wife?"

Groom: "I do."

The couple may also make the statement of agreement themselves in addition to answering with an acceptance. For example:

Bride: "Joseph, I accept your hand in marriage. I pledge myself to you as your wife. I will love and honor you all the days of my life."

However, with few exceptions, when the couple make a statement of acceptance I strongly advise that the celebrant prompt them, preferably in short increments. When prompting the couple, I prefer to speak quietly to the bride and groom so that the focus is on *their* words, not on my prompting. When I use a PA system, I do not speak into the microphone. I keep the microphone poised by the couple so that their words are heard clearly.

Part One:
The Questions and Agreements

The questions of agreement and acceptance can be simple and short, leaving the more creative and poetically written questions for the "statement of acceptance" which the celebrant will break down into small increments and then proceed to prompt the couple.

Question and Agreement 1:

Celebrant: "Do you, (name), take (name) as your wife (husband)?"
Groom (Bride): "I do."

Question and Agreement 2:

Celebrant: "Will you, (name), accept (name) as your wife (husband), your true love and your life partner?"
Groom (Bride): "I will."

Question and Agreement 3:

Celebrant: "Will you, (name), accept (name) as your wife (husband), your greatest love and your lifelong partner?"
Groom (Bride): "I will."

Question and Agreement 4:

Celebrant: "Will you receive (name) as your wife (husband), your deepest love and your cherished life partner?"
Groom (Bride): "I will."

Question and Agreement 5:

Celebrant: "Do you, (name), take (name) to be your wife (husband)? Do you promise to love, honor, cherish, and protect her (him), forsaking all others and holding only unto her (him)?"
Groom (Bride): "I do."

Question and Agreement 6:

Celebrant: "(Name), do you come here freely and without reservation to take (name) to be your wife (husband)?"
Groom (Bride): "I do."

Question and Agreement 7:

Celebrant: "(Name), do you promise to share your life with (name) as your wife (husband), to live together in all honesty and faithfulness? Do you promise also to join together in the spirit of tolerance, sharing your hopes and dreams, your joys and sorrows?"
Groom (Bride): "I do."

Part Two:
The Statement of Acceptance

The statement of acceptance is repeated after the celebrant's prompt.

Statement of Acceptance 1:

"I, (name), take you, (name), for my lifelong wife (husband) and partner in holy matrimony."

Statement of Acceptance 2:

"I, (name), take you, (name), as my wife (husband) and dearest friend in marriage."

Statement of Acceptance 3:

"I, (name), take you, (name), as my wife (husband), best friend, and partner for life."

Statement of Acceptance 4:

"I, (name), choose you, (name), as my wife (husband), my dearest love, and my partner in life."

Statement of Acceptance 5:

"I, (name), receive you, (name), as my beloved wife (husband) and my deepest friend."

Statement of Acceptance 6:

"I, (name), take you, (name), to be my wife (husband), my partner in life, and my one true love."

Statement of Acceptance 7:

"I, (name), choose you, (name), to be my wife (husband), to respect you in life's successes, and to support you in life's challenges, to care for you, in sickness and in health, to nurture you, and to grow with you throughout all the seasons of life."

Statement of Acceptance 8:

"I, (name), take you, (name), as my wife (husband). In the presence of God and these witnesses I promise to be a loving, caring, faithful, and loyal wife (husband), to you, for as long as we both shall live."

Statement of Acceptance Read by the Celebrant

I will occasionally encounter a bride or groom who will request that they not do a statement of acceptance since this involves a prompt-and-response format. Sometimes they are so nervous that all they wish to say is "I do" or "I will." The following is a statement read by the celebrant, requiring only the statement of agreement.

Celebrant: "As you join with (name) today in marriage, do you promise to love, honor, respect, cherish, and care for her (him) in times of good and bad; in times of joy and sorrow; promising to be true, faithful, and honorable partners to one another; cherishing each other for all the days of your lives?"

Groom (Bride): "I do."

Part Three:
The Declarations and Promises

Now that the legal part of the vows has been written, the structuring of the third part of the vows, the declarations and promises, allows for much latitude in creative personalization. Some witty and humorous couples include the mutual exchange of bargains in this portion of their vows. Remember Lisa and Kip from the previous chapter? They actually combined the statement of acceptance (part two), and the declarations and promises (part three). Their vows were unique in content and humor. Remember, Lisa promised to flatter Kip's music profusely, providing he make her a cup of tea and give her a back rub at the end of a hard day. I recall another wedding where the groom promised to always take out the garbage if the bride allowed him to watch the Monday night football game. From traditional to unpredictable, the variations are infinite. So why not be creative?

Declarations and Promises 1:

Groom (Bride): "I, (name), promise you, (name), to cherish our union, to love you more each day, allowing our love to grow fuller and deeper, to trust and respect you, to celebrate our successes, to be supportive during our challenges, to love you faithfully through good times and bad, regardless of the obstacles we may together face. I give you my hand, my heart, and my love, from this day forward, for as long as we both shall live."

Declarations and Promises 2:

Groom (Bride): "I, (name), in the presence our friends and family, promise (with Divine assistance) to be a loving and faithful husband (wife) to you, (name). I vow to be a constant friend to you during the ebb and flow of life's changing tides. I will love you in times of celebration and triumph, in times of challenge and unpredictability. I promise to stand by you, to cherish you, to respect you, to care for and protect you, to comfort and encourage you, and to stay with you, from this day forward. This is my solemn pledge to you."

Declarations and Promises 3:

Groom (Bride): "I, (name), offer you, (name), these promises: As your husband (wife) and true love, I will nurture and love you from the depths of my heart. I will listen to you, respect you, and honor your hopes and dreams, I will support your highest aspirations, and love you during the sunshine of abundance and the shadow of uncertainty. These promises I make to you now and for all the days of our lives."

Declarations and Promises 4:

Groom (Bride): "I, (name), solemnly pledge to love, honor, respect, cherish, and be faithful to you, to listen to you, to support and honor your goals and aspirations, to hold you sacred in my heart, to stand by you through good times and bad, through times of joy and times of sorrow, for as long as we both shall live."

Declarations and Promises 5:

Groom (Bride): "I, (name), offer you, (name) these vows before all that is Sacred and Divine and before all gathered here as witnesses. You cannot possess me for I belong to God alone, but I give you these promises: With you, I will share my love. You cannot command me, for I am free, but I will listen to your needs. I will give you my trust. I will support your aspirations. I will offer my wisdom and council when needed. I will stand beside you as an equal. I will walk with you as a companion. I will care for you as a friend. I will offer you my deepest devotion. I will give you my greatest respect. These things I offer you from the depth of my heart."

Declarations and Promises 6:

Groom (Bride): "In the presence of God, our family and friends, I, (name), offer you, (name), my solemn vow to be your faithful partner, in sickness and in health, in good times and in bad, and in joy as well as in sorrow. I promise to love you, to support your goals, to honor and respect you, to celebrate your successes, and to stand by you through life's disappointments, to love and to cherish you for as long as we both shall live."

Declarations and Promises 7:

Groom (Bride): "I, (name), take you, (name), to be my lawfully wedded wife (husband), my life partner, and my true love. Before Almighty God, before family and friends as witnesses, I solemnly pledge to love, honor, respect, cherish, and be faithful to you, to stand by you through good times and bad, through times of joy and times of sorrow, for as long as we both shall live."

Declarations and Promises 8:

Groom (Bride): "I, (name), promise to you, (name), to support and stand by you in your successes and in your disappointments, to care for you in sickness and in health, to nurture you and to grow with you throughout the seasons of life, loving what I know of you, and anticipating what I am yet to learn of you as we grow together on the path of life and marriage. My fervent wish and aspiration is that we each fall deeper and deeper in love with one another, day by day, as the years go by. I promise to love and cherish you through whatever life may bring us. You are my true love and my deepest friend."

Declarations and Promises 9:

Groom (Bride): "I, (name), affirm my love to you, (name). I invite you to share your life with me and anticipate sharing my life with you. I promise always to love, respect, and listen to you with kindness, compassion, and trust. I will honor your uniqueness and individuality as we create our life together. May our marriage be built on love's exquisite attributes—understanding and deep respect—as we work side by side to create a marriage that is based on true and unending love."

Declarations and Promises 10:

Groom (Bride): "I, (name), love you, (name). You are my best friend, my dearest partner, and my one true love. I offer myself to you in marriage. I promise to encourage and inspire you, to laugh with you in times of wonder and joy, and to comfort you in times of sorrow and struggle. I promise to love you in good times and in bad, during the ebb and the flow of life's changing tides. I promise to cherish you, and to always hold you in highest regard and respect. These things I offer to you today, and all the days of our lives."

Declarations and Promises 11:

Groom (Bride): "I, (name), am honored to receive you, (name), as my wife (husband), to share life's joys and sorrows, to stand firmly side by side, to walk hand in hand through the unpredictable journey of life. I humbly offer you my hand, my heart, my respect, and unending regard as I pledge my faith and love to you. You are my true and dearest love."

Declarations and Promises 12:

Groom (Bride): "I, (name), with all my love, take you, (name), to be my wife (husband). I will love, cherish, and respect you, through life's joys and life's sorrows. I will strive to be an understanding, caring, compassionate, and trusting friend. Together we will join our dreams, aspirations, and goals. I promise I will be your equal partner in a loving, honest relationship, for as long as we both shall live."

Declarations and Promises 13:

Groom (Bride): "I, (name), promise to love you, (name), to be your best friend, to respect and support you, to be patient with you, to work together with you to achieve our individual and our mutual goals, to accept and respect your unique and special gifts, to communicate openly, to listen carefully, to inspire and to uphold, to celebrate our similarities, to respect our differences, to be infinitely creative in expressing my love for you, to always be in awe and full of gratitude for the gift of this love that we both share. These are my fervent and heartfelt promises that I offer you today and always."

Declarations and Promises 14:

Groom (Bride): "I, (name), take you, (name), as my wife (husband), and my dearest friend and my true love. I promise to honor you, to respect you, and to listen to you. From this day forward, I join my life with your life. I join my heart with your heart. I promise to stand by you in good times and in bad, in times of joy and times of sorrow, for all the days of our lives together. You are my eternal love."

Declarations and Promises 15:

Groom (Bride): "I, (name), am the luckiest man (woman) in the world. From the moment I saw you, you amazed me, and I knew then that we were brought together by our deepest yearning for one another and by a force greater than both of us. The depth and freedom of your love for me truly allows the liberating and open expression for me to be who I really am. I pledge to you this day that my love for you will also allow you the freedom to be who you truly are. From the depths of my soul, I want you to know that as long as we are together I am fully and completely devoted to you. I promise to always listen to you with an open heart and mind without judging you. I fully realize that you are a reflection of me, as I am a reflection of you. As we formally join together our lives this day, let us reflect in one another the deepest and the best that we already are. Let us acknowledge that the purest and the best that we are is not only a reflection of one another but also the seed of the inner spirit of infinite and eternal love."

Declarations and Promises 16:

Groom (Bride): "I, (name), accept you as my wife (husband). As a measure of my love, I make these promises to you from the depth of my heart: I will do my best to keep our love vital and alive. I will honor you, respect you, nurture you, and listen to you. I will honor your growth as well as my own. I will share your dreams and support your aspirations. I will hold you precious in my heart as I share my life with your life, and my heart with your heart. These promises I make to you this day, for all of the days of our life together."

Declarations and Promises 17:

Groom (Bride): "I am blessed to receive you as my cherished wife (husband). I treasure you as my beloved life companion and dearest friend. As we embark upon our life's journey together today, I pledge to you these promises: To love, honor, respect, encourage, and listen to you. I will uphold you in all your endeavors. I will rejoice at your successes. Throughout the sunshine and shadows of life, I will do my utmost to be a tower of strength for you. I will offer you a soft shoulder to lean on, a warm embrace to comfort you, and a strong hand to support you. These promises I make to you this day before God and these witnesses."

Declarations and Promises 18:

Groom (Bride): "I, (name), choose and accept you, (name), as my wife (husband). I promise to be a kind and loving friend to you, to be true to you and to respect you, to stand by you when you need comfort and understanding. I will continue to respect and care for you. When you are assailed with discouragement, I will offer you encouragement. When you are blessed with life's successes, I will celebrate and rejoice with you. Together the strength of our love will help build a solid marriage. A marriage built on love is unshakable, as the depth of this love is unbreakable."

Declarations and Promises 19:

Groom (Bride): "As I receive you as my husband (wife), I (name) promise you, (name), to always love you as I do today. I promise to respect you as the beautifully unique person that you are, knowing that your needs, desires, interests, and aspirations are no less important than mine. I promise to do my best to stay open and receptive to you, especially when I feel hurt, insecure, or fearful. I promise to do my best to be a strong, caring, compassionate, and reliable friend to you, particularly at the times when life's difficulties and challenges assail you. I promise to be a joyful ally and champion when life's successes honor and bless you. I promise to listen to you. I promise to always show you in both words and actions of the depth of my love for you. I promise to share my life with you as you share your life with me, remembering that love of this magnitude can never be limited. For this love that we share is an extension of the infinite and unlimited love of God the Creator."

Part Four:
The Ring Blessing and the Exchange of Rings

The Ring Blessing

I feel that as symbols of a lifelong union, rings deserve to be blessed. For an informal, less religious service, there are alternative rituals that place more emphasis on honoring the meaning of the rings, which to me still constitutes a subtle blessing. The ring blessing may be done as a prelude, directly before the exchange of rings. The blessing can also be done at the very beginning of the exchange of vows. I personally prefer the latter because of the uninterrupted flow from the exchange of vows to the exchange of rings, but either way will work beautifully.

Think of the style and theme of your ceremony as you make your choices.

The Ring Blessing 1:

Celebrant: "Marriage is a state in which two people come together and create a union based on love and mutual respect. Love is beginningless, endless, and eternal, as is a circle, and as are these rings."

(Rings are handed to celebrant.)

Celebrant: "Lord, bless these rings and the two who will wear them. May they stand together in a circle of eternal love. Amen."

The Ring Blessing 2:

Celebrant: "From time immemorial, a circle of metal has been a symbol of the durability of a couple's love for one another and their union. As these rings of precious metal encircle upon themselves, so do those who commit their lives to one another encircle each other with their love, throughout the years of a lasting marriage. As precious metal is solid and strong, so is a committed marriage pledged in love solid and strong."

(Rings are handed to celebrant.)

Celebrant: "May these rings be blessed and the two who will wear them. May they stand together steadfast in a circle of unbreakable love. Amen."

The Ring Blessing 3:

Celebrant: "The ring is a symbol of the sincerity and permanence of a couple's love for one another. The circle is also a symbol of eternal love that, like a circle, is without beginning and without end."

(Rings are handed to celebrant.)

Celebrant: "Bless these rings, O Lord, and the two who will exchange them, in the spirit of endless and eternal love. Amen."

The Ring Blessing 4:

Celebrant: "Since ancient times, rings have symbolized the commitment of married love. An unbroken and never-ending circle symbolizes a love that is eternal and never-ending."

(Rings are handed to celebrant.)

Celebrant: "We ask that God bless these rings and this union of souls. May they be encircled in divine blessings and may all their years together be hallowed. Amen."

The Ring Blessing 5:

Celebrant: "The circle is a symbol of wholeness, holiness, perfection, and peace."

(Rings are handed to celebrant.)

Celebrant: "Almighty God, we ask for Your blessing upon these rings and upon the bride and groom who will wear them. May they be blessed with wholeness of body and mind. May they be blessed with holiness, perfection, and peace of spirit. May these rings symbolize the eternity of their love. Amen."

The Ring Blessing 6:

Celebrant: "The ring is a circle, a symbol of love and eternity. Like the infinite universe, love is endless. May you enter into the circle of married love. May your devotion to each other grow ever stronger, building a sanctuary of love that expands and grows with the passing years."

(Rings are handed to celebrant.)

Celebrant: "Lord, may these rings be blessed and may this bride and groom stand steadfast and secure in a circle of ever-growing love. Amen."

The Ring Blessing 7:

Celebrant: "The ring is a symbol of commitment and everlasting love that, like a circle, is without beginning and without end. In eastern traditions, the circle symbolizes the wheel of life, around which we each travel throughout our lives, experiencing life's joys and life's sorrows. when we stand steadfast and firm within the circle of life, we are less affected by life's unpredictable circumstances."

(Rings are handed to celebrant.)

Celebrant: "May these rings be blessed and may the wearing of them be a reminder, from this day forward, to stand together at the center of the circle of your lives; to be a source of reliability, dependability, and constancy with and for one another, throughout your lives together. Amen."

The Exchange of Rings

In selecting the words to accompany the exchange of rings, choose carefully. Be cognizant of maintaining a common theme and flow. Remember that the exchange of vows and exchange of rings comprise the pivotal moments of a wedding ceremony; everything has been leading up to this moment.

The Exchange of Rings 1:

Couple (repeated after the celebrant prompts): "I give you this ring as token of my devotion that—like a circle—is eternal and endless, as is my love for you."

The Exchange of Rings 2:

Couple (repeated after the celebrant prompts): "In token and pledge of our constant faith and abiding love, I give you this to wear upon your hand as a symbol of our unending love."

The Exchange of Rings 3:

Couple (repeated after the celebrant prompts): "This ring I give you is a circle that has no beginning and no end and is unbroken, as is our love. Wear it as a token and symbol of my love for you."

The Exchange of Rings 4:

Couple (repeated after the celebrant prompts): "This ring that I offer you is a circle without end and is eternal, as is my love for you. It is created of the strength of precious metal, as our love is precious and the strength of my commitment to you will never fail. With this ring, I thee wed."

The Exchange of Rings 5:

Couple (repeated after the celebrant prompts): "This ring is a circle, unbroken, just as my love for you is unbroken and complete. I offer you this ring as a token of the promises that I have made to you this day. Wear it as a symbol of our eternal commitment to one another."

The Exchange of Rings 6:

Couple (repeated after the celebrant prompts): "I offer you this ring to wear upon your hand as a reminder that from this moment on, our lives are joined and encircled in an unbreakable and infinite bond of love. With this ring, I thee wed."

The Exchange of Rings 7:

Couple (repeated after the celebrant prompts): "As a pledge of my constant faith and abiding devotion to you, I offer you this ring. As I place it upon your hand, I give you my promise that from this day forward, our hearts are joined and our lives are united."

The Exchange of Rings 8:

Couple (repeated after the celebrant prompts): "As a token of my deepest and eternal love, I give you this ring and pledge my constant faith and abiding love. Wear it forever as a symbol of my endless and eternal love."

The Exchange of Rings 9:

Couple (repeated after the celebrant prompts): "This ring is a circle, whole and fully complete, as is my love for you. Take this ring I give you, and wear it as a symbol of my devotion and sincerity. With this ring, I wed my dearest friend. Wear it eternally, for my love for you is endless and eternal."

The Exchange of Rings 10:

Couple (repeated after the celebrant prompts): "You are my deepest and most beloved friend. Accept this ring as a token of my unending devotion, love, and commitment to you. With this ring that I offer to you this day, I wed my lifetime companion and my dearest friend."

The Exchange of Rings 11:

Couple (repeated after the celebrant prompts): "This ring I offer you is made of the strength of precious metal, which is solid and strong, as is my committed pledge and my love for you. I offer you this ring as a promise that the strength of my love for you is eternal."

The Exchange of Rings 12:

Couple (repeated after the celebrant prompts): "This ring I offer you is round like the glowing sun that radiates light and warmth. It is a circle like loving arms that encircle and embrace. As I commit my life to you, I encircle you with my love, I embrace you with comfort and warmth, now and throughout the years of our lives. With this ring, I thee wed."

A Liturgy of Standard Traditional Vows

The vows included below are the standard exchange of vows drawn from the specific marriage rite liturgies of many denominations and faiths. With the exception of the Hindu and Muslim standard vows, most of them include all four parts of the exchange of vows outlined above: the questions and agreements, the statement of acceptance, the declarations and promises, and the ring blessing and exchange of rings.

Obviously, a standard, pre-scripted outline precludes the creation of a unique ceremony. However, standard vows can work beautifully when combined with an otherwise unique, creative, and custom ceremony.

For those of you who love the poetic flow of King James English, you may want to consider the Lutheran, Methodist, Presbyterian, or Episcopal wedding vows. The subtle distinctions among them are insightful and reflect the style and spirit of each denomination. If you are a non-Jewish couple, yet you prefer the wonderful flow of the Jewish wedding vows, why not consider incorporating them anyway?

Baptist Vows:

Celebrant: "Will you, (name), have (name) to be your wife (husband)? Will you love her (him), comfort and keep her (him), and, forsaking all others, remain true to her (him) as long as you both shall live?"

Groom (Bride): "I will."

Groom (Bride): "I, (name) take thee, (name), to be my wife (husband), and before God and these witnesses, I promise to be a faithful and true husband (wife)."

(Rings): "With this ring I thee wed, and all my worldly goods I thee endow. In sickness and in health, in poverty or in wealth, 'til death do us part."

Catholic Vows 1:

Celebrant: "(Name), will you take (name), here present, for your lawful wife (husband), according to the rite of our Holy Mother, the Catholic Church?"

Groom (Bride): "I will."

Groom (Bride): "I, (name), take you, (name), for my wife (husband), to have and to hold, from this day forward, for better, for worse, for richer, for poorer, in sickness and in health, until death do us part."

(Rings): "With this ring, I thee wed, and pledge thee my troth."

Catholic Vows 2:

Celebrant: "(Name), will you take (name), here present, for your lawful wife (husband), according to the rite of our Holy Mother, the Catholic Church?"

Groom (Bride): "I will."

Groom (Bride): "I, (name), take you, (name), to be my wife (husband). I promise to be true to you in good times and in bad, in sickness and in health. I will love you and honor you all the days of my life."

(Rings): "With this ring, I thee wed, and pledge thee my troth."

Civil Ceremony Vows 1:

Celebrant: "(Name), do you take (name) to be your wife (husband)?"

Groom (Bride): "I do."

Celebrant: "Do you promise to love, honor, cherish, and protect her (him), forsaking all others and holding only unto her (him) forevermore?"

Groom (Bride): "I do."

Groom (Bride): "I, (name), take thee, (name), to be my wife (husband), to have and to hold, in sickness and in health, for richer or for poorer, in joy and in sorrow, and I promise my love to you."

Civil Ceremony Vows 2:

Celebrant: "(Name), do you take (name) to be your lawfully wedded wife (husband)? To have and to hold, from this day forward, in sickness and health, for as long as you both shall live?"

Groom (Bride): "I do."

Groom (Bride): "I, (name), take you, (name), to be my lawfully wedded wife (husband). Before these witnesses, I solemnly promise to love you and care for you as long as we both shall live. I love you just as you are, as I offer myself to you just as I am. I anticipate knowing you more and loving you deeper throughout the years that stretch out before us. You are the one that I choose as the person with whom I will spend my life."

Episcopal Vows:

Celebrant: "(Name), wilt thou have this woman (man) to be thy wedded wife (husband), to live together after God's ordinance in the Holy Estate of matrimony? Wilt thou love her (him), comfort her (him), honor and keep her (him), in sickness and in health, and forsaking all others keep thee only unto her (him), as long as you both shall live?"

Groom (Bride): "I will."

Groom (Bride): "I, (name), take thee, (name), to be my wedded wife (husband), to have and to hold, from this day forward, for better or for worse, for richer or for poorer, in sickness and in health, to love and to cherish, 'til death do us part, according to God's ordinance, and thereto I pledge thee my troth."

(Rings): "With this ring, I thee wed, in the name of the Father, and of the Son, and of the Holy Ghost. Amen."

Hindu Vows:

"Let us take the first step to provide for our household, keeping a pure diet and avoiding those things that might harm us.

"Let us take the second step, to develop our physical, mental, and spiritual powers.

"Let us take our third step, to increase our wealth by righteous and proper means.

"Let us take our fourth step, to acquire knowledge, happiness, and harmony by mutual love, respect, and trust.

"Let us take the fifth step, so that we may be blessed with strong, virtuous, and heroic children.

"Let us take the sixth step, for self-restraint and longevity.

"Let us take the seventh step, to be true companions and remain lifelong partners by marriage."

Jewish (Reform) Vows:

Celebrant (to groom): "Do you, (name), take (name) to be your wife?"

Groom: "I do."

Celebrant (to groom): "Do you promise to love, cherish, and protect her, whether in good fortune or in adversity, and to seek with her a life hallowed by the faith of Israel?"

Groom: "I do."

Celebrant (to bride): "Do you, (name), take (name) to be your husband?"

Bride: "I do."

Celebrant (to bride): "Do you promise to love, cherish, and protect him, whether in good fortune or in adversity, and to seek with him a life hallowed by the faith of Israel?"

Bride: "I do."

Celebrant (to groom): "(Name), as you place this ring upon the finger of (name), speak to her these vows: 'With this ring be thou consecrated unto me as my wife according to the law of God and the faith of Israel.'"

Celebrant (to bride): "(Name), as you place this ring upon the finger of (name), speak to him these vows: 'With this ring be thou consecrated unto me as my husband according to the law of God and the faith of Israel.'"

Jewish (Conservative) Vows:

Celebrant (to groom): "Do you, (name), take (name) to be your lawfully wedded wife, to love, honor, and cherish?"

Groom: "I do."

Celebrant (to bride): "Do you, (name), take (name) to be your lawfully wedded husband, to love, honor, and cherish?"

Bride: "I do."

Celebrant (to groom): "(Name), as you place this ring upon the finger of (name), speak to her these vows: 'With this ring be thou consecrated unto me as my wife according to the law of God and the faith of Israel.'"

Celebrant (to bride): "(Name), as you place this ring upon the finger of (name), speak to him these vows: 'With this ring be thou consecrated unto me as my husband according to the law of God and the faith of Israel.'"

Lutheran Vows 1:

Celebrant: "(Name), wilt thou have this woman (man) to be thy wedded wife (husband), to live together after God's ordinance in the Holy Estate of matrimony? Wilt thou love her (him), comfort her (him), honor and keep her (him), as long as ye both shall live?"

Groom (Bride): "I will."

Groom (Bride): "I, (name), take thee, (name), to be my wife (husband), and pledge thee my troth, so long as we both shall live."

(Rings): "Receive this ring as a token of wedded love and faith."

Lutheran Vows 2:

Celebrant: "(Name), wilt thou have this woman (man) to be thy wedded wife (husband), to live together after God's ordinance in the Holy Estate of matrimony? Wilt thou love her (him), comfort her (him), honor and keep her (him), as long as ye both shall live?"

Groom (Bride): "I will."

Groom (Bride): "I, (name), take you, (name), to be my wife (husband), and these things I promise you: I will be faithful to you and honest with you; I will respect, trust, help, and care for you; I will share my life with you; I will forgive you as we have been forgiven; and I will try with you to better understand ourselves, the world, and God; through the best and the worst of what is to come, as long as we live."

(Rings): "Receive this ring as a token of wedded love and faith."

Lutheran Vows 3:

Celebrant: "(Name), wilt thou have this woman (man) to be thy wedded wife (husband), to live together after God's ordinance in the Holy Estate of matrimony? Wilt thou love her (him), comfort her (him), honor and keep her (him), as long as ye both shall live?"

Groom (Bride): "I will."

Groom (Bride): "(Name), our miracle lies in the path we have chosen together. I enter into this marriage with you knowing that the true magic of love is not to avoid changes, but to navigate them successfully. Let us commit until death parts us."

(Rings): "Receive this ring as a token of wedded love and faith."

Methodist Vows 1:

Celebrant: "(Name), wilt thou have this woman (man) to be thy wedded wife (husband), to live together after God's ordinance in the Holy Estate of matrimony? Wilt thou love her (him), in sickness and in health, and forsaking all others, keep thee only unto her (him), so long as ye both shall live?"

Groom (Bride): "I will."

Groom (Bride): "I, (name), take thee, (name), to be my wife (husband), to have and to hold, from this day forward, for better, for worse, for richer, for poorer, in sickness and in health, to love and to cherish, till death do us part, and thereto I pledge thee my faith."

(Rings): "In token and pledge of the vow between us made, with this ring I thee wed; in the name of the Father, and of the Son, and of the Holy Spirit. Amen."

Methodist Vows 2:

Celebrant: "(Name), wilt thou have this woman (man) to be thy wedded wife (husband), to live together after God's ordinance in the Holy Estate of matrimony? Wilt thou love her (him), in sickness and in health, and forsaking all others, keep thee only unto her (him), so long as ye both shall live?"

Groom (Bride): "I will."

Groom (Bride): "I, (name), take thee, (name), to be my wedded wife (husband), to have and to hold, from this day forward, for better, for worse, for richer, for poorer, in sickness and in health, to love and to cherish, till death do us part, according to God's holy ordinance, and thereto I pledge thee my faith."

(Rings): "In token and pledge of the vow between us made, with this ring I thee wed; in the name of the Father, and of the Son, and of the Holy Spirit. Amen."

Muslim Vows:

Bride: "(Name), I offer you myself in marriage in accordance with the instructions of the Holy Koran and the Holy Prophet, peace and blessings be unto Him. I pledge in honesty and in sincerity to be for you an obedient wife."

Groom: "(Name), I pledge, in honesty and sincerity, to be for you a faithful and helpful husband."

Presbyterian Vows:

Celebrant: "(Name), wilt thou have this woman (man) to be thy wife (husband), and wilt thou pledge thy faith to her (him), in all love and honor, in all duty and service, in all faith and tenderness, to live with her (him) and cherish her (him), according to the ordinance of God, in the holy bond of marriage?"

Groom (Bride): "I will."

Groom (Bride): "I, (name), take thee, (name), to be my wedded wife (husband), and I do promise and covenant, before God and these witnesses, to be thy loving and faithful husband (wife); in plenty and in want, in joy and in sorrow, in sickness and in health, as long as we both shall live."

(Rings): "This ring I give thee, in token and pledge of our constant faith and abiding love."

Quaker Vows 1:

Groom (Bride): "In the presence of God and these our Friends, I take thee to be my wife (husband), promising with Divine assistance to be unto thee a loving and faithful husband (wife), as long as we both shall live."

(Certification): "On this the (day) of (month), in the year of our Lord (year), (name) and (name) appeared together, and (husband's name) taking (wife's name) by the hand, did, on this solemn and joyous occasion, declare that he took (wife's name) to be his wife, promising with Divine assistance to be unto her a loving and faithful husband; and then, in the same assembly, (wife's name) did in like manner declare that she took (husband's name) to be her husband, promising with Divine assistance, to be unto him a loving and faithful wife. And moreover they, (husband's name) and (wife's name), did,

as further confirmation thereof, then and there to this certificate set their hands.

(Husband's name) _____

(Wife's name) _____

And we, having been present at the marriage, have as witnesses hereunto set our hands."

Quaker Vows 2:

Groom (Bride): "In the presence of God and these our Friends, I take thee to be my wife (husband), promising with Divine assistance to be unto thee a loving and faithful husband (wife), as long as we both shall live."

(Certification): "Whereas (husband's name) of (city), (state), son of (husband's father's name) and (husband's mother's name), and (wife's name) of (city), (state), daughter of (wife's father's name) and (wife's mother's name), having declared their intentions of marriage with each other to the (name of meetinghouse) monthly meeting of the Religious Society of Friends held at (city and state of meetinghouse), their proposed marriage was allowed by that Meeting. Now this is to certify to whom it may concern, that for the accomplishment of their intentions, this (day) of (month), in the year of our Lord (year), they, (husband's name) and (wife's name), appeared in a meeting for worship of the Religious Society of Friends, held at (city), (state), and (husband's name), taking (wife's name) by the hand, did on this solemn occasion declare that he took her, (wife's name), to be his wife, promising with Divine assistance to be unto her a loving and faithful husband so

long as they both shall live, and then, in the same assembly, (wife's name) did in like manner declare that she took him, (husband's name), to be her husband, promising with Divine assistance to be unto him a loving and faithful wife so long as they both shall live. And moreover, they, (husband's name) and (wife's name) did as further confirmation thereof, then and there, to this certificate set their hands.

(Husband's name) _____

(Wife's name) _____

And we, having been present at the marriage, have hereunto set our hands."

Unitarian Universalist Vows 1:

Celebrant: "(Name), will you take (name) to be your wife (husband)? Will you love, honor, and cherish her (him) now and forever more?"

Groom (Bride): "I will."

Groom (Bride): "I, (name), take you, (name), to be my wife (husband), to have and to hold, from this day forward, for better, for worse, for richer, for poorer, in sickness and in health, to love, cherish, honor, and respect, always and forever."

Unitarian Universalist Vows 2:

Celebrant: "(Name), will you take (name) to be your wife (husband)? Will you love, honor, and cherish her (him) now and forever more?"

Groom (Bride): "I will."

Groom (Bride): "I, (name), joyfully receive you, (name), into my life as my wedded wife (husband), to live together and work together, to create a marriage built on love and mutual respect. I promise to honor, comfort, and cherish you, in sickness and in health, in sorrow and in joy, from this day forward."

United Church of Christ Vows:

Groom (Bride): "I, (name), take you, (name), to be my wife (husband), and I promise to love and sustain you in the bonds of marriage from this day forward, in sickness and in health, in plenty and in want, in joy and in sorrow, till death shall part us, according to God's holy ordinance."

Special Ceremonies and Celebrations

During each ceremony I officiate, I suggest to the couple that we find ways to honor parents or those who have played a significant role in their lives. Sometimes the parents are blessed or honored with a few simple, heartfelt words of thanks. It saddens me so when this is not an option due to family difficulties, disagreements, or turmoil. When parents are deceased, I often suggest that a sibling stand in proxy for the deceased parent (or parents), to receive the honor on their behalf. A proxy may also stand in for a deceased parent to assist in a Family Permission and Community Support Ceremony, a Candle Lighting Ceremony, a Sand Ceremony, a Wine Ceremony, or a Hand-Fasting or Hand-Joining Ceremony.

A personalized wedding ceremony offers the opportunity to give thanks and offer gratitude to God and to loving family members and friends. This can be the most cherished and special experience for the couple and their loved ones, particularly when the ceremony is personalized. Building a unique ceremony reflects the bond shared by the couple, making the day a celebration of their special uniting. Though the ceremony is about the bride and groom, the role of beloved family members can be immeasurable and needs to be acknowledged and honored; only then is there true participation and rejoicing for all involved. Many of the following special ceremonies and celebrations include the option of family participation.

The Parental Blessing Ceremony (optional)

Celebrant (to the parents of the bride and groom): "The bride and groom wish to offer you their heartfelt gratitude for the guidance, support, encouragement, nurturance and most of all, for the all-embracing love you have given them over the years, without which they could not have grown to become who they are today. You have passed on to them your ethics and values, not only through your words, but through your actions. Your love is unending. Therefore it is fitting as this union and new family is about to be formed, that we offer each of you this blessing:

"We call upon all that is holy, sacred and divine to bless these parents, without whom this sacred union would not have been possible. Lord, as these parents celebrate this union today we ask that you continue to bless their lives as the years stretch forward and as this marriage grows and matures. We know that their sheer goodness and caring assures that they continue to be a positive influence in the lives of their grown children. May all that they have given in love from the depth of their own hearts flow back as blessings into their lives to be shared with those they love. Amen."

Family Permission and Community Support

Marriage is not only the joining together of two individuals; it is the uniting of two families. When a couple is blessed with loving and supportive families, this ritual is a gracious way of thanking, acknowledging, and honoring these blessed family members who have cared for and nurtured the bride and groom for so many years. Some client couples convey a little reluctance at putting their parents "on the spot," feeling that this ritual may evoke an overly emotional response. Other clients express a concern for parents who tend to be rather shy. When this is the case, I assure them that there are many ways to arrange and configure a parental permission and community support ceremony, none of which require that the parents stand up or join the bride and groom at the altar. Of course, that is certainly an option for those who so wish. Though "family permission" and "community support" represent two separate parts of the ceremony, I have opted to join them together in the following examples. They could certainly be separated if the couple so choose.

Family Permission and Community Support 1:

Celebrant: "Independently, the family of the bride and the family of the groom have loved, supported, and nurtured these two throughout their lives. Now, as these separate families are to be joined as one loving family unit, the bride and groom have requested that they each join together in their support for the bride and groom. We ask each of these families to unite in their loving wishes and highest hopes and dreams for this couple as they are joined in marriage."

Celebrant to families: "Therefore, I ask you as family members of the bride and groom: Do you support the choice the bride and groom have made to be joined in marriage this day?"

Family members: "We do."

Celebrant to families: "Will you stand by them, offering your love, support, caring, and compassion?"

Family members: "We will."

Celebrant to families: "Will you rejoice with them in times of celebration, and when life is beset with difficulties will you, with their consent, offer them your loving support, comfort, and words of wisdom?"

Family members: "We will."

Celebrant: "I now call upon the entire community gathered here to silently declare your support. From the depths of your hearts, send love and compassion. From the clarity of your minds, send inspiration and encouragement. From the stillness of your spirits, send benedictions and prayers. Amen."

Family Permission and Community Support 2:

Celebrant: "Although today is a great and significant day in the lives of the bride and groom, this day is also a tribute to these families who are here because of their love for the bride and groom who stand before us. Without these caring families, none of us would be witnessing this ceremony today. They have nurtured, cared for, taught, guided, influenced, and most of all, loved these two. We also acknowledge the role of considerate and supportive friends. A wedding ceremony without a community of loving witnesses is bereft of support."

Celebrant to families: "Therefore, to the families of (name) and (name), I ask you: From this day forward, will you encourage, love, and support them?"

Families: "We will."

Celebrant to families: "Will you be there when they need you, yet maintain the wisdom to allow them space and freedom when required?"

Families: "We will."

Celebrant to community and families: "I now call upon you, the community and friends of the bride and groom, to declare your support. Therefore, I ask you: Do you each, from the depths of your hearts, through your love for them, offer your greatest support for a marriage filled with joy, peacefulness, fulfillment, and infinite blessings?"

Community and families: "We do."

Family Permission and Community Support 3:

Celebrant: "Today the bride and groom will cross the threshold of this ceremony and enter a lifetime of love and commitment. They will unite in a marriage knowing the true magic of love and the promise to commit to the miracle of making each day work together. These promises and pledges they make are made before God and each one gathered as witnesses. Thus, as each of these families joins together in their support for the bride and groom, the blessings bestowed upon them today will be doubled."

Celebrant to families: "Therefore, to the families of (name) and (name), I ask you: Will you offer your loving support throughout the days of their marriage?"

Families: "We will."

Celebrant to families: "Will you promise to encourage them, love them, guide and support them, in remaining unwavering in the promises they have made this day?"

Families: "We will."

Celebrant to community and families: "Each gathered here who are honored friends of the bride and groom and who mutually honor the bride and groom with their friendship and love, I ask you now: Will you be there for the bride and groom, offering your love and support as their marriage matures and grow as the years go by?"

Community and families: "We will."

Honoring and Joining Children

When a child or children are joining a marriage because of a divorce, or the death of a parent, there are many ways to involve and honor them in the ceremony. It is vital that they be recognized and included in some aspect of the ceremony itself. Children are often reluctant or unable to express their complicated emotions or the fears and insecurities they may be experiencing regarding a parent marrying a new spouse. Involving children in the ceremony helps them to transition into, and bond with, the new family unit.

Don't expect children to share your sense of excitement about the wedding. They most likely will not understand the significance of a wedding ceremony and will consider it more of a party than a life passage. If they are given a role in the ceremony, please keep their participation simple and uncomplicated. Be sensitive to the involvement of teenagers. Be aware of this awkward age and be realistic enough to know that they may not even want to be addressed as "children." I am generally a bit reluctant to have teenagers participate in a children's vows ceremony. Do not include or involve them in anything that makes them feel embarrassed or silly. Be sure to take time to talk to them about the wedding day. And please don't suddenly spring this life-changing event on them, without including and preparing them. Finally, remember to thank them for their participation.

Including the Children by Naming Them

The names of the children can be included during certain ceremonial sections. For instance, the celebrant can include their names during the opening and closing benediction as she invokes God's blessings upon the bride and groom. There is also a perfect opportunity to mention children during the marriage foundation address or the opening welcome.

Ceremony Participation of Children

There are a number of ways of including children in the ceremony, in addition to—or instead of—naming them. They can participate in the unity sand ceremony. Older children can join in the unity candle lighting ceremony. Younger children can be included in the vows for children ceremony. Children can function as ring bearers, flower girls, train holders, and page boys. Older children can read a Bible passage or a poem.

Gifts for Children

An additional subtle way of honoring children is by giving them a gift. This can be woven into the ceremony, and for children who tend to be rather shy, the gift can be presented in silence. There are a number of appropriate gifts—a ring, wristwatch, or family medallion. Some couples like to offer a family heirloom to a child during the ceremony.

Vows for Children 1:

Celebrant: "Though this is a significant day in the lives of the bride and groom, this day also marks the joining and creation of a new family. The bride and groom have requested that these children are honored and welcomed into this new family unit by the following 'children's vows' ceremony."

Celebrant to bride and groom: "You are now about to create and build a new family. Included in this new family unit are these children who will also be joining you as members of this union. As you join in the bond of a marriage built on love and respect, I ask you: Will you love and honor these children?"

Bride and groom: "We will."

Celebrant to bride and groom: "Will you respect their individual beauty as the lovely and unique souls that they already are?"

Bride and groom: "We will."

Celebrant to bride and groom: "Will you do your best to create a home where love and peace prevail?"

Bride and groom: "We will."

Celebrant to bride and groom: "Will you guide their lives with wisdom and compassion, to help them reach their greatest and highest potential?"

Bride and groom: "We will."

Celebrant to bride and groom: "By the power vested in me, in the presence of all that is Sacred and Divine and before all who are gathered here, I now pronounce that from this moment on, you are one family, joined and united in God's abiding love."

Vows for Children 2:

Celebrant to bride and groom: "With the help of God, will you promise to love, respect, and honor these children (this child)?"

Bride and groom: "We will."

Celebrant to bride and groom: "Will you do your best to guide their lives with wisdom, compassion, and tenderness?"

Bride and groom: "We will."

Celebrant to bride and groom: "Will you try your utmost to be honorable and loving examples for them?"

Bride and groom: "We will."

Celebrant to bride and groom: "Will you do your best to create a loving home where peace and love prevail, to help them realize the depth and fullness of their potential?"

Bride and groom: "We will."

Celebrant to bride and groom: "Before God and before this

company, I pronounce that you are now one family, united in God's love."

Celebrant to children: "I now pronounce you brothers (sisters) (brothers and sisters)."

The Universal Ecumenical Wine Ceremony

The universal ecumenical version of the wine ceremony—though adapted from the classic Jewish wine ceremony—offers a lovely addition to any marriage ceremony. This ritual adds visual beauty, meaning, and significance. The phrasing of some of the following samples is identical to that of the classic Jewish wine ceremonies I outlined in the section on incorporating multicultural traditions (see page 288). Notice that the Hebrew transliterated and translated prayers have been eliminated to convey a more versatile, universal feeling and style.

Universal Ecumenical Wine Ceremony 1:

Celebrant: "Throughout history, in many traditions, the sharing of a cup of wine has symbolized the central moment of sharing during significant celebrations. In ancient cultures, wine has symbolized the fruit of our labors and the gathering of the harvest after the years of work, dedication, and sacrifice. It is fitting in this moment of celebration that the bride and groom now take their first sip of wine together to celebrate all that has taken place in their lives up to this point. The sharing of the wine also serves as a symbol and expression of all hope and faith in the harvest of their lives from this point forward."

Celebrant to bride and groom: "As you each sip from this

single cup of wine, you partake in an ancient ritual of sharing. From this moment on, your two lives have become as one. Drink from the cup of life and may your lives be sweet and full, and may they bring forth abundance."

Universal Ecumenical Wine Ceremony 2:

Celebrant: "The fruit of the vine symbolizes the fullness of the spirit. Wine is a symbol of the sacredness that lies within in each of us. It is a symbol of life itself. The bride and groom wish to share a glass of wine in this ceremony, as a symbol of the sharing and the joining of their lives, their fates, and their futures. As witnesses, each of us gathered here, by our very presence, shares with them this very sacred moment."

Celebrant to bride and groom: "Many days will you sit at the same table, and eat and drink together. As you share this wine, share also the sacred cup of life that will flow throughout all the days of renewal and growth that are yet to come. May the cup of your lives pour forth blessings that are sweet and full to running over."

Universal Ecumenical Wine Ceremony 3:

Celebrant: "It is fitting, in this moment of celebration, that the bride and groom now take their first sip of wine together to celebrate all that has taken place in their lives up to this point. This is also a symbol and expression of all hope and faith in the harvest of their lives from this point forward."

Celebrant to bride and groom: "As you participate in the wine ceremony and drink from this cup, may you, under God's guidance, draw contentment, peace, strength, and solace from the cup of life. May you find life's joys doubled and life's bitterness halved, because you share them together, and may all things be blessed and sanctified by companionship and love. May your lives give forth abundance, health, joy, and blessings."

Universal Ecumenical Wine Ceremony 4:

Celebrant to bride and groom: "As you each share wine from this common chalice, from this day forward you will share a lifetime together. You will share both the sweetness and the bitterness of life. You will share the joys and the sorrows of life. May each of you now, in this sacred moment of beginnings, as in all the days of renewal and growth that lie before you, drink from the sacred cup of life, and drink with consecration and with joy. May all things be hallowed and may the cup of your lives be sweet and full to overflow with love. Amen."

Universal Ecumenical Wine Ceremony 5:

Celebrant to bride and groom: "This cup represents the common cup of life—the token of a full life of harmony and of mutual sharing. The sharing of wine from this cup serves to impress upon you both that from this moment on, you will share fully life's joys and sorrows, life's bitterness and sweetness. Together, sweetness and bitterness represents the journey of two souls in love, and all of the experiences that flow naturally from that mutual joined love. When you share and bear one another's burdens, your joys are doubled and your sorrows halved, because they are shared and held by two. Those with a loving heart and a courageous spirit invite the full range of the challenges of life's journey and drink deeply from the cup of life. May your lives be blessed. Amen."

The Rose Ceremony

I preface the following rose ceremony selections with a word about my own special love for roses and for wedding ceremony elements that include these timeless beauties. While growing up in North England, I cultivated a great love for roses. My father tended our rose garden patiently and lovingly and he was the recipient of prizes and honors for his glorious blooms. I remember particularly an exquisite rose species named Lavender Lassie. Alas! I was not successful locating similar roses when planning my daughter's wedding, though we did select lovely roses in varying shades of lavender-pink. From April or May through November, the magnificent variations of full-headed roses in our English rose garden were dazzling in the daylight and in the evening the perfume was indescribable.

Depending on the color and type of rose, the meaning or symbolism will differ. A red rose signifies love, respect, and beauty. A red rosebud signifies purity and loveliness. The offering to one another of a long-stemmed red rose or rosebud speaks the perfect message, which can be interchangeable for bride or groom: "I love and respect you, my beautiful (handsome) one. You are pure and lovely (wonderful)." Some couples like to present a long-stemmed red rose to one another at the conclusion of the exchange of vows. They are then creatively placed on the altar with the stems crossed, symbolizing the entwining of the lives of the bride and groom, from this moment on.

Including Mothers in the Rose Ceremony

During a wedding ceremony, the offering of roses to mothers is always one of those particularly tender and memorable moments. A note (which can be wrapped around the stems) may be attached, upon which special words of love and gratitude have been penned by the bride and groom. Some couples ask me to read these notes to the mothers during the rose ceremony, while other couples read them directly to their mothers. These notes may also be read by the mothers after the ceremony, in private. Some couples feel that including a note is not necessary, as a perfect rose carries its own exquisite message. Personally, I agree.

My own preference in terms of when to present roses to mothers is generally sometime during mid-ceremony, after the marriage foundation address and before the exchange of vows.

An alternative and touching way of including mothers in the rose ceremony is for the bride and groom to swiftly offer each mother a rose during the recession at the conclusion of the ceremony as they make their exit. The bride and groom may also offer their mothers the same roses that they themselves exchanged to one another during the ceremony.

Including a Remembrance in the Rose Ceremony

The placing of a rose upon the altar by the bride and groom is a way of offering a tribute and remembrance to those beloveds who have passed on. As the roses are placed, the celebrant can offer an appropriate blessing; for example, "This rose, placed upon the altar, is offered in memory of those beloveds who no longer share this world with us. The deep and everlasting love that we hold for them remains precious in our hearts. Our tribute to those we loved is that we never forget them. We hold, eternal and sacred, a place for them in our minds and our hearts. They survive in the freshness of our memories, for that of Spirit is Eternal. Amen."

The Candle-Lighting Ceremony

The unity candle ceremony is nondenominational, ecumenical, with no specific religious affiliation. The beauty of this ceremony is its adaptability, meaningfulness, and the exquisite visual effect of candles.

Candle ceremonies have become popular in recent years. The ceremonious lighting of candles enhances and adds atmosphere to a ceremony. A flame represents the presence of the Spirit, or spark of divinity that lies at the very core of all beings. The overall tone and level of religious wording is optional. A unity candle set generally consists of a center column candle and two outer taper candles. More candles can be added to represent the including of children.

Generally, during a conventional candle ceremony, the two outer tapers are lit, often by the mothers, then together they light the center column.

Frankly, this version has never quite made sense to me, since the center column, to me, represents God. The two outer tapers symbolize the bride and groom (or the bride and groom and their families). Therefore my suggestion is that the taper candles are lit from the column candle. In this representation, the bride and groom are receiving from God, the source of all light. When the bride and groom light their taper candles from the center candle, they bring their individual candle flames together to form one flame. Symbolically, this represents the "greater flame" of their marriage. The merging and unifying of two flames also provides a magnificent visual image. This version of the candle ceremony was not my own idea but a version I adapted from the wedding booklet I spoke of in the introduction. My friends (and ceremony deans) Reverend Jon Mundy and Reverend Diane Berke wrote this helpful booklet. This adaptation of the candle ceremony makes infinitely more sense to me. In the event that the conventional candle ceremony is your preference, I have included a version, which follows the general formula of igniting the center column candle with the two outer taper candles. (See Bride and Groom Candle-Lighting Ceremony 8.)

For a couple with children who are planning a second wedding, the candle ceremony can be a beautiful representation and acknowledgement of children. By adding an additional candle for each child, that child is acknowledged, honored, and received into the newly formed family.

Tips and Cautions on Candle Lighting

You may have noticed that I haven't yet encouraged the participation of the mothers of the bride and groom in the candle ceremony. If the couple wishes to honor mothers by including them in the ceremony, my suggestion is: keep it simple! Have the mothers light the candles and then pass them to the bride and groom to continue the ritual themselves. I have witnessed both near and actual disasters involving nervous mothers handling candles, particularly when those mothers are wearing flowing and flammable clothing. There is a way of avoiding such disasters when the bride and groom participate in this part of the ceremony. This involves the strategic positioning of the couple in relationship to the altar or ceremonial table. There are many ceremonial alternatives available for the honoring of mothers (see section on Unity Sand Ceremony, page 261.)

When planning an outdoor ceremony, the use of hurricane lamps can be a helpful solution to the volatility of weather conditions. I have officiated ceremonies by the ocean which included the candle ceremony. In order to diffuse any disappointment on the part of guests and the couple, I simply announce that the candle flame is *symbolic* and regardless of the weather, the Light of Divinity still remains inextinguishable.

Though I have made this suggestion in a previous chapter, it is worth repeating here: before the ceremony, please remember to check the candlewicks to be sure they work.

I generally like to begin each candle ceremony with the following quote from Baal Shem Tov. Rabbi Yisroel (Israel) ben Eliezer (1698 -1760) was often called Baal Shem Tov or Besht. He was a highly revered Jewish mystical rabbi, and is considered to be the founder of Hasidic Judaism. I had originally suggested this reading for an interfaith couple whose ceremony I officiated eleven years ago. They were considering a candle-lighting ceremony *and* a Jewish wine ceremony. The groom pointed out that this reading, because of its reference to light, would be a beautiful addition to a candle-lighting ceremony. The bride agreed. I thought that both his observation and idea were brilliant; I have incorporated this ever since. Thank you, Bob and Frances.

> *From every soul there is a light*
> *that reaches straight to heaven.*
> *When two souls who are destined*
> *to be together find one another,*
> *Their streams of light flow together*
> *and a single, brighter light flows forth*
> *from their united being.*

Bride and Groom Candle-Lighting Ceremony 1:

Celebrant: "'From every soul there is a light that reaches straight to heaven. When two souls who are destined to be together find one another, their streams of light flow together and a single, brighter light flows forth from their united being.' Baal Shem Tov. When two people love one another with deep devotion and with freedom, they honor, nurture, and kindle the Inner Light in each other as nothing else quite can do. (Name) and (name), as you promise to love and honor one another today, I ask that you promise to acknowledge and honor that light within your partner as best you can each day—particularly when you forget to see that light or when you or your partner doubts its existence."

Celebrant to bride and groom: "Please light your individual candles from the center candle. These separate candle flames symbolize the individual spark of Divinity inherent within each of you as separate and unique beings. As you bring together and merge these individual flames, you create the one greater flame of your marriage. Never forget that the light of your union is made up of your connection to the Eternal Light of God, the source. (*Option:* the light of Eternal Love) The joining of these candle flames also symbolizes the joining and uniting of two families into one." (Bride and groom hold their candle flames together to form one flame.)

Bride and Groom Candle-Lighting Ceremony 2:

Celebrant: "'From every soul there is a light that reaches straight to heaven. When two souls who are destined to be together find one another, their streams of light flow together and a single, brighter light flows forth from their united being.' Baal Shem Tov. Throughout the ages among many cultures, a lighted candle is a symbol of the sacredness of life and the individual spark of divinity that lies at the heart of all beings."

Celebrant to bride and groom: "As you each light your individual candles, you acknowledge the divinity within your partner. Throughout your years together, remember and hold sacred the inner light that radiates from within the heart of your beloved. As you bring together your individual flames to form the greater flame of your union, never forget that at the center of your union lies your connection to the Ever-loving God, the source of all Life. In addition, the merging of two flames symbolizes the coming together of two families who unite as one."

Bride and Groom Candle-Lighting Ceremony 3:

Celebrant: "'From every human being, there rises a light that reaches straight to heaven. And when two souls who are destined to be together find one another, their streams of light flow together and a single, brighter light goes forth from their united being.' Baal Shem Tov. A candle flame is a symbol of the light of infinite and eternal love, born of all that is Divine. Love is what brought you together. Love is what will sustain you throughout your lives together. From love you are created, to love you will return."

Celebrant to bride and groom: "Please light your individual candles from this center candle. Now, bring your lighted candle flames together, acknowledging and symbolizing your union. As the two flames merge into one, your love for one another grows stronger and brighter. Always remember the radiant light of your union represents your connection to God, the source of all light. Amen."

Bride and Groom Candle-Lighting Ceremony 4 (includes children):

Celebrant: "The light of this center candle represents the inextinguishable light of love and unity. These separate outer candles symbolize your two separate lives and your families as they existed separately until this moment. I ask that each of you take one of these individual candles and together light them from the center candle. Bring your individual flames together to symbolize the uniting of your lives and of your families. As these two flames merge and unify, they symbolize the joining of these children into one family, bonded and united by the strength and radiance of your love for one another and for each of them."

Bride and Groom Candle-Lighting Ceremony 5:

Celebrant: "The center column candle has been ignited, symbolizing the unity of love, which binds and unites. Love is what created us and is what sustains us throughout our lives. Love impels us to tap the deepest place within our own hearts. Love builds and creates the depth and strength of the best that we can be. These individual candles symbolize the two distinct lives of two in love."

Celebrant to bride and groom: "As you light these candles from the unity candle, you draw to you the fire of infinite love. Hold your individual flames together to form the one greater flame of your union in marriage and of the inextinguishable love that brought you—and will hold you—together. Amen."

Bride and Groom Candle-Lighting Ceremony 6:

Celebrant to bride and groom: "This unity candle flame is a symbol of the oneness of this union and the eternal flame of love that burns within your two hearts. (Name) and (name), please light your candles from the unity candle. The individual candles represent your lives before today, the love and the care that nurtured you as you grew. They represent all that you can be from this day on, all of your possibilities as individuals. As you light your candles from the unity candle and join the separate flames together, your individual hopes, dreams, and futures will now be entwined and united. May the sacred and eternal flame of love continue to burn within your hearts."

Bride and Groom Candle-Lighting Ceremony 7:

Celebrant to bride and groom: "'From every human being, there rises a light that reaches straight to heaven. And when two souls who are destined to be together find one another, their streams of light flow together and a single, brighter light goes forth from their united being.' Baal Shem Tov. The candles you are about to light symbolize the flame of two people in love and the flame of the spirit, which is the source of that love. The flame of these candles also represents the flame of commitment, because it takes the two of you, working together, to keep the inner fire of the spirit of love alive and burning. Please light your individual candles from the center unity candle, a symbol of the Divine and unifying force in each of you that unites you in love and your marriage."

Bride and Groom Candle-Lighting Ceremony 8:

The celebrant has previously lighted the two taper candles.

Celebrant to bride and groom: "The unity candle that you are about to light represents the flame of love that will shine throughout your lives—the central source of all love, which by its very nature is an attribute of the Spirit. The two outer candles symbolize your separate lives. Within your two separate lives, there have existed separate dreams, hopes, and aspirations. Please each of you take an outer candle and together light the center unity candle. As you do so, you are joining your separate lives to one life—united, vivified, and unified by the burning fire of your love for one another. May the joining of your hearts and your lives create a home where the light of love, harmony, and joy prevail. Amen."

Bride and Groom Candle-Lighting Ceremony 9:

Celebrant: "The bride and groom have requested that they share in a candle-lighting ceremony, symbolizing the special flame that burns at the heart of all beings."

Celebrant to bride and groom: "As you light these candles today, may the brightness of the flame shine throughout your lives as a great beacon of light, lighting the way for you. May this light give forth illumination in times of darkness. May it radiate warmth and comfort in the cold. May it offer you strength, courage, and assurance in times of uncertainty. As you bring together your individual flames, they merge together, becoming one flame—the radiant flame of your union in marriage. Never forget that the light of your union will be ever sustained by the Sacred Light of Divine Love. Amen."

Bride and Groom Candle-Lighting Ceremony 10:

Celebrant to bride and groom: "As you light these candles and draw together the two flames we call upon the Sacred Light of the Holy Spirit to bless you. (*Alternatives:* the Sacred Light of God, the Sacred Light of Love) May the light of these candles shine eternally in your lives. May it add clarity to every goal and brilliance to every achievement. May it be a beacon of light to guide and protect you. May it radiate the light of blessings and benedictions throughout your marriage. May it illuminate the darkest moments. May it lighten the heaviest burden. May it give each of you strength and vitality. May all that is virtuous, honorable, and beautiful remain with you always. Amen."

The Unity Sand Ceremony

If your preference is a unity candle ceremony, but your wedding ceremony is scheduled for outdoors, you might want to consider this beautiful alternative to the candle ceremony. Even with the use of hurricane lamps, you may feel more at ease with the sand ceremony. The unity sand ceremony is really rather simple. The wording and symbolism can be similar to that of the unity candle ceremony. The effortless format goes as follows:

- A large, empty glass container or chalice is placed in the center of the altar table.

- Flanking this empty chalice, on either side, are two smaller containers filled with sand, each of different colors chosen by the bride and groom.

- At the appropriate time, the bride and groom, each in turn, pour and blend alternate layers of the contents of their own designated containers into one larger chalice, creating beautiful layers of colored sand.

This unity chalice can become a souvenir of your wedding ceremony. The sand ceremony is also a wonderful way of symbolically honoring and welcoming the children of the bride and groom into a new family unit. When rewritten, this ceremony works beautifully as a vows renewal ceremony. For example, Elaine and Walter (see page 340) used a sand ceremony in their vows renewal. The sand ceremony was conducted to symbolically honor three generations of a loving family. We began by having Walter and Elaine each pour the first two layers of sand, representing themselves as matriarch and patriarch, the "foundation" of the family. Then, in turn, each grandchild (who also represented their parents) poured a layer of sand—each using a different color—into the unity chalice.

Unity Sand Ceremony 1:

Celebrant to bride and groom: "These two separate vessels of sand represent the past. They also represent your separate lives and your separate journeys up until this moment. Each of your lives also include separate families and separate friends. The center chalice is empty, and represents all that the future holds for you. In a moment, your lives will change. The two of you are about to create and shape your future lives. I now ask that you each take your separate vessels and, in turn, pour the sand into the center chalice. As these grains of sand blend together, you are now joining your individual lives and journeys into one life of companionship and love. This also represents the joining of these friends and family members.

As these grains of sand can never be separated nor can they be rearranged back into their original formation, nor can you ever be separated in your love for one another. May you walk forward joined as one in a strong and loving union, blessed and joined on the path of love and marriage."

Unity Sand Ceremony 2 (includes children):

In addition to the two separate vessels of colored sand, which represent the bride and groom, there is also one vessel for each child. The bride and groom may each choose separate earth tones that represent their role as the strength and foundation in the lives of their children.

Celebrant to bride and groom: "These separate vessels of sand represent the past. They also represent your separate lives and separate journeys up until this moment. Each of your lives also includes these wonderful children who are about to be joined together, forming a new and united family. The center chalice is empty and represents all that the future holds for you. In a moment your lives will be forever change."

Celebrant to bride: "I now ask that you take your separate vessel and pour the sand into the center chalice."

Celebrant to groom: "Please take your separate vessel and pour the sand into the center chalice."

Celebrant to children: "Please each take your separate vessels and pour the sand into the center chalice."

Celebrant: "As these grains of sand have now been joined into one unit, so are your lives now joined as one family. As these grains of sand can never be separated and rearranged back to their original formation, nor can this family ever be separated in love, blessings, and unity."

Special Remembrances, Dedications, and Acknowledgements

The emotional charge of a wedding ceremony often draws upon those special childhood memories, particularly of those beloveds who are no longer with us to share in the joys and celebrations of the ceremony. Understandably, many couples wish to acknowledge and remember those beloveds. The perfect time for a remembrance, dedication, or acknowledgement is at the beginning of the ceremony, before the opening benediction. When a remembrance or dedication is specific to one or more named beloveds who have passed on, this can be offered silently or in words, as the following examples illustrate.

Remembrances

There are many ways to remember those beloveds who are no longer with us. I prefer to keep a remembrance brief and simple. Most couples want to honor these loved ones without overshadowing or weighing down the ceremony with sadness and melancholy. A wedding ceremony alone generates deep and tender memories and feelings. It is vital to be sensitive to these highly charged emotions and attempt to not create unnecessary emotional overload. However, it is essential and respectful to offer a fitting and dignified remembrance. The key, then, is to say a great deal in very few words. A few carefully chosen words can say volumes. Expressed correctly, these words can honor and *celebrate* the memory of a loved one, thereby diffusing overt sadness and adding a note of respect, thankfulness, and gratitude to the ceremony.

In addition to a dedication or a remembrance, some of my clients opt to honor a loved one by placing a photo on the altar, or by including a moment of silence, a special reading, or a favorite song in their memory. Also, the choice of wedding flowers can be intentionally selected to honor a beloved one who has passed on and it may be mentioned in the program.

Dedications

A dedication is a simplified remembrance. Often it is offered as a generalized statement, sometimes requiring only one sentence. The intended purpose is to dedicate the ceremony to a person or persons who have passed. The beloved can be named or go unnamed.

Acknowledgments

Acknowledgements offer a loving way to honor those friends and family members who cannot attend the ceremony due to diverse circumstances. Whether their absence is due to illness, geographical constraints, or scheduling conflicts, if their presence is missed, they can be acknowledged. Once again, my suggestion is to keep the acknowledgement short and brief.

Remembrance 1 (specific):

Celebrant: "At this time, we take a moment to remember those beloveds who no longer share this world with us, (name)(s). We hold them eternally in our hearts and memory, so that their presence is felt here with us today. Amen."

Remembrance 2 (specific):

Celebrant: "Let us remember the life (lives) of (name)(s). Our greatest tribute to those who no longer share this world with us is that their memory lives on in our hearts.

Remembrance 3 (specific):

Celebrant: "We give thanks for the life of (name). We hold him (her) precious in our hearts and eternally alive in our memories. May he (she) live on in the in the eternal home within the loving heart of God. Amen."

Remembrance 4 (specific):

Celebrant: "At this time, I would ask that we remember (name) (s) and our love for him (her) (them). We hold precious in our hearts each moment that we shared with him (her) (them). We offer up gratitude for the great privilege to have known and loved him (her) (them). We honor his (her) (their) life (lives) and memory which we will hold eternally sacred. Amen."

Remembrance 5 (specific):

Celebrant: "Let us open our hearts as we take a moment to remember and honor all of those beloveds who no longer share our lives in this world: (name)(s). Our memories of him (her) (them) are precious and sacred to us. Our lives will forever be blessed for having known and having shared our love with him (her) (them). Our greatest tribute to those we loved is that we keep them eternally alive in our hearts. Amen."

Remembrance 6 (general):

Celebrant: "At this time, we take a moment to pay tribute and remember all of those beloveds who are no longer here with us in this world. Let us remember that they live on in our memories and in the love we hold for them in our hearts. For that born of Spirit is eternal. Amen."

Remembrance 7 (general):

Celebrant: "Since this ceremony is a celebration of a marriage, it is appropriate and fitting that we remember and celebrate the lives of those beloveds who meant so much to the bride and groom and their families. Though they no longer share this world with us, their presence is felt here with us today. Our love for them lives on in our hearts, for love is eternal and never dies. Amen."

Remembrance 8 (Rose Ceremony, general):

Celebrant: "The bride and groom will now offer one another a red rose. These roses signify the depth of the love and respect they hold for one another. They will now place these roses on the altar in memory of those beloveds who are no longer with us. The deep and eternal love that the bride and groom hold for them is precious and eternal. Our tribute to those we loved is that we never forget them. We hold them in the sanctuary of our hearts. They survive in the freshness of our memories. For that born of Spirit is Eternal. Amen."

Dedication 1 (specific):

Celebrant: "The bride, groom, and their families have

requested that this ceremony be dedicated to the memory of (name)(s). Our love for him (her) (them) and the precious memories of him (her) (them) that we hold sacred in the depths of our hearts will live on eternally. May he (she) (they) abide in the loving light of the eternal and ever-living God. Amen."

Dedication 2 (specific):

Celebrant: "This ceremony is dedicated to the loving memory of: (name)(s). Our memories of him (her) (them) are precious to us. For love lives on eternally. Amen."

Dedication 3 (general):

Celebrant: "The families of the bride and groom dedicate this ceremony to the memory of all of those beloveds who no longer share this world with us. Our greatest tribute to them is that we hold them forever precious in our memories and in the quiet sanctuary our hearts. Amen."

Dedication 4 (general):

Celebrant: "This ceremony is dedicated to all of those beloveds who are no longer with us, so that their presence and our love for them is felt and acknowledged today. May they be held forever in the precious arms of God. For that born of Spirit is eternal and never dies. Amen."

Dedication 5 (general):

Celebrant: "We dedicate this ceremony to those who are no longer sharing this earthly life with us, so that their presence is honored and felt here today. Our love for them will live on eternally. Amen."

Dedication 6 (specific):

Celebrant: "The bride, groom, and their families are dedicating this ceremony to all those who perished on September eleven, two thousand and one. May they be carried to their eternal abode in the loving Light of God. May their families find peace and solace. Amen."

Acknowledgement 1 (general):

Celebrant: "We acknowledge all those friends and family members who could not attend this ceremony today due to the great distance between us. Their love and support is carried to us over the miles, as on the wings of love. For love transcends all barriers, obstacles, time, and space. We acknowledge our love for them and hold them deeply in our hearts."

Acknowledgement 2 (general):

Celebrant: "We acknowledge those who could not attend this ceremony due to previous unbreakable commitments. Though they are not here today to share this celebration, we acknowledge their loving and heartfelt wishes for us. We bless them and hold them in the depths of our hearts."

Acknowledgement 3 (specific):

Celebrant: "We would like to acknowledge the Burwell family at this time. Today they celebrate the wedding of their daughter. They send us their well-wishes and blessings. Though their physical presence is missed, their love and support is ever present."

Acknowledgement 4 (specific):

Celebrant: "At this moment, we offer our heartfelt congratulations to Jennifer and Joe Gomersal and their families. They are not attending this ceremony due to the arrival of their baby daughter, who was born during the early hours of this morning. We shower them with love, sincere blessings, and congratulations."

The Closing Benediction

A closing benediction is a final blessing that may be offered in a number of ways. Final thoughts and advice can be offered to the couple within these closing words, though I feel it preferable to steer away from "preachy"-sounding verbiage. A closing benediction can be a simple blessing offered to the couple, their joined new life, and their families. The tone may be religious, spiritual, or nonreligious, and can be as traditional as the following priestly blessing:

• May God bless you and keep you.

• May God's light shine upon you and give you peace. Amen.

The closing benediction is the optimum time and opportunity to offer a wedding charge as a closing benediction. Points and themes that have already been covered during the ceremony can be reiterated. I sometimes adapt and repeat parts of the exchange of vows that may have been particularly poignant, memorable, or even humorous.

Closing Benediction 1:

Celebrant: "May your hearts be open, your love be full, your lives be joined, your fates be sealed, your union be strong, your home be sheltered, and your marriage be blessed. Amen."

Closing Benediction 2:

Celebrant: "We give thanks for the great miracle of love and for this union born out that Divine love. May the sacred blessings of this day continue to flow down upon the two of you, like a river of pure light, showering forth peace, joy, strength and encouragement upon and into your lives. And may you remember never to hold these blessings only to yourselves but let them pour forth like wine to nourish, make sacred, and bless all who touch your lives. Amen."

Closing Benediction 3:

Celebrant: "The Lord bless you and keep you, the Lord make His face shine upon you, and be gracious to you. The Lord lift up His countenance upon you, and give you peace. Amen."

Closing Benediction 4
(A Native American Wedding Blessing, Version 1):

by Maureen Burwell Pollinger.

Celebrant: "May the healing sun that watches over the earth warm you.

May the soft breeze that whispers over the plains cool you.

May your home give you shelter from the storm and may the soft rain nourish your pastures.

May the stars in the heavens be your blanket of blessings and may the silver moon light your way over the long night's waters.

Let your words to one another be as sacred as the songbird's song and clear as call of the loon.

May your hearts shine as brilliantly as the northern lights over the mountain peaks and as beautifully as the summer rainbow.

May your embrace be as gentle as the morning dove and your love as mighty as the roaring buffalo.

May blessings linger above you as the humming bird hovers over the cobweb thistle, and may abundance rain upon you.

May your love be as powerful as the mountain thunder, as vast as the endless sky and as deep as the greatest ocean.

Be a soft pillow for your beloved to fall upon in times of sadness and celebrate together in times of gladness.

Proclaim your union, from the highest mountain to the deepest valley, that those who hear may also be so blessed.

Walk together hand-in-hand upon life's unpredictable journey.

Rejoice at sunrise, for one more day with your beloved and when the sun sets deeply over the plains offer a prayer of gratitude, for another day together.

For your two lives are now woven together as one life and your love will live forever in the heart of The Great Spirit."

Closing Benediction 5
(Adapted from A Native American Wedding Blessing, Version 2):
by Maureen Burwell Pollinger.

    Celebrant: "May the healing sun that watches over the earth warm you.

May the soft breeze that whispers over the plains cool you.

May your home give you shelter from the storm and may the soft rain nourish your pastures.

May the stars in the heavens be your blanket of blessings and may the silver moon light your way over the long night's waters.

May your love be as powerful as the mountain thunder, as vast as the endless sky and as deep as the greatest ocean.

Be a soft pillow for your beloved to fall upon in times of sadness and celebrate together in times of gladness.

Proclaim your union, from the highest mountain to the deepest valley, that those who hear may also be so blessed.

Walk together hand-in-hand upon life's unpredictable journey.

Rejoice at sunrise, for one more day with your beloved and when the sun sets deeply over the plains offer a prayer of gratitude, for another day together.

For your two lives are now woven together as one life and your love will live forever in the heart of The Great Spirit."

Closing Benediction 6
(Celtic blessing, adapted from ancient Gaelic runes):

Celebrant: "Deep peace of the running wave to you. Deep peace of the flowing air to you. Deep peace of the quiet earth to you. Deep peace of the shining stars to you. Deep peace of the Son of Peace to you."

Closing Benediction 7
(Adapted from the *Irish Blessing*, version 1):

Celebrant: "May the road rise to meet you. May the wind be always at your back. May the sun shine warm upon your face, the rains fall soft upon your fields. And until we meet again, may God hold you in the hollow of his hand."

Closing Benediction 8
(Adapted from the *Irish Blessing*, version 2):

Celebrant: "May God be with you and bless you; may you see your children's children. May you be poor in misfortune, rich in blessings. May you know nothing but happiness from this day forward."

Closing Benediction 9
(Adapted from the *Irish Blessing*, version 3):

Celebrant: "May the road rise to meet you. May the wind be always at your back. May the warm rays of sun fall upon your home. And may the hand of a friend always be near. May green be the grass you walk on. May blue be the skies above you. May pure be the joys that surround you. May true be the hearts that love you."

Closing Benediction 10
(Adapted from the *Irish Blessing*, version 4):

Celebrant: "May the raindrops fall lightly on your brow. May the soft winds freshen your spirit. May the sunshine brighten your heart. May the burdens of the day rest lightly upon you. And may God enfold you in the mantle of His love. But rich or poor, quick or slow, may you know nothing but happiness, from this day forward. May the joys of today be those of tomorrow."

Closing Benediction 11:

Celebrant: "May all that you have already become—through your separate life journeys, which have brought you to this moment of the joining of the two—and all that you will become—as a consequence of the promises you have made and the life that you will now continue to develop—expand and grow in love for all of your days together. Amen."

The Universal Hand-Joining Ritual

The universal hand-joining ritual is an adaptation of Celtic hand-fasting. It is intended to precede the final pronouncement. I chose to include this ritual simply because it lends itself so exquisitely to the closing phases of most, if not all, ceremonies. In an attempt to create a universal version of this lovely ceremony, I reworked the traditional hand-fasting, creating a more generic representation. My suggestion is to have the final pronouncement directly follow this ritual, more or less without a pause.

Universal Hand-Joining Ritual 1:

Celebrant: "Below you, the earth; above you, the sky. As time passes, remember, as you tread the sacred path of marriage, your lives will be held strong and secure, as the sacred earth below holds you now. As time passes, remember also that your love for one another is as infinite as the vast sky above. (Name) and (name), as I tie your hands together, may your lives, fates, and futures be so tied entwined and wrapped in the Infinite Love of God. For it is your love for each other that brought you together and it is the entwining of that love which will hold this bond unbroken. May the Divine hand of God be upon you, bless you and hold you, even as you are held and tied together today. Amen."

Universal Hand-Joining Ritual 2:

Celebrant: "Today your lives are joined in a union of love and trust. Above you are the stars and below you is the earth. Like the stars, may your love illuminate and bless each other. Like the earth, may your love provide a firm foundation upon which to build a strong marriage. (Name) and (name), as your hands are tied together today, let the vastness of this love infinitely bless you. For it is your love that brought you together, and it is your love that will hold and keep you together. Amen."

Universal Hand-Joining Ritual 3:

Celebrant: "(Name) and (name), as I tie together your hands, may your lives be held steadfast and firmly by your love for one another. These promises you have declared this day will greatly strengthen your bond and your union throughout the coming years, as you embark upon a life joined in love. May the lives of those whom the Loving God has brought and tied together be held securely with the ties that are forever unbroken. Amen."

Universal Hand-Joining Ritual 4:

Celebrant: "(Name) and (name), as your hands are joined together, may your lives be held securely joined by your commitment to one another and by the infinite spirit of love. Let the Divine Hand of God be upon you today and always. For those whom God and love hath brought and held together, let no-one put asunder."

Universal Hand-Joining Ritual 5:

Celebrant: "(Name) and (name), with the entwining of this knot do I tie and hold together all of your hopes and dreams; all of the prayers, benedictions, and well-wishes of each one gathered here today; all of the vows and promises that you have made to one another this day; and as this knot is tied, we speak also our intentions to God. These promises made today and the ties that are bound will greatly strengthen your bond and your union throughout the years of your life journey, as you embark upon a life joined together as husband and wife. May those whom the loving hand of God has brought and tied together remain entwined in a love that is forever unbroken."

Universal Hand-Joining Ritual 6:

Celebrant: "With the entwining of this knot, we tie all of the love and joy wished by each witness to this ceremony. In the joining and tying of these hands, so are your lives now held and tied one to another. By this cord woven of many threads are you thus bound to your vows. Your lives are now threaded and woven together. May this knot remain tied to the end of your days. May this cord draw your hands together in love, never to be used in displeasure. You two are entwined in love, bound by commitment and joy. May you be strong over hardship and victorious over difficulties, drawing together in a greater bond all the promises you have made today. Hold tightly to one another throughout life's journey together. May this cord be a symbol of two lives now unbreakably tied."

The Final Pronouncement

The final pronouncement is an official proclamation and public statement by the officiating celebrant that the bride and groom are now legally husband and wife. Regardless of the ceremony content and style, I prefer to include in the final pronouncement a statement of the legal authority, which grants the celebrant the right to make such a proclamation. This is a way of offering respect and acknowledging the importance and awesomeness of each and every marriage.

Final Pronouncement 1:

Celebrant: "As you have each made this commitment to one another in the Holy bond of marriage before God and this loving community of witnesses, it is my legal right as a minister by the powers vested in me—and it is also my greatest joy—to pronounce you husband and wife."

Final Pronouncement 2:

Celebrant: "(Name) and (name), though I have officiated your ceremony, it is beyond my power to sanctify your relationship— because the two of you have already done so, in your hearts, through the love you share with one another. Since love is a direct attribute of God, only God alone can truly and fully bless this marriage. Therefore, in the name of Almighty God before these loving witnesses, it is my legal right and my greatest privilege to pronounce that you are, indeed, husband and wife."

Final Pronouncement 3:

Celebrant: "By the powers vested in me as a minister, and as witness to the solemn vows you have made and to the love between you, it is my greatest joy and my legal right to now pronounce that from this moment on, you are now joined in the bond of marriage."

Final Pronouncement 4:

Celebrant: "As each of you have declared your love for one another by the exchange of your vows and the promises you have made this day, and by affirming your acceptance of the responsibilities of this union before these witnesses and before all that is Sacred and Divine, it is my legal right as a celebrant by the powers vested in me, and it is also my greatest joy, to now pronounce that you are husband and wife."

Final Pronouncement 5:

Celebrant: "As you walk forth together today, joined in love and bonded in marriage through the vows and promises you have given to one another before these loving witnesses, it is my legal right by the powers vested in me by the State of New York and it is my greatest privilege to pronounce before all that is Sacred and Divine that you are now husband and wife."

Final Pronouncement 6:

Celebrant: "You have chosen each other to love, you have given your solemn vow to one another for all of your days together, therefore before Almighty God and before this community of loving witnesses, it is my legal right by the powers vested in me—and it is my greatest blessing and privilege—to pronounce that you are now husband and wife."

Final Pronouncement 7:

Celebrant: "As your joined lives stretch out before you, know that you are committed and dedicated to each other because of the vows you have exchanged this day, born of the love you share. Therefore, because of these promises you have made to one another today, before God and these witnesses, it is my legal right and my greatest pleasure to pronounce that you are now legally married."

Final Pronouncement 8:

Celebrant: "Having witnessed your vows and the promises made this day before all assembled here as witnesses and as a community of loving friends and family members: by the powers vested in me, it is my legal right and duty—as it is also my greatest honor—to pronounce and make known that you are now husband and wife."

Review Checklist

❑ Review "points to remember" at the beginning of this chapter.

❑ Review the lists of words and phrases at the beginning of this chapter.

❑ Decide on your preferences regarding:

    ❑ Words of promises

    ❑ Descriptive words

    ❑ Verbs

    ❑ Phrases

    ❑ Words of personal endearment

    ❑ Negative words

❑ Decide on your preferences and comfort level in terms of invoking God's name.

❑ Review all ceremony components and samples, from invocation to final pronouncement.

❑ Make a written record of your choices.

❑ If either the bride or the groom has children and is planning on involving them in the ceremony, read the section on "honoring and joining of children," then decide on how you would prefer to include and honor them:

    ❑ By honoring them by name during an appropriate segment of the ceremony

    ❑ By their participation in parts of the ceremony

    ❑ By inviting them to participate in the procession

    ❑ By including them in a "vows for children" ceremony

    ❑ By presenting them with a special gift

Chapter Nine

Multicultural and Interfaith Traditions

Incorporating Multicultural and Interfaith Traditions

Generally, though not always, an interfaith ceremony necessitates the co-participation of two celebrants. This can work well, providing the two personalities do not clash or compete. The practical problem for many couples is that having two celebrants can be prohibitively expensive. There is, however, a practical alternative: an ecumenical-interfaith minister/celebrant. She or he can to some measure be a representative of both traditions. It is important to bear in mind that the ecumenical-interfaith celebrant cannot be *entirely* knowledgeable about all religious traditions. But it is possible, with the awareness of a few simple rules, that this alternative to engaging two celebrants can work beautifully.

- Though an interfaith ceremony addresses both religious traditions, the ceremony will flow more smoothly when the general tone of the ceremony is not excessively religious.

- There needs to be equal and fair acknowledgement of both traditions.

- During the ceremonial components of some religious traditions, the celebrant may require the participation of a family member or friend.

This last point is vital. Ecumenical-interfaith ministers are familiar with some of the sacred texts and traditions of many major religious traditions, but not necessarily all of them. The celebrant may find that some ceremonies may be complicated and unfamiliar to her or him, particularly those involving ceremonial rites conducted in foreign languages. It may be preferable to invite a family member or friend as assistant or participant. By the way, inviting someone to participate is also a wonderful way of honoring that person.

The following outline of interfaith and multicultural traditions is, from my experience, listed in order of the frequency in numbers of these traditions that I personally officiate. This is my own opinion, based entirely on my own ministerial practice and personal experience as a celebrant.

Jewish Traditions

The *Shehekhianu* as an Opening Prayer

Rabbi Reuben Modek, founder and director of the Hebrew Learning Circles in Nyack, New York, explains that the *Shehekhianu* is a blessing recited when something is done or occurs for the first time within the cycle of one year. Rabbi Modek describes the *Shehekhianu* in his own poetic way as "a blessing of firsts." He goes on to explain, "Let us take the two first nights of Passover, for example. Candles are lit and blessed to mark the onset of all Jewish festive nights, including those of Passover. However, on the very first evening of Passover, in addition to the blessing over candle lighting, the *Shehekhianu* is recited as an additional blessing, marking the first night of Passover within the cycle of that year. We can also apply the same principle to the eating of a specific seasonal food. Fruit is an example: in addition to the customary blessing offered each time we eat fruit, on the occasion of eating a particular fruit for the first time in that year's cycle, we also recite the *Shehekhianu*. The ancient Hebrew sages knew, as do we, that any conscious first is a 'wow' that deserves special extra gratitude to the Creator."

Transliteration: Barukh atah Adonai, Eloheynu, melekh ha-olam she-hekheeyanu v'keey'manu v'heegeeyanu la-z,man ha-zeh.

Translation: Blessed are you, Lord, our God, ruler of the universe, who has kept us alive, sustained us, and enabled us to reach this season.

The Seven Blessings 1:

- Blessed art Thou, O lord our God, King of the Universe, who hast created the fruit of the vine.

- Blessed art Thou, O lord our God, King of the Universe, who has created all things for His glory.

- Blessed art Thou, O lord our God, King of the Universe, creator of man.

- Blessed art Thou, O lord our God, King of the Universe, who hast made man in his image, after his likeness, and hast prepared for him, out of his very self, a perpetual fabric. Blessed art Thou, O Lord, creator of man.

- May she who was barren be exceedingly glad and rejoice when her children are united in her midst in joy. Blessed art Thou, O Lord, who makes Zion joyful through her children.

- Lord, make these beloved companions greatly rejoice even as Thou didst rejoice at Thy creation in the Garden of Eden as of old. Blessed art Thou, O Lord, who makest bridegroom and bride to rejoice.

- Blessed art Thou, O lord our God, King of the Universe, who has created joy and gladness, bridegroom and bride, mirth and exultation, pleasure and delight, love and brotherhood, peace and fellowship. Soon may there be heard in the cities of Judah and in the streets of Jerusalem the voice of joy and gladness, the voice of the bridegroom and the voice of the bride, the jubilant voice of the bridegrooms from the canopies, and of youths from their feasts of song. Blessed art Thou, O Lord who makest the bridegroom to rejoice with the bride.

The Seven Blessings 2:

- Blessed are You, Eternal our God, Sovereign of the Universe, Creator of the fruit of the vine.

- Blessed are You, Eternal our God, Sovereign of the Universe, who created everything for Your glory.

- Blessed are You, Eternal our God, Sovereign of the Universe, who formed the first human.

- Blessed are You, Eternal our God, Sovereign of the Universe, who created humanity in Your image, patterned after Your image and likeness, and enabled them to perpetuate this image. Blessed are You, Eternal, who created humanity.

- Bring joy and exultation to the barren one [Israel] as her children are joyfully gathered to her. Blessed are You, Eternal, who makes Zion glad with her children.

- Grant great joy to these loving companions, as You once gladdened your creations in the Garden of Eden. Blessed are you, Eternal, who gladdens the groom and bride.

- Blessed are You, Eternal our God, Sovereign of the universe, who created joy and gladness, groom and bride, mirth, glad song, pleasure and delight, love and harmony, peace and companionship. May it be your will, Eternal our God, that there will soon be heard in the cities of Judah and streets of Jerusalem the voice of joy, the voice of gladness, the voice of groom, and the voice of bride, the sound of grooms rejoicing under the wedding canopy and of youths feasting and singing. Blessed are You, Eternal, who gladdens the groom with the bride.

The Breaking of the Glass

In Jewish ceremonies, at the conclusion of the final blessing, final pronouncement, and the nuptial kiss, the groom breaks a glass by crushing it with his right foot. Traditionally, this is the same glass from which the couple partook of the wine during the wine ceremony. This glass is thereby destroyed to ensure that no one else can drink from it, as a remembrance of the destruction of the Holy Temple in Jerusalem. Traditionally, this custom was also incorporated into the ceremony to remind everyone that even at the height of one's personal joy, we must nevertheless remember the destruction of the Temple in Jerusalem. Some interpretations maintain that the shattering of the glass symbolizes the breaking of our hearts as we remember the destruction of the Temple.

The *Chuppah*

A Jewish wedding ceremony takes place beneath a *chuppah*. This visually beautiful canopy frames and "contains" the wedding party, similarly to the aesthetic function of a picture frame, as it focalizes and draws attention to its contents in order to enhance and honor them. The *chuppah* symbolizes the home, particularly the first home that is created as the couple embarks upon their married life together. A home, like the *chuppah*, is open to and supported by friends, family, and community. The open sides and temporary nature of the *chuppah* are also reminiscent of Abraham and Sarah's tent, as described in Genesis.

The Priestly Blessing

The Lord bless you and keep you; the Lord make His face shine upon you, and be gracious to you; the Lord lift up His countenance upon you, and give you peace. Amen.

The Jewish Wine Ceremony

I have a particular love of the Jewish wine ceremony and often encourage my non-Jewish couples to consider including this exquisite and universally spiritual tradition in their ceremony. This ceremony is visually so beautiful that the ritual speaks for itself and can even be done without explanation or words.

The Sharing of the Wine 1:

The Hebrew blessing of the wine: Bar-uch' A-tah' Adonai El-o-hei-nu me'-lech ha-o-lam' bo-re' pe-ri' ha-ga'-fen.

Translation: Blessed are you, Lord, Our God, King of the universe. You created the fruit of the vine.

Celebrant: "The years of our lives are as a cup of wine poured out for us to drink. Within this cup, there is contained all that is sweet, joyful, and hopeful. This same cup also holds the bitter wine of life's struggles and difficulties. Those who are courageous draw fully upon life, drinking deeply, and inviting the full range of experiences into their being."

Celebrant to bride and groom: "As you drink from this cup, acknowledge that your separate lives have become as one vessel from which you share your joys and your sorrows, and from which together you will receive mutual strength, support, and sustenance for all the unpredictable days of your lives. Amen."

The Sharing of the Wine 2:

The Hebrew blessing of the wine: Bar-uch' A-tah' Adonai El-o-hei-nu me'-lech ha-o-lam' bo-re' pe-ri' ha-ga'-fen.

Translation: Blessed are you, Lord, Our God, King of the universe. You created the fruit of the vine.

Celebrant: "Throughout the ages, among many people and traditions, wine has symbolized the fullness of life. Drinking wine from a common chalice also represents a deeper sharing of life and love. The bride and groom have asked that they share a glass of wine in this ceremony, symbolizing their union with each other, with each one of us gathered here as witnesses, and with the sacred flow of life itself."

Celebrant to bride and groom: "Many days you will sit at the same table, eat, and drink together. Drink now, and may the cup of your lives be full to running over. Amen."

The Sharing of the Wine 3:

The Hebrew blessing of the wine: Bar-uch' A-tah' Adonai El-o-hei-nu me'-lech ha-o-lam' bo-re' pe-ri' ha-ga'-fen.

Translation: Blessed are you, Lord, Our God, King of the universe. You created the fruit of the vine.

Celebrant to bride and groom: "As you each share wine from this common chalice, from this day forward you will share a lifetime together. You each will share the sweetness and the bitterness of life. You will share the joys and the sorrows of life. You will support one another through times of sorrow. You will rejoice with one another through times of joy. May each of you now, in this sacred moment of beginnings, as in all the days of renewal and growth that are yet to come in your life together that lies before you, drink from the sacred cup of life, and drink with consecration and with joy. May the cup of your lives be sweet and full and overflow with love. Amen."

The Sharing of the Wine 4:

The Hebrew blessing of the wine: Bar-uch' A-tah' Adonai El-o-hei-nu me'-lech ha-o-lam' bo-re' pe-ri' ha-ga'-fen.

Translation: Blessed are you, Lord, Our God, King of the universe. You created the fruit of the vine.

Celebrant: "Throughout history, in many traditions, the sharing of a cup of wine has symbolized the central moment of sharing during significant moments of celebration. In ancient cultures, wine symbolized the fruit of our labors and the gathering of the harvest after the months of work, dedication, and sacrifice. It is fitting in this moment of celebration that the bride and groom now take their first sip of wine together to celebrate all that has taken place in their lives up to this point. This is also a symbol and expression of all hope and faith in the harvest of their lives from this point forward."

Celebrant to bride and groom: "(Name) and (name), may your lives give forth abundance, health, joy and blessings."

The Sharing of the Wine 5:

The Hebrew blessing of the wine: Bar-uch' A-tah' Adonai El-o-hei-nu me'-lech ha-o-lam' bo-re' pe-ri' ha-ga'-fen.

Translation: Blessed are you, Lord, Our God, King of the universe. You created the fruit of the vine.

Celebrant: "The fruit of the vine symbolizes the fullness of the spirit. Wine is a symbol of the sacredness that lies within each of us. It is a symbol of life itself. The bride and groom wish to share a glass of wine in this ceremony, as a symbol of the sharing and the joining of their lives, fates, and futures. They also include each of us gathered here as witnesses, who share with them this very sacred moment."

Celebrant to bride and groom: "Many days will you sit at the same table, and eat and drink together. As you share this wine, share also the sacred cup of life throughout all the days of renewal and growth that are yet to come. May the cup of your lives pour forth blessings that are sweet and full to running over."

The Sharing of the Wine 6:

The Hebrew blessing of the wine: Bar-uch' A-tah' Adonai El-o-hei-nu me'-lech ha-o-lam' bo-re' pe-ri' ha-ga'-fen.

Translation: Blessed are you Lord Our God, King of the universe. You created the fruit of the vine.

Celebrant to bride and groom: "As you share the wine from this chalice, so may you share your lives. May you explore the mysteries of this union and share in the reflection of love in one another's souls. From love all things are born, and unto love they return. And as you sip this wine, you partake in an ancient ritual of sharing. May you find life's joys increased and life's bitterness sweetened, and all of life deepened, enriched, and hallowed by God's blessings upon you. From this moment on, your two lives have become one. Drink from the cup of life and may your lives bring forth abundance. Amen."

The Sharing of the Wine 7:

The Hebrew blessing of the wine: Bar-uch' A-tah' Adonai El-o-hei-nu me'-lech ha-o-lam' bo-re' pe-ri' ha-ga'-fen.

Translation: Blessed are you, Lord, Our God, King of the universe. You created the fruit of the vine.

Celebrant to bride and groom: "This cup represents the common cup of life; the token of a full life of harmony and of mutual sharing. The sharing of wine from this cup serves to impress upon you both that from this moment on, you will share fully life's joys and sorrows, life's bitterness and sweetness. Together, sweetness and bitterness represent the journey of two souls in love, and all of the experiences that flow naturally from that mutual joined love. When you share and bear one another's burdens, your joys are doubled and your sorrows halved, because they are shared and held by two. Those with a loving heart and a courageous spirit invite the full range of the challenges of life's journey and drink deeply from the cup of life. May your lives be blessed. Amen."

Jewish Exchange of Vows:

Celebrant to groom: "Do you, (name), take (name) to be your wife?"

Groom: "I do."

Celebrant to groom: "Do you promise to love, cherish, and protect her, whether in good fortune or in adversity, and to seek with her a life hallowed by the faith of Israel?"

Groom: "I do."

Celebrant to bride: "Do you, (name), take (name) to be your husband?"

Bride: "I do."

Celebrant to bride: "Do you promise to love, cherish, and protect him, whether in good fortune or in adversity, and to seek with him a life hallowed by the faith of Israel?"

Bride: "I do."

Celebrant to groom: "(Name), as you place this ring upon the finger of (name), speak to her these vows: 'With this ring, be thou consecrated unto me as my wife, according to the law of God and the faith of Israel.'"

Celebrant to bride: "(Name), as you place this ring upon the finger of (name), speak to him these vows: 'With this ring, be thou consecrated unto me as my husband, according to the law of God and the faith of Israel.'"

Celtic Traditions

Celtic websites abound on the Internet, reflecting the recent revival and popularization of all things Celtic, including Celtic jewelry, Celtic music and dance, and most particularly Celtic wedding traditions. The Celtic ceremony is abundantly vibrant, especially when kilts of the family clan's tartan are worn and the bride is escorted to and from the altar by a bagpiper.

Many traditional elements connected with Celtic weddings date back to the ancient Druids, including the casting and conse-cration of the circle and the passing of pebbles, and are impracti-cal in a modern or an indoor ceremony. However, other elements can be incorporated beautifully in an otherwise typical wedding setting, particularly the *Anam cara* (Loving Cup) Ceremony, the Four Directions and the Four Elements Ceremony and the Hand-Fasting Ceremony. My own personal fondness for these wonder-ful rituals lies in their versatility and easy incorporation into most ceremonies. Notice how they all blend and flow so exquisitely.

The *Anam Cara* (Loving Cup) Ceremony

Most people are unaware of the Celtic alternative to the Jewish wine ceremony, the *Anam cara* or loving cup ceremony. The sym-bology of both is practically identical.

The ancient Celts believed that when a couple joined in mar-riage, they celebrated the spirit of *anam cara*. *Anam* is the Gaelic word for soul and *cara* is the Gaelic word for friend; hence, *anam cara* translates as "soul friend." *Anam cara* was the term given to a trusted friend, confidant, confessor, or a beloved partner with whom the deepest secrets of the heart could be entrusted.

The use of the wine cup or chalice at a wedding is an ancient Celtic tradition. By the fifteenth century, it was common for the Celts to toast one another with a ceremonial loving cup. In Scotland, this cup is known as a *quaich,* a name which originates from the Celtic word *cuach,* meaning "cup." The most poetic clarification of *anam cara* that I have come across is that of the Irish poet, author, philosopher, and Catholic priest, John O'Donohue, who explains: "...You are joined in an ancient and eternal union with humanity that cuts across all barriers of time, convention, philosophy and definition. When you are blessed with an *anam cara,* the Irish believe, you have arrived at that most sacred place: home."

Today there are versions of the loving cup in many designs, shapes, sizes, and colors. The traditional cup is shaped like a double-handled bowl and often has inlaid Celtic designs. A couple I worked with recently produced a large wooden chalice with a tall stem, ornately carved with Celtic designs. They had located this wonderful cup on a Celtic wedding website. Some couples use a wine glass and have their names and the date of their wedding etched on the glass.

Drinking from the loving cup symbolizes the uniting of wife and husband and, in addition, can include the joining of families, by passing the cup to other family members to sip from, as a toast to the couple. My preference is to limit the cup solely to use by the couple during the ceremony and to leave the family toasting to the appropriate time during the reception. Notice that the ceremony wording is almost identical to that of the Jewish wine ceremony outlined above, and the universal-ecumenical wine ceremony featured on page 248.

Loving Cup Ceremony 1:

Celebrant: "Wine is a symbol of life. The years of our lives are as a cup of wine. The wine contained within this cup represents all of life's qualities, both sweet and bitter. Together, the sweet and the bitter represent the journey of life and all of the experiences that are a part of it. Those who drink deeply from this cup, with love and courage, invite the full range of challenges and experiences into their lives. As you drink from this cup, you share this life together, supporting and upholding one another throughout the unpredictable journey of life. May your life together be full and rich with love and blessings. Amen."

Groom (offering a sip of wine to the bride): "As you sip this wine, remember that from this day forward, you are my *anam cara*, my soul friend. From this moment on, you and I have become 'we'."

Bride (offering a sip of wine to the groom): "As you sip this wine, remember that from this day forward, you are my *anam cara*, my soul friend. From this moment on, you and I have become 'we.'"

Loving Cup Ceremony 2:

Celebrant: "From time immemorial, wine has symbolized life and a life of fullness and plenty. This loving cup represents all that you share within this life, from this day forward. It represents all that the future holds for you, both the sweet and the bitter, the blessings and joys as well as the sorrows. As you drink from this cup, you acknowledge to one another that your lives, separate until this moment, have now become one. As you drink from this cup, you share this life together, supporting and strengthening one another throughout the unpredictable journey of life. As you each acknowledge one another as life partner and soul friend: your *anam cara,* you have awakened and fostered in one another a deep and sacred companionship. May you be forever blessed. Amen."

Loving Cup Ceremony 3:

Celebrant: "Wine is the symbol of life. This loving cup in which it is contained symbolizes both of your lives, which are to be joined together today, as will your fates and your futures be so joined in a union of body and soul.

Celebrant to bride and groom: "Please face your beloved and repeat: 'Today I recognize you as my *anam cara,* my soul friend. You have become a part of my life in the sacred kinship of marriage. I will share with you my thoughts and deepest longings. I will share with you my heart, my love, and my life. In times of fear and uncertainty, I offer you my courage to help strengthen you and my compassion to help comfort you. In times of abundance and plenty, we will joyfully celebrate our gratitude together as clan and kinfolk. We have found one another, our *anam cara,* and a new beginning has dawned in our lives. From this moment on, we two have become one."

Loving Cup Ceremony 4:

Celebrant: "The sharing of wine from this cup serves to

impress upon you both that from this moment on, you will share fully life's joys and sorrows, life's bitterness and sweetness. Together, sweetness and bitterness represent the journey of two soul-friends in love, and all the experiences that flow naturally from that mutual joined love. When you share and bear one another's burdens, your joys are doubled and your sorrows halved because they are shared and held by two. Those with a loving heart and a courageous spirit invite the full range of the challenges of life's journey and drink deeply from the cup of life. May your lives be blessed."

Groom (offering a sip of wine to the bride): "As you sip this wine, remember that from this day forward, you are my *anam cara,* my soul friend. From this moment on, you and I are linked together as kinfolk. We two have now become one."

Bride (offering a sip of wine to the groom): "As you sip this wine, remember that from this day forward, you are my *anam cara,* my soul friend. From this moment on, you and I are linked together as kinfolk. We two have now become one."

Loving Cup Ceremony 5:

Celebrant: "It is fitting, in this moment of celebration, that the bride and groom now take their first sip of wine together, to celebrate all that has taken place in their lives up to this point. Wine is an ancient symbol of the fruits of our labors and sacrifices. Wine symbolizes the abundance and flow of life. Wine is the result of years of hard work and careful and loving tending. Wine is a symbol of celebration, joy, and the uniting of two."

Celebrant to bride and groom: "As the two of you sip from this one loving cup, acknowledge that this wine you share together is a symbol of your lives that are about to be joined and shared as clan and kinfolk. You are now soul friends and life partners. From this moment on, these two lives have become one. You now each become the *anam cara*—the soul friend to one another. Drink from this loving cup of life, that each of you have awakened in one another a rebirth, a new beginning. You are now home within each other's hearts."

Loving Cup Ceremony 6:

Celebrant to bride and groom: "Today you will be partaking of an ancient custom. Wine represents the sweetness and the potency of life. Drinking from a common cup symbolizes the life the two of you will share from this day forward as you join together in the kinship of marriage. May this loving cup filled with wine be a symbol of your lifelong communion of body, mind, and spirit. As you share from this loving cup, you undertake to share all that the future holds for you. The bitterness that life holds will be less bitter because you share it together. The sweetness that life holds will be much sweeter because you share it together. As you now sip from this cup, you are joined together as *anam cara*—soul friends."

The Four Directions and the Four Elements

According to Celtic spirituality, God is present not only within the human heart, but in all of His creations. The ancient Celts incorporated into the marriage ceremony the calling forth of the four elements of Earth, Fire, Air, and Water to bless the couple. This ritual offers a way of honoring the current of life within the bride and groom, it reminds them of their inter-connectedness with all of life and with the energies of the living earth. The couple are united in their love for one another and their respect for the natural world as they join together with a mutual understanding of Mother Nature and her elements.

Each of the directions is associated with one of the elements. The following associations are intended for the Northern hemisphere:

North represents the Earth element. It stands for birth, life, death, and rebirth. It is nurturing and stable, solid and firm, full of endurance and strength.

East represents the element Air. It stands for the soul and breath of life, and the spoken word.

South represents Fire. Fire is purifying and connected to strong will, energy, passion, and vitality. Fire both creates and destroys.

West represents the element Water. Water stands for healing, cleansing, and purification. Water is associated with emotion.

The Four Directions and the Four Elements Ceremony
The couple may wish to turn and face each direction that is honored and addressed by the celebrant.

Celebrant to the bride and groom: "We ask for the blessing of the North: the element of Earth. May we never forget the gifts of the earth upon which we stand. May you each be fed and nurtured, enriched and supported, by this beloved earth. May the foundation of your union be firm and stable as the rocks upon which you build your life and your home.

"We ask for the blessing of the East, the element of Air.

Through the spoken word, may you each communicate freely, truthfully, compassionately, and openly, carrying forth blessings upon your lips for your beloved.

"We ask for the blessing of the South, the element of Fire. May this union be blessed with energy, passion, enthusiasm, creativity, and inspiration. May you each be a beacon of light for one another through the inextinguishable fire of compassionate hearts.

"We ask for the blessing of the West, the element of Water. May your hearts be pure and clear as the mountain stream and your lives be blessed with the courage to feel and express your deepest emotions. May the soft summer rains bring forth blessings."

Hand-Fasting and Universal Hand-Joining

An old adage states: "A picture speaks a thousand words." Without a doubt, the most memorable rituals are those that are richly visual. There is something timeless in the ancient rituals that move us deeply. Hand fasting is an ancient Celtic wedding ritual in which the couple's hands are tied ("fasted") together with a ceremonial ribbon, rope, or piece of cloth made of the family clan's traditional tartan. This is one of the rituals from which the terms "giving one's hand in marriage" and "tying the knot" originated. (According to folklore, this ritual has additional origins.) The modern version of this ritual is performed with a cord or ribbon chosen by the couple. My preference is to use my ministerial stole, which I tie in a loose knot. I also ask the bride and groom to bring their hands together palm-to-palm, in what I refer to as a Celtic knot.

I have made a distinction between hand-fasting and universal hand-joining. The former adaptation, though versatile, represents the more classic, traditional ritual, whereas universal hand-joining offers a wider adaptability.

The Hand-Fasting Blessing of the Hands

Though the hand-fasting tradition of blessing of the hands may be fully integrated into the hand-fasting tradition itself, couples sometimes prefer this hand-blessing ritual to precede the actual fastening (fasting) of the hands. When I question my clients as to why this is their preference, their general response is that the wording is so exquisite, it should be separated from the body of the ritual to be fully appreciated. Though there are many versions of the actual spoken blessing, the following versions are my own adaptations. Any one of them may be separate and may precede, or lead into, the actual hand-joining ritual.

Hand Fasting 1 (with a separate blessing of the hands):

Celebrant: "These are the hands that will passionately hold, love, and cherish you through the years together, for a lifetime of joy and happiness. These are the hands that will wipe the tears from your eyes—tears of sadness and sorrow, and tears of celebration and joy. These are the hands that will comfort and hold you securely in times of discomfort and insecurity. These are the hands that will hold you steadily and calm you, through the unpredictable ups and downs of life's changing tides. These are the hands that offer blessings and healing. These are the hands that will support and encourage you in your deepest endeavors and your highest dreams. These hands are conduits of God's infinite and Divine love. When you reach out your hands in love, these hands are emissaries of God."

Celebrant (as the right hands are loosely tied together): "(Name), and (name), below you is the earth. Like the earth, may your love provide a strong and firm foundation upon which your lives are built. Above you is the sky. Like the sky, may your love be endless and infinite. It is your love that brought you together and it is the infinite power of your love that will hold you together ever as you are held together this day."

Hand Fasting 2 (combined with the blessing of hands):

Celebrant (as the right hands are loosely tied together): "May these hands be blessed. These are the hands that will love you and cherish you over the years. These are the hands that will wipe the tears from your eyes—tears of sorrow and tears of joy. These are the hands that will hold you in times of fear and in times of fearlessness. These are the hands that will comfort you in times of sickness and health. These are the hands that will offer encouragement in times of discouragement. These are the hands that will hold you in times of celebration and accomplishment. From these hands pours forth love for a lifetime of caring. As your hands are tied today, may your fates and future be so tied. For it is your love for one another that brought you together, and it is this love that will hold you together, ever as you are held together this day. Amen."

Hand Fasting 3 (combined with the blessing of hands):

Celebrant (as the right hands are loosely tied together): "May these hands be blessed. These hands are the messengers of the heart. They are the emissaries of love. They are the hands that softly comfort in times of sadness. They hold, uplift, and support in times of uncertainty. They join together in times of celebration, joy, and happiness. They wipe away the tears of sorrow and joy. They will hold you steadfast as you walk forward on your life journey together. As your hands are tied together this day, may your lives be woven together as are the fibers of this cord. For it is your love that brought you together, and it is this love that, like this cord, will hold you together for an eternity of tomorrows. Amen."

Hand Fasting 4 (combined with the blessing of hands):

Celebrant (as the right hands are loosely tied together): "These are the hands that will hold, support, love, and cherish you throughout the years of your lives for a lifetime of happiness. These are the hands that you will reach for in times of joy and in times of need. For these hands are messengers of the heart. This cord, woven of many fibers, symbolizes the weaving together of your hopes, dreams, fates, and futures. As this knot is tied, so are your lives now tied and woven together today. As this knot is tied, you are thus bound to your vows. Your love for one another brought you together and it is that love that will hold you and keep you together."

Hand Fasting 5 (combined with the blessing of hands):

Celebrant (as the right hands are loosely tied together): "As these hands are fasted today, each of us gathered are privileged witnesses to an ancient rite. These hands are the hands that you will reach for during the ups and downs of life. These are the hands that will steady and comfort. These are the hands that will love and bless. For these hands are messengers of the heart. The promises made today and this cord that fastens you will greatly strengthen, bind, and secure your union. These promises made today will cross the years of your soul journey, secured by the fasting of these hands. These promises made today speak not only of your intentions to each other. They speak your intentions to God. For those whom God and love hath brought together, let no one put asunder."

The Universal Hand-Joining Ritual

Since the following universal hand-joining rituals can serve as simplified versions of the traditional Celtic hand-fasting ritual (see above, page 301, I have opted to also feature them here as alternative adaptations.

Universal Hand-Joining Ritual 1:

Celebrant: "Below you, the earth; above you, the sky. As time passes, remember, as you tread the sacred path of marriage, your lives will be held strong and secure, as the sacred earth below holds you now. As time passes, remember also that your love for one another is infinite as the vast sky above. (Name) and (name), as I tie your hands together, may your lives, fates, and futures be so tied, entwined and wrapped in the Infinite Love of God. For it is your love for each other that brought you together, and it is the entwining of that love which will hold this bond unbroken. May the Divine Hand of God be upon you, bless you and hold you ever as you are held and tied together today. Amen."

Universal Hand-Joining Ritual 2:

Celebrant: "Today your lives are joined in a union of love and trust. Above you are the stars and below you is the earth. Like the stars, may your love illuminate and bless one another. Like the earth, may your love provide a firm foundation upon which to build a strong marriage. (Name) and (name), as your hands are tied together today, let the vastness of this love infinitely bless you. For it is your love that brought you together and it is your love that will hold and keep you together. Amen."

Universal Hand-Joining Ritual 3:

Celebrant: "(Name) and (name), as I tie together your hands, may your lives be held steadfast and firmly by your love for one another. These promises you have declared this day will greatly strengthen your bond and your union, throughout the coming years, as you embark upon a life joined in love. May the lives of those whom the loving God has brought and tied together be held securely with the ties that are forever unbroken. Amen."

Universal Hand-Joining Ritual 4:

Celebrant: "(Name) and (name), as your hands are joined together, may your lives be held securely joined by your commitment to one another and by the infinite spirit of love. Let the Divine Hand of God be upon you today and always. For those whom God and love hath brought and held together, let no-one put asunder."

Universal Hand- Joining Ritual 5:

Celebrant: "(Name) and (name), with the entwining of this knot do I tie and hold together all of your hopes and dreams; all the prayers, benedictions and well-wishes of each one gathered here today; all the vows and promises that you have made to one another this day. And as this knot is tied, we speak also our intentions to God who will greatly strengthen your bond and your union, throughout the years of your life journey, as you embark upon a life joined together as husband and wife. May those whom the loving hand of God has brought and tied together remain entwined in a love that is forever unbroken."

Universal Hand-Joining Ritual 6:

Celebrant: "With the entwining of this knot, we tie all of the love and joy wished by each witness to this ceremony. In the joining and tying of these hands, so are your lives now held and tied one to another. By this cord woven of many threads, you are thus bound to your vows. Your lives are now threaded and woven together. Symbolically, may this knot remain tied to the end of your days. May this cord draw your hands together in love, never to be used in displeasure. You two are entwined in love, bound by commitment and joy. May you be strong over hardship and victorious over difficulties, drawing together in a greater bond all the promises you have made today. Hold tightly to one another throughout life's journey together. May this cord be a symbol of two lives now unbreakably tied."

Quaker Traditions

Quakerism is a term used to describe members of the Religious Society of Friends. This movement began in the mid-seventeenth century as a splinter group that broke from the mainstream Christian Church of England. The name "Religious Society of Friends" implies the rejection of clerical hierarchy. The Quakers also resisted political hierarchy. Many early Quakers were militant religious dissenters. Nowadays they are pacifists, and are known as conscientious objectors during times of war. However, they still quietly challenge established religion. They believe that a spark of God resides in everyone, and that God works individually through each person. Therefore, the Quakers have no ministers or vicars. Quaker services, which are called meetings, are mostly conducted in silence.

There are four fundamental indications, or testimonies, associated with Quakerism: peace, equality/community, simplicity, and integrity. Members try to live their lives by these precepts. Since there is no celebrant required at a Quaker wedding ceremony, it seems rather futile to include a Quaker outline here, but there *is* a way that elements of this custom can be included in a traditional ceremony.

In the following Quaker wedding ceremony outline, the described "period of silence" may be modified and included in the beginning of a typical ceremony. My advice would be to shorten the overall ceremony because of the inclusion of the period of silence. From experience, I would tend to doubt that this could work realistically at a banquet or wedding hall, where each moment of the wedding celebration has to adhere to a meticulously timed schedule.

During a Quaker wedding ceremony, guests may be invited to the meeting, regardless of whether or not they are Quakers. The ceremony itself takes place during the meeting for worship and meditation. The atmosphere of quiet and reverence is the setting in which the promises of the bride and groom are made to one another without the help or the prompts of a third person. The bride and groom sit at the front of the group and face the guests. At the beginning of the meeting, it is customary for a "friend" to briefly explain the procedures of a Quaker wedding ceremony. Members of the congregation are free to stand up and speak. If they choose to speak, their contributions are considered to be both prompted and inspired by Spirit. They may also choose to remain silent. Since the bride and groom enter the meetinghouse together, there is no formal processing or recessing, no wedding party, no music and, as stated, no minister present. When they feel that the time is right, they will stand together, take one another's hand and thus, before God and in the presence of their friends, make their solemn declaration of marriage. The bride and groom will say the following words: "Friends, I take this my friend, (name), to be my husband (wife), promising, through Divine assistance (or with God's help), to be unto him (her) a loving and faithful wife (husband), so long as we both on earth shall live."

Traditionally, it was not customary for Quakers to exchange rings; however, in recent years, many Quaker couples now participate in this custom.

When they are again seated, the marriage certificate is brought forward to the couple for their signatures. It is customary for the bride to adopt the surname of her husband. The certificate is read to the meeting by a person who has been asked in advance to do so. At the close of the meeting or during the reception, the certificate is placed on a table. Those who have been present are asked to sign the certificate as witnesses. The marriage certificate is considered a beautiful part of the Quaker ceremony. It is usually written out on a large piece of parchment paper by a calligrapher. The certificate states the declarations of the couple, including their vows. Quakers will then frame this certificate and often hang it in their home as a reminder of their wedding day and their friends' support for them.

Latin American/Hispanic/Filipino Traditions

The coin, veil, cord, and candle-lighting ceremonies were traditionally and exclusively an important part of the wedding rites of the branch of the Roman Catholic Church in the Philippine Islands. Nowadays, other Christian churches have also adopted these traditions. It is up to the couple to ask their officiating celebrant to include these traditional elements.

The Spanish colonization period in the Philippines (1521-1898) brought the Roman Catholic religion to the islands. The Spanish friars brought these special wedding rites to the Philippines, and similar wedding rites are found in Mexico today. Spain ruled the Philippines through Mexico, and a scheduled route of merchant trade ships joined the cultures of these three countries in many ways. Latin American, Hispanic, and Filipino weddings reflect the strong traditions of family and extended family and are rich in symbolism. Typically, many people participate in the ceremony, all of whom are significant in the couple's life.

The main problem with the full Latin American/Hispanic/Filipino ceremony is the lengthiness. The full traditional ceremony is so visually rich in these meaningful rituals that I ponder including smaller, watered-down segments of this beautiful tradition in an ecumenical ceremony (unless you are planning on having a sixty- to ninety-minute ceremony, which I strongly advise against). Remember also that a ceremony that includes all of these elements and participants may, by necessity, require narration and explanation, which will mean more time is required!

The combined complicated and lengthy elements of the Hispanic/Filipino ceremony may not transition or condense well into an otherwise standard wedding ceremony. If your heart is set on including these traditions in an ecumenical or typical ceremony, it is essential to shorten them and remain alert to the time issue. Rather than attempt to squeeze in abbreviated versions of all four ceremonies, my suggestion is to choose only one, or at the most two, of these rituals. Recently, I officiated the wedding of a lovely Mexican couple that included a slightly abbreviated version of the unity wedding coins—it worked beautifully.

The Principal or Main Sponsors

The principal or main sponsors are women and men whom the bride and groom wish to honor. They attest to the couple's characters in terms of their maturity and readiness for marriage.

Often aunts and uncles or close friends of the family are chosen. In the Philippines, they also function as official witnesses of the state and they sign the marriage license. Outside of the Philippines, their participation is symbolic and is offered as support and encouragement for the newlyweds. The principal sponsors are part of the bridal procession. At the nuptial blessing, they may also be invited to come up with the celebrant and to extend their right hands to join in the prayer of blessing and benediction. In doing so, they are fulfilling their roles as sponsors.

The Secondary Sponsors

The secondary sponsors are women and men selected to participate in the ceremony because of their mutual respect and friendship. They are typically relatives or close friends. There are four sets of secondary sponsors: the unity wedding coin sponsors, the veil sponsors, the cord sponsors, and the candle-lighting sponsors.

The Unity Wedding Coins *(Arras)* Ceremony and the Unity Wedding Coin Sponsors

The unity wedding coins (or *arras*) have traditionally symbolized prosperity shared by the new couple, and the groom's promise to provide for the new family. The thirteen coins used in this ritual represent the twelve disciples and Christ. Nowadays, the coins represent more than the groom's ability to support his wife financially, since most couples share in this responsibility. They may also represent various aspects and qualities of marriage—love, commitment, respect, trust, wisdom, and cooperation.

Traditionally, the coins are blessed first by the officiating priest. Though there are some variations on the traditional passing of the wedding coins, the priest generally hands them to the groom, who in turn "pours" the coins into the bride's hands. The bride "pours" the coins back into the groom's hands. The groom then lets them drop or 'rain down' onto a ceremonial platter, which is held by an altar server. Some brides hold their hand over the hand of the groom as he pours the coins onto the platter.

The unity wedding coin sponsors are those who present the unity wedding coins. Often, they also purchase and provide the coins. A child coin bearer, similar to the ring bearer who brings the rings to the altar, may also bring the coins to the altar.

The Veil Ceremony and Veil Sponsors

Veil sponsors are those who will carefully pin a large white veil on the top of the bride's head and onto the shoulder of the groom. The couple's veil has become a symbol of unity and purity. It originally symbolized the presence of the Lord, because a white cloud was a symbol of His presence. As it is placed over the shoulders of the couple, it signifies their joining and uniting into one blessed union.

The Cord Ceremony and Cord Sponsors

Cord sponsors place a knotted cord over the heads of the couple, to lie on their shoulders. This generally occurs after the veil is placed on both the bride and groom, though some couples reverse this sequence. The cord symbolizes the lifelong bond and unbreakable tie between the couple, signifying that they are no longer two but are joined together and united as one in their new life together. The white cord is loosely tied around the necks of the couple in a figure eight or "symbol of infinity" configuration.

The Candle-Lighting Ceremony and Candle-Lighting Sponsors

The unity candle is identical to the traditional Christian unity candle set: two long taper candles flank a thick column candle. The candles symbolize the Light of God, the light of the Holy Spirit, the Light of Christ, the same light that they received at the sacrament of their baptism and which they now receive again.

Since these combined ceremonies involve a variety of elements, in order for the congregation to comprehend the meaning of these many and varied symbols:

- The celebrant may preface each symbolic component with an explanation.

- The couple may choose another person to read an explanatory commentary.

- The couple may wish to print out a short explanation in their program.

Greek Wedding Traditions

The wedding ceremony of the Greek Orthodox Church is an ancient and meaningful ceremony and is steeped in ritual and symbolism, reflecting the theology of the Church. Traditionally, upon the altar table are placed the Holy Gospel, a cup of wine, the betrothal rings, and the wedding crowns. Two candles are lit as a reminder that Christ is "the Light of the world" who offers Himself as illumination for the couple that they will not walk in darkness but will have the light of life.

The ceremony consists of prayers and petitions, the crowning, New Testament readings, the offering and sharing of the common cup, the ceremonial walk, and the benediction. At the conclusion of the prayers, the celebrant joins the hands of the bride and the groom. The hands remain joined until the end of the service to symbolize the uniting of the couple.

The ceremony consists of two parts:

- The betrothal ceremony, with the official blessing and exchange of the rings

- The marriage service, including the crowning of the bride and groom, the sharing of the common cup, and the ceremonial walk.

The Betrothal Ceremony

The celebrant begins the ceremony with the opening benediction.

Celebrant: "Blessed is our God, always, now and ever, and to the ages of ages. Amen."

This is followed by the litany in which the celebrant beseeches the Lord for the salvation of the bride and groom. She or he prays for perfect and peaceful love for the two of them, along with the preservation of steadfast faith and the blessings of a blameless life, and asks that they be granted an honorable marriage. The litany concludes by glorifying God.

Celebrant: "For to You belong all glory, honor, and worship, to the Father, the Son, and the Holy Spirit."

More prayers are offered, beseeching God to set a unity upon the couple that is unbreakable. Then there is a blessing of peace, oneness of mind, and a spirit of truth and love. The betrothal is a double ring ceremony. The celebrant holds the rings, and with them makes the sign of the cross on the forehead of the groom, saying:

Celebrant: "The servant of God, (name), is betrothed to the servant of God, (name), in the name of the Father, and of the Son, and of the Holy Spirit. Amen." *(Celebrant repeats three times.)*

At the conclusion of this prayer, the rings are placed on the ring finger of the couple's right hands. The best man then steps forward and, crossing his hands first, takes the rings and exchanges them, over and under, on the same fingers, three times.

The celebrant then calls upon God to bless the exchanging of rings with a heavenly blessing, requesting that an angel of the

Lord will go before these, God's servants, all the days of their lives. This concludes the betrothal service.

The Marriage Service

Including:

> *The crowning of the bride and groom*
>
> *The common cup ceremony*
>
> *The ceremonial walk*

The Crowning Ceremony

Within the Greek Orthodox wedding ceremony is a form of coronation service, similar to those conducted for kings and queens. Since the bride and groom are regarded as part of the "royal family" of God, they are crowned king and queen of their new home and family within God's family.

The crowns are usually braided or plaited of lemon blossoms or flowers. Some are made of silver or gold. These crowns, also known as *stefana,* symbolize the bond between the bride and groom and represent the glory and honor which God bestows upon them.

The celebrant takes the two crowns and blesses the bride and groom, in the name of the Father, and of the Son, and of the Holy Spirit, then places the crowns on their heads. The best man then steps behind the bride and groom and interchanges the crowns three times, functioning as a witness to the sealing of this sacred union. With the crowns upon the heads of the bride and groom, the celebrant offers Bible readings.

The Sharing of the Common Cup

This ritual is *not* Holy Communion. Rather, it is a symbol of the "common cup of life," a ritual symbolically denoting the mutual sharing of life's joy and sorrow. As in the Jewish wine ceremony or the Celtic loving cup ceremony, the drinking from a common cup represents a deep sharing of all that life will bring—the sweetness of life as well as the bitterness of life. Symbolically, sipping from the same cup signifies the agreement of the bride and groom to *equally* share life's joys and life's burdens. The celebrant offers three sips of the cup, first to the groom and then to the bride.

The Ceremonial Walk

The celebrant leads the couple in a circle around the altar table. The bride and groom are now taking their first steps together as husband and wife. The Holy Gospel and the cross lie upon the altar table. This expresses the Church's desire that the life of the couple will revolve around the infallible and secure Word of Almighty God.

The Removal of the Crowns

At the conclusion of the ceremonial walk, the celebrant removes the crowns from the bride and the groom. She or he prays to the Lord that He grant to the newlyweds a long, joyful, and blessed life together. He then lifts up the Gospel and separates their joined hands, reminding them that only God can separate the couple from one another.

Review Checklist

If you are planning an interfaith ceremony, hold in mind the following points:

❏ It is better to keep the overall tone of the ceremony not excessively religious, to avoid competing traditions.

❏ Be sure there is fair and equitable acknowledgement of both traditions.

❏ If you are planning on dual officiation by two separate clergy members, select carefully, taking into consideration their personality compatibility.

❏ If you decide to have an interfaith–multi-faith–ecumenical celebrant officiate your ceremony as one representative of both religious traditions, consider inviting a friend or family member to be an assistant or co-participant; for example, during the reciting of Hebrew prayers.

❏ If an assistant or co-participant is necessary, choose someone whom you respect and love. Remember that being asked to assist in a wedding ceremony is considered a great honor for that person.

❏ Review the religious and cultural ceremonies that you wish to include and incorporate them.

❏ Try to simplify and abbreviate those elements that are ornate, complex, and lengthy when integrating two religious traditions in one ceremony.

Chapter Ten

The Vows Renewal Ceremony and the Commitment Ceremony

The Vows Renewal Ceremony

The beauty of marriage is the blending of two individual lives into one union and the infinite possibilities that exist within that union. The healthy growth and development of this unique union depends completely on the couple. This is really where the mystery of a strong marriage lies: in the commitment of the couple to their marriage. In the end, only they can create their marriage.

One of the many gifts marriage offers us is the potential for spiritual and character development. Without a doubt, loving and supporting one another builds selflessness and maturity of character. Marriage nowadays is becoming increasingly difficult for so many couples. I am reassured and inspired by those who, under immense pressure and stress, still manage to maintain a happy and faithful union.

Therefore, it is important to take the time to honor and celebrate those marriages that have steadfastly endured the test of time. One of the most meaningful ways to give thanks and celebrate such a marriage is the vows renewal ceremony, particularly for a significant anniversary.

This can be a time to pause and look back nostalgically at the passing years—the joys experienced and the challenges endured.

It is such a positive example and inspiration for family members, particularly children, to witness the real possibilities that a loving union can offer. It's rather surprising that we don't acknowledge and celebrate these marriages more often.

Pointers and Practicalities

For vows renewal ceremonies, most couples tend to prefer a state-registered wedding celebrant, particularly a member of the clergy. Obviously, the choice of an experienced clergyperson can ensure that the ceremony is spiritually based. Some couples feel a clergyperson lends the appearance of authenticity to the ceremony. However, a registered wedding celebrant is not legally necessary for a vows renewal ceremony. A secular celebrant or even a dear friend can function as the celebrant.

The ceremony can be scheduled at the couple's regular place of worship or at a reception site. The reception—and ceremony—can be scheduled at any typical venue, from a large conventional banquet or wedding hall to an intimate home setting. Invitations may be mailed to guests in the same manner as conventional wedding invitations.

Because of the nostalgia associated with a long and loving marriage, it may be worth considering only close family members and intimate, caring friends as invited guests. The typical and customary procession for an already married couple is for the husband to escort his wife down the aisle or entranceway. However, you may want to consider including grandchildren in the procession. They could walk down the aisle *with* Grandma and Grandpa. Alternatively, a lovely idea is to have them escort

Grandma down the aisle as Grandpa waits at the altar or ceremony site.

Consider including a bridal bouquet of the same flowers that were carried in the original ceremony. You may prefer a smaller version of this bouquet, to have processing granddaughters carry an even smaller version of the bouquet or just one flower of the same species, or have grandsons wear a similar boutonnière.

A vows renewal ceremony can be formal and ornate, or informal and casual. The decision is yours.

The use, or re-giving, of the original rings is customary; some couples opt to give another special anniversary ring to one another.

Include traditions that correspond with your spiritual beliefs and convictions. Include as much family participation as possible, especially of grandchildren. Though a candle-lighting ceremony may offer a way of including children, I tend to be a little cautious with children and candles. The sand ceremony is a wonderful alternative.

Try to include elements from your original wedding ceremony. Set up photographs of your original wedding. Include some of the music from your original ceremony; for example, a favorite hymn. If you remember your original processional anthem, include that. Include your "special song" or the first song you danced to at your reception.

Some elements of a vows renewal ceremony—particularly the vows themselves—really should be personalized. So, think of what you would like to say to one another. These words can be broken down into a question-and-answer or prompt-response format.

The Vows Renewal Ceremony Questionnaire

Read through and then answer following questions:

- What life lessons have you learned from your years together?

- Over the years, how have you personally grown and matured in ways that you can directly attribute to being together?

- How do you see your partner in terms of her or his personal growth that you attribute to the years of being together?

- What are (and always were) your partner's strengths and positive characteristics?

- How have those strengths and positive characteristics helped build a strong marriage?

- What was it that attracted you to your partner?

- How would you describe how you felt about your partner when you first met.? (Try to focus on the actual feelings rather than on your thoughts.)

- How would you describe the defining moment when you knew you were in love, and how that felt?

- How would you describe the proposal, and once again, try to remember how you felt at that moment?

Vows Renewal Ceremony Samples

Opening Benediction

Celebrant: "We thank you, Lord, for the great love and continuing joy that has brought—and held—(name) and (name) together in the union of lasting marriage. We ask for your continued blessings upon them and support as they reaffirm their lasting commitment as partners in love and life. May they continue to treat this love with deep gratitude and awe, and may each of us gathered here as witnesses be overjoyed and encouraged in our own lives and relationships; may this be an inspiration for each of us gathered here."

Opening Welcome

Celebrant: "(Name) and (name), we are gathered here today to celebrate (number) years of marriage and your continuing love for one another. Each of us gathered is truly privileged to witness the possibilities that a union can offer. We are indeed inspired by the strength and deep commitment that has brought you to this moment. Today, on this momentous anniversary, you will re-declare to one another that, despite life's challenges and difficulties, you will continue to love and be faithful to one another. Once again, you commit yourselves to one another in marriage. This time each of you is blessed to have amassed the wisdom of experience of a life spent together.

As you once again make this covenant today before God, do so with the knowledge that He is the creator of this life you share together and He is the creator of the special and unique love you hold and have held for each other. May this special love continue to expand, intensify, and be ever sustained by God."

Reading

Celebrant: "When the one man loves the one woman and the one woman loves the one man, the very angels desert heaven and sit in that house and sing for joy. *Brahma Sutra.*"

The Ring Blessing

Celebrant: "The ring is a token of your love and, like a circle, is a symbol of peace. It also symbolizes unity and infinity. This circle is beginningless and endless, as is love. As this ring is created from precious gold, so your love is created, nourished, and sustained by the precious love of God.

"Once again, as you exchange rings, you affirm that, like a circle, your love is without beginning and without end. Your lives are held within the circle of a union that is unbreakably joined by God, the source of all love. May these rings be blessed and the two who wear them. May they continue to stand together steadfast in a circle of Divine protection and love. Amen."

Reading

Celebrant: "Where thou goest, I will go, and where thou livest, I will live. Your family is my family, and your God my God." *From The Book of Ruth.*

Celebrant Pre-Vows Statement

Celebrant to bride and groom: "(Name) and (name), years ago, you each stood together and made your vows to one another. As you stand here today, reflect back to those two people who loved and trusted in that shared love. At that time, your love had not yet stood the test of time. Now, as you stand together, you have shared your dreams and deepest aspirations throughout the ups and downs of life. The years have passed and time has brought you even closer. The promises that you are about to make reaffirm, acknowledge, and pay tribute to the depth of that love and respect that has continued to develop, blossom, mature, and

324

grow over these years. These promises declare your continuing love to be a special gift that you two have honored and treasured, which will strengthen your lives for whatever situations you may face with strength and courage forever."

Exchange of Vows Renewal (Ecumenical/Interfaith/Non-denominational)

Celebrant to groom: "Therefore I ask you, (name), after the passing of these years, do you receive (name) as your beloved wife?"

Groom: "I do."

Celebrant to groom: "Will you continue to love, honor, respect, and cherish her? Will you give thanks to her and for her—not only in your words, but also in your actions? Will you continue to honor and support her growth and aspirations?"

Groom: "I will."

Celebrant to bride: "Therefore I ask you, (name), after the passing of these years, do you receive (name) as your beloved husband?"

Bride: "I do."

Celebrant to bride: "Will you continue to love, honor, respect, and cherish him? Will you give thanks to him and for him—not only in your words, but also in your actions? Will you continue to honor and support his growth and aspirations?"

Bride: "I will."

Traditional-Standard Choices for Renewed Vows

For couples who prefer traditional-standard vows, the following choices include Episcopal, Baptist, Catholic, Lutheran, Methodist, Presbyterian, and Jewish vows, each appropriately re-worded to fit a vows renewal ceremony. Once again, notice the subtle distinctions among them, reflecting the style and spirit of each denomination.

Exchange of Vows Renewal (Episcopal)

Celebrant to groom (bride): "(Name), once again I ask you, wilt thou have this woman (man) to continue to be thy wedded wife (husband), to continue to live together after God's ordinance in the holy estate of matrimony? Wilt thou love her (him) as you have throughout these years together? Wilt thou continue to comfort, honor, and keep her (him), in sickness and in health, and forsaking all others, keep thee only unto her (him), as long as you both shall live?"

Groom (bride): "I will. I, (name), once again take thee, (name), to be my wedded wife (husband), to have and to hold, from this day forward, as we have throughout our years together, for better, for worse, for richer or for poorer, in sickness and in health, to love and to cherish, 'til death do us part, according to God's ordinance; and thereto I again pledge thee my troth."

(Rings): "With this ring I reaffirm these promises to thee, in the name of the Father, and of the Son, and of the Holy Ghost. Amen."

Exchange of Vows Renewal (Baptist)

Celebrant to groom (bride): "Will you, (name), after the passing of these years together, have (name) to be your wife (husband)? Will you continue to love her (him), comfort and keep her (him), and forsaking all others, remain true to her (him), as long as you both shall live?"

Groom (bride): "I will. I, (name), after the passing of these years together, am honored to take thee, (name), to be my wife (husband), and before God and these witnesses, I promise to continue to be a faithful and true husband (wife)."

(Rings): "Once again, I promise that with this ring I thee wed, and all my worldly goods I thee endow. In sickness and in health, in poverty or in wealth, 'til death do us part."

Exchange of Vows Renewal (Catholic)

Celebrant to groom (bride): "(Name), after the passing of these years together, will you take (name), here present, for your lawful wife (husband), according to the rite of our Holy Mother, the Catholic Church?"

Groom (bride): "I will. I, (name), after the passing of these years together, again take you, (name), for my wife (husband), to continue to have and to hold, from this day forward, for better, for worse, for richer, for poorer, in sickness and in health, until death do us part."

(Rings): "Once again, with this ring I thee wed, and continue to pledge thee my troth."

Exchange of Vows Renewal (Lutheran)

Celebrant to groom (bride): "(Name), after these years together, wilt thou have this woman (man) to be thy wedded wife (husband), to live together after God's ordinance in the holy estate of matrimony? Wilt thou continue to love her (him), comfort her (him), honor, and keep her (him), as long as ye both shall live?"

Groom (bride): "I will. I, (name), after these years together, continue to take thee, (name), to be my wife (husband). I therefore re-pledge thee my troth, so long as we both shall live."

(Rings): "Receive this ring as a token of the continuation of wedded love and faith."

Exchange of Vows Renewal (Methodist)

Celebrant to groom (bride): "(Name), after these years together, wilt thou continue to have this woman (man) to be thy wedded wife (husband), to live together after God's ordinance in the holy estate of matrimony? Wilt thou love her (him), in sickness and in health, and forsaking all others, keep thee only unto her (him), so long as ye both shall live?"

Groom (bride): "I will. I, (name), am honored to continue to take thee, (name), to be my wife (husband), to have and to hold, from this day forward; for better, for worse; for richer, for poorer; in sickness and in health; to love and to cherish; till death do us part, and thereto I pledge thee my faith."

(Rings): "In token and pledge of the vows once again spoken between us and re-affirmed again, with this ring, I thee wed; in the name of the Father, and of the Son, and of the Holy Spirit. Amen."

Exchange of Vows Renewal (Presbyterian)

Celebrant to groom (bride): "(Name), wilt thou, as promised once before, have this woman (man) to be thy wife (husband), and wilt thou re-pledge thy faith to her (him), in all love and honor, in all duty and service, in all faith and tenderness, to continue to live with her (him), and cherish her (him), according to the ordinance of God, in the holy bond of marriage?"

Groom (bride): "I will. I, (name) as promised once before, take thee, (name), to be my wedded wife (husband), and I do promise and covenant, before God and these witnesses, to continue to be thy loving and faithful husband (wife); in plenty and in want, in joy and in sorrow, in sickness and in health, as long as we both shall live."

(Rings): "This ring given thee once before in token and pledge, I give once again as I reaffirm our constant faith and abiding love."

Exchange of Vows Renewal (Jewish)

Celebrant to groom: "Do you, (name), as promised once before, take (name) to be your wife?"

Groom: "I do."

Celebrant to groom: "Will you, (name), continue to love, cherish, and protect her, whether in good fortune or in adversity, and continue to seek with her a life hallowed by the faith of Israel?"

Groom: "I will."

Celebrant to bride: "Do you, (name), as promised once before, take (name) to be your husband?"

Bride: "I do."

Celebrant to bride: "Will you, (name), continue to love, cherish, and protect him, whether in good fortune or in adversity, and continue to seek with him a life hallowed by the faith of Israel?"

Bride: "I will."

Celebrant to groom: "(Name), once again place this ring upon the finger of (name). As you reaffirm your promises, speak to her these vows: 'With this ring, be thou consecrated unto me as my wife, according to the law of God and the faith of Israel.'"

Celebrant to bride: "(Name), once again place this ring upon the finger of (name). As you reaffirm your promises, speak to him these vows: 'With this ring, be thou consecrated unto me as my husband, according to the law of God and the faith of Israel.'"

Walter and Elaine: a Fifty-Year Love Story

The following vows renewal ceremony outline is that of my in-laws Walter and Elaine, the paternal grandparents of my granddaughter Rachel Elaine. Walter and Elaine are also dear and wonderful friends. I hereby acknowledge my indebtedness to them for inspiring me to include this section on wedding vows renewal. I was considering doing so, but had not quite decided, when I received a call from Elaine and Walter from their home in Boca Raton, Florida, requesting my services for officiating their fiftieth anniversary and vows renewal ceremony at the magnificent Mohonk Mountain House in New Paltz, New York. At that moment, I became inspired to start the process of working on this segment.

Each love story is unique and beautifully touching in its own distinct way. There are some love stories that are especially tender and heart-stirring, as is theirs. First of all, I must preface their story by describing Elaine: She is probably as beautiful, youthful, and eternally slender as she ever was in her youth. In fact, it is inconceivable to imagine that she and Walter are old enough to celebrate fifty years together. They are Jewish, yet universally spiritual, open minded, openhearted, and lovingly accepting of all. They are both spiritually "well-developed," and extraordinarily kind and dedicated to friends, family, and their community. Their actions bear this out: For some time now, their routine Sunday morning ritual, after a busy six-day work week, has included cleaning up litter on a local beach in Florida.

They actually knew *of* one another as teens growing up in the same New York City neighborhood. During the late nineteen-fifties, Walter was serving in the military and Elaine was attending modeling school. Their official meeting occurred during a short personal leave Walter had been granted in order to attend the funeral services of a family member. He was driving from downtown Manhattan to his family's neighborhood. Elaine commuted home from modeling school and was waiting at a bus stop at the precise moment that Walter drove by in his yellow convertible. During the late nineteen-fifties, the immaculately accessorized Jackie Kennedy and Doris Day-styles were birthed: tightly clinging sheath dresses and pencil-line skirts were in vogue. Elaine had—and still has—the perfect tall, slim figure to carry off these meticulous, and very unforgiving, styles. On the day they met, she wore a two-piece suit, stiletto heels, and white kid gloves. A small pillbox hat was perched on her pretty head. It was this perfectly lovely image that prompted Walter to slow to a snail's pace in order to get a better look at Elaine. Not only was he immediately attracted to her, he also realized that he recognized and knew her—*they had grown up and lived in the same neighborhood!* He quickly seized this opportunity to make verbal contact with her. Smartly dressed in his military uniform, he stopped the car and politely offered Elaine a ride home. Walter is still to this day a perfect gentleman. Since Elaine recognized Walter as a neighbor, she graciously accepted. Within three months, they were engaged to be married.

The following are highlights from their vows renewal ceremony. As a limerick writer, I feel privileged to be able to add a unique rhyme to a unique, personalized ceremony. Components of this ceremony will be found in the section on vows renewal ceremony samples, on page 322. Note the beautiful interweaving of elements from Judaism in an essentially universal-ecumenical ceremony.

Walter and Elaine's Vows Renewal

For the following ceremony, a perfect outdoor location was selected: the beautiful Mohonk Mountain House gardens. At the end of a long, covered colonnade of creeping vines, we chose the ceremony site, complete with a wrought-iron altar flanked by treehouses, a privet-hedge maze, and lovingly tended flower beds boasting extra-tall hollyhocks and lupines. We gathered together in the fragrantly scented shade.

Walter escorted Elaine to the ceremony site. Elaine had searched for, and found, a white eyelet cotton dress. This A-line style is timeless and classic and she looked astonishingly beautiful in it. (When I commented later on the lovely dress, she informed me it was almost identical to the one in which she was originally married.)

Walter and Elaine insisted on family participation in the ceremony, particularly that of their grandchildren. Their grandchildren opened the ceremony, each in turn reading one of the following passages.

I Ching

"When two people are at one in their inmost hearts, they shatter even the strength of iron or bronze."

The Book of Ruth

"For where thou goest, I will go, and where thou livest, I will live. Your family is my family, and your God, my God."

Aztec Wedding Poem

I know not whether thou have been absent:
I lie down with thee, I rise up with thee,
In my dreams thou art with me.
If my eardrops tremble in my ears,
I know it is thou moving within my heart.

Inuit Wedding Vow

"You are my partner. My feet shall run because of you. My feet dance because of you. My eyes see because of you. My mind thinks because of you. And I shall love because of you."

Oath of Friendship (Anonymous, China, 1st Century B.C.)

I want to be your friend for ever and ever

Without break or decay.
When the hills are all flat
And the rivers are all dry,
When it lightens and thunders in winter,
When it rains and snows in summer,
When Heaven and Earth mingle
Not 'til then will I part from you.

The traditional Jewish prayer, the Shehecheyanu (see page 284), expressing thanksgiving and gratitude to the Lord who "has brought us to this season," is a perfect opening prayer of ceremonial thankfulness. It was read aloud by the two youngest grandchildren, Rachel Elaine and Max.

Opening Prayer: The *Shehecheyanu*

Transliteration from the Hebrew: Barukh atah Adonai, Eloheynu, melekh ha-olam she-hekheeyanu v'keey'manu v'heegeeyanu la-z,man ha-zeh.

Translation: Blessed are you, Lord, our God, Ruler of the universe, who has kept us alive, sustained us, and enabled us to reach this season.

A note for classic limerick aficionados: Though referred to as a limerick—since the rhyming pattern is identical—the following rhyme does not quite fit the cadence of a typical limerick, since the first, second, and fifth lines include one extra beat. It was read aloud by the older grandchildren: Sophie, Rubin, and Sam.

A Love-imerick

*It was fifty years past, young Elaine and young Walter
Knew a love that grew vast, that would last and not falter
And this love that, though new,
they avowed to be true
For they knew a love true, no mortal could alter.*

*As we gather today, we each are elated
For we witness the union God has created
A marriage anointed
This lifetime appointed
Not only in body, in soul they are mated*

*A friendship developed through loving and caring
Supporting each other, commitment unsparing
Though fifty years dated,
Those vows now re-stated
To honor their life of respect and deep sharing*

*For you, dearest Walter and dearest Elaine
May your blessed union be ever sustained
Through life's ebbing and flowing
Your love ever growing
Each one of us knowing this God did ordain*

Opening Benediction

Celebrant: "We thank you, Lord, for the great love and continuing joy that has brought and held Walter and Elaine together in the union of lasting marriage. We ask for your continued blessing upon them, and support as they reaffirm their lasting commitment as partners in love and life. May they continue to treat this love with deep gratitude and awe, and may each of us gathered here as witnesses so be inspired and overjoyed, that this may be an inspiration for each of us."

Opening Welcome

Celebrant: "Walter and Elaine, we are gathered here today to celebrate fifty years of marriage and your continuing love for one another. Each of us gathered is truly privileged to witness the possibilities that a union can offer. We are indeed inspired by the strength and deep commitment that has brought you to this moment. Today on this momentous anniversary, you will re-declare that throughout all the seasons of life, you will continue to love and be faithful to one another. Once again you commit yourselves to one another in marriage. This time, each of you are blessed to have amassed the wisdom of experience of a life spent together. As you once again make this covenant today before God, do so with the knowledge that He is the creator of this life you share together, and He is the creator of the special and unique love you hold for each other. May this special love continue to expand, intensify, and be sustained by God."

The following wine ceremony, from the opening words of Baal Shem Tov to the closing words from the *Brahma Sutra,* was read aloud by Walter and Elaine's children: Neil, Craig, and June.

Reading from Baal Shem Tov (see page 255)

"From every human being, there rises a light that reaches straight to heaven, and when two souls who are destined to be together find one another, their streams of light flow together, and a single, brighter light goes forth from their united being."

The Sharing of the Wine

"The years of our lives are as a cup of wine poured out for us to drink. Within this cup there is contained all that is sweet, joyful, hopeful. This same cup also holds the bitter wine of life. But those who are courageous—as are the two of you, Elaine and Walter—drink deeply of life, inviting the full range of experience into their being. As you drink from this cup, acknowledge that your separate lives have become as one vessel from which you share your joys and your sorrows, and from which, together, you will receive mutual strength, support, and sustenance. Many more days, you will sit at the same table and eat and drink together."

The Blessing of the Wine

Transliteration: Bar-uch' A-tah' Adonai El-o-hei-nu me'-lech ha-o-lam' bo-re' pe-ri' ha-ga'-fen.

Translation: Blessed are you, Lord, Our God, King of the universe. You created the fruit of the vine.

Celebrant: "Walter and Elaine, drink now with consecration and with joy, and may the cup of your lives continue to be sweet and full to running over."

Reading from the *Brahma Sutra*

"When the one man loves the one woman and the one woman loves the one man, the very angels desert heaven and sit in that house and sing for joy."

The Ring Blessing

Celebrant: "The ring is a token of your love and, like a circle,

337

is a symbol of peace. It also symbolizes unity and infinity. It is beginning-less and endless, as is love. As this token is created from precious gold, so your love is created, nourished, and sustained by the precious love of God.

Once again, as you exchange rings, you affirm that, like a circle, your love is without beginning and without end. Your lives are held within the circle of an amalgamation that is unbreakably joined by God, the circle—the source of all love.

"May these rings be blessed and the two who wear them. May they continue to stand steadfast in a circle of divine protection and love. Amen."

Pre-Vows Statement

Celebrant: "Elaine and Walter, fifty years ago you each stood together and made your vows to one another. As you stand here today, reflect back to those two people who loved and trusted in that love that you shared. At that time, your love had not yet stood the test of time. You have shared your dreams and deepest aspirations through the ups and downs of life. The years have passed, time has brought you even closer. The promises that you are about to make re-affirm, acknowledge, and pay tribute to the depth of that love and respect that has continued to develop, blossom, and mature and grow over these years. These promises declare your continuing love to be a special and Divine gift that you two have developed, tended, and treasured, and which will continue to strengthen your lives and your future together as you grow even more in your love for one another."

Exchange of Renewal Vows

Celebrant to groom: "Therefore I ask you, Walter, after the passing of these years, do you receive Elaine as your beloved wife?"

Groom: "I do."

Celebrant to groom: "Will you continue to love, honor, respect, and cherish her? Will you give thanks to her and for her—not only in your words, but also in your actions? Will you continue to honor and support her growth and aspirations?"

Groom: "I will."

Celebrant to bride: "Therefore I ask you, Elaine, after the passing of these years, do you receive Walter as your beloved husband?"

Bride: "I do."

Celebrant to bride: "Will you continue to love, honor, respect, and cherish him? Will you give thanks to him and for him—not only in your words, but also in your actions? Will you continue to honor and support his growth and aspirations?"

Bride: "I will."

Celebrant to groom: "Walter, once again place this ring upon the finger of Elaine. As you re-affirm your promises, speak to her these vows: 'With this ring, be thou consecrated unto me as my wife, according to the law of God and the faith of Israel. Elaine, you are my deepest friend and my eternal love.'"

Celebrant to bride: "Elaine, once again place this ring upon the finger of Walter. As you re-affirm your promises, speak to him these vows: 'With this ring, be thou consecrated unto me as my husband, according to the law of God and the faith of Israel. Walter, you are my deepest friend and my eternal love.'"

Sand Ceremony

Celebrant: "Walter and Elaine, now pour together the sand from these separate containers into this one vessel. This symbolizes each one as two separate individuals, yet joined in one blessed union. These colors you have chosen represent the rocks, stones, the earth beneath you; a symbol of strength, security, power, and dependability. This symbolizes your marriage, a perfect model and example for these future generations to behold.

"I now ask each of your grandchildren to come forward, the oldest first. Each one of you also represents your parents. Please, in turn, pour a layer of sand into this vessel as a symbol of the lives and families that have been created in the ever-renewing and continuing regenerations and cycles of life, born because of the union of your grandparents. As these containers of sand are now joined, the individual containers no longer exist; they are joined together as one. Just as these grains of sand can no longer be poured again into separate containers, nor can each of you be separated as loving members of this one family, and Elaine and Walter as loving members of this marriage, without whom this family would not exist.

"May your lives be good and long, and as lasting as the stars of the heavens and the sands of time. Amen."

The Commitment Ceremony

Commitment ceremonies show the bond of love between two people who choose to have a commitment ceremony as a public declaration and celebration of their love and commitment to one another. Contrary to what most people think, there are a number of reasons for a commitment ceremony besides the most obvious, a same-sex commitment ceremony. There are heterosexual couples who are not candidates for a legal marriage, or who choose not to enter into a legal commitment for a number of reasons.

As in a marriage ceremony, the style, tone, and degree of religiosity of a commitment ceremony can vary vastly, and is the choice and preference of the couple. A commitment ceremony can follow the same formulation as a marriage ceremony and all that is required are a few creative changes in overall phraseology, particularly in the final pronouncement. With a little innovative modification of terms, the ceremony can flow beautifully. Comparable or alternate wording for a final pronouncement could be expressed as follows:

- Bonded together as lifetime lovers and faithful partners
- Committed to one another in a lifetime union of love
- Friends, lovers, and partners for life, joined in the sacred bond of eternal love
- Joined in a union and bond of eternal love
- Joined in an avowed commitment to one another for life
- Joined together and united as partners for life

- Joined together as partners for life

- Life mates and partners joined in a bond of love

- Life partners joined in a pledge of unending love

- Sacred union of two beloveds joined as one and blessed by God

- Two beloved souls united for a lifetime commitment of mutual love and support

- Two persons joined together as one and united for life in the sacred bond of love

- Two souls and two destinies now joined and united as one true and faithful union

- Two united as one in a life commitment of undying love

- Two whose lives are now unified and bonded in a lifelong commitment of avowed love

- Unbreakably joined in a lifetime partnership of love and commitment

- United and bonded as beloved life partners

- United and joined for a lifetime of love and commitment

- United as partners in a lifetime union

- United companions and lovers joined unbreakably for life

- United in a lifetime partnership and bond of love

- United life partners

A "Golden Years" Commitment Ceremony

An example comes to mind of a commitment ceremony I officiated for an older retired couple, whose mutual meager pensions would have been substantially reduced to even less of the pittance that they already were, if they had become legally married. They described their decision for a commitment ceremony thus: "Since we are both knocking on a bit in years, we feel at our age we should make our relationship look respectable." In addition, a non-legal union ensured that both of their respective family's inheritances, such as they were, were not placed in jeopardy.

The Temporary (by necessity) Commitment Ceremony

On a few occasions, I have "officiated" the meticulously planned ceremonies of couples who fully intended to be legally married. Unfortunately, through no fault of their own, the final divorce decree of one member of the union had been delayed. I remember that on one occasion, it was intentionally delayed by a jealous and malicious ex-wife. I have also "officiated" ceremonies where the bride and groom have forgotten to bring the license. The only recourse, in either of these situations, is for the celebrant to preside over what appears to be a legal wedding ceremony, when in fact, it is a non-legally binding commitment ceremony. Often in these situations, the guests are not informed of the true nature of the ceremony. The solution to these unpredictable situations is for the celebrant to meet with the couple at a later date to legally solemnize the marriage. However, the marriage license will reflect the date and time of the legal solemnization of the marriage, rather than that of the ceremony.

The Commitment Ceremony that Progressed into a Legal Wedding Ceremony

Sandy and Sam had been together for ten years when Sandy suffered an unexpected illness. Although I did not inquire about the nature of her condition, her debilitation resembled that of a stroke victim. She suffered partial deafness and nerve damage, and her verbal responses were delayed. In spite of her condition, I found her delightfully aware and interactive, though her speech sometimes faltered and was slightly slurred. Because of her illness, her family was given power of attorney and they began making decisions regarding her medical care, which resulted in her being placed in a medical type of institution. Since she and Sam were not legally married, he had no recourse but to abide by their decision to place her in this facility, a decision to which he was opposed. In addition, her family refused to agree to a marriage, stating that she was not of "sound mind" to be married, due to her illness. Sam wanted desperately to bring Sandy home where he could oversee her care. He began exploring alternative courses of action and hired an attorney. Regardless of the outcome of the legal situation, they decided to have a commitment ceremony. This decision was twofold:

Sandy and Sam are both very spiritual. They felt that by having a commitment ceremony, they would be declaring their love for one another formally. Doing so, they would be petitioning God's help by officially—though not legally—declaring their love for each other. In speaking these intentions, they were, in fact, sending forth prayers and petitions to the Loving God. They also pointed out that they would be "acting out" a marriage ceremony.

The second reason for the commitment ceremony was that Sam's lawyer was planning to attend this very intimate event. He felt that if Sandy appeared clear and alert in her responses to the legal questions, we should go forward with a legal marriage. It also required that the small group of witnesses would need to be willing to testify in court in the event that this became necessary. We each agreed. Sam had taken Sandy out of the facility for an hour in order for them to apply for and secure the marriage license, which he brought along with him, just in case. In the end, the commitment ceremony became a legal marriage ceremony. Not only did Sandy understand and answer the questions clearly, she stated extemporaneous, on-the-spot wedding vows that were concise and heartfelt, and that flowed more beautifully than any that a wedding celebrant could have composed, including me! The last time I heard from the couple, Sandy's physical health had improved, and her family—witnessing her improvement—had accepted and supported the marriage.

Domestic Partnerships/Civil Unions

Today a number of states offer <u>civil unions</u>, which, like California's domestic partnerships, are equivalent to marriage in all but title.

For legal benefits in the United States, same-sex couples should check to see if their city or state has any <u>domestic partnership</u> laws. <u>Vermont</u> and <u>Connecticut</u> residents can be joined in a civil union. Hawaii residents can use the <u>reciprocal beneficiaries law</u>. Domestic partnership laws can be very confusing, so make sure you fully understand the laws before entering into any binding contract. At the time of writing this text, only <u>six states</u> allow same-sex couples to marry; however, due to restrictive federal law, these marriages offer couples no more rights than other states' civil unions.

Some municipalities in Massachusetts provide domestic partnerships as an alternative option to marriage.

Requirements for Entering into a Domestic Partnership/ Civil Union

My wedding ministry, though based in New York, allows for easy access to neighboring states, particularly the state of New Jersey, where I officiate many wedding ceremonies. Therefore, the following information on civil union/domestic partnership law applies to the state of New Jersey.

For two people to establish a civil union in New Jersey, they must satisfy all of the following requirements:

- Not be a party to another civil union, domestic partnership, or marriage in this state or that is recognized by this state.

- Be of the same sex.

- Be at least eighteen years of age, except that applicants under eighteen may enter into a civil union with parental consent. Applicants under age sixteen must obtain parental consent and have the consent approved in writing by any judge of the Superior Court, Chancery Division, Family Part.

Same sex couples who meet the above requirements and are registered as domestic partners may enter into a civil union with the same person without terminating their domestic partnership first. If the domestic partnership was registered in New Jersey, it automatically terminates when the civil union is registered. If the domestic partnership was registered in another state, that state's laws determine the impact on the domestic partnership. A couple that has previously entered into a civil union or a same-sex marriage shall apply for a Reaffirmation of Civil Union License.

You may apply in the New Jersey municipality in which either person resides. The license is valid throughout the state. If neither applicant lives in New Jersey, submit the application in the municipality where the civil union ceremony will be performed. The license is only valid in the issuing municipality.

When you apply for a civil union license, bring with you:

- If you are divorced or have dissolved a previous civil union, terminated a domestic partnership, or annulled a civil union, bring the decree(s) or the civil annulment documents

- If your former spouse, civil union partner, or domestic partner is deceased, bring the death certificate.

- A copy of your birth certificate, driver's license, passport, or state-issued I.D.

- Proof of your residency

- Your social security card or social security number—your social security number is required by law and will be kept confidential

- A witness, eighteen years of age or older

- The application fee

Any documents in a foreign language must be accompanied by a certified English translation.

After you apply:

- There is a seventy-two-hour waiting period before the license is issued. The waiting period begins when the application is filed with the local registrar.

- The civil union license application is valid for six months from the date accepted, unless the registrar has given prior approval to extend the validity of the application to a maximum of one year.

- Only one civil union license may be granted from a civil

union application. If the license expires before being used, a new application must be made and another fee remitted.

- The only exception to this requirement is in the case where a civil and a religious ceremony are to be performed on the same day. In this case, the local registrar will photocopy the civil union application, marking one "A" and one "B," and issue the corresponding civil union licenses, marking them "A" and "B" as well. One copy will be used for the religious ceremony and the other for the civil ceremony.

For same-sex couples, there are many benefits to becoming domestic partners. Partnership provides the right to many of an ex- or late spouse's benefits, including:

- Social Security pension

- Veteran's pension

- Indemnity compensation for service-connected deaths, medical care, and nursing home care

- Right to burial in veterans' cemeteries

- Preferential hiring for spouses of veterans in government jobs

- Tax-free transfer of property between spouses (including on death) and exemption from "due-on-sale" clauses

- Special consideration to spouses of citizens and resident aliens

Review Checklist

If you are considering a vows renewal ceremony, note the following advice and pointers:

❑ Decide on the celebrant: A state-registered wedding celebrant is not legally necessary. A secular celebrant or even a dear friend can function quite well as the celebrant.

❑ Decide on the location of the ceremony: the couple's general place of worship or a reception site.

❑ Decide on the reception: The reception can be scheduled at any location, from a banquet or wedding hall to an intimate home setting.

❑ Consider sending out invitations: They may be mailed to guests in the same manner as conventional wedding invitations.

❑ Decide on the tone of your ceremony: A vows renewal ceremony can be formal and ornate or informal.

❑ Because of the nostalgia associated with a long and loving marriage, it may be worth inviting only close family members and intimate caring friends as guests.

❑ Decide if you would like to process and if so, how. It is customary for an already married couple to have the husband escort his wife down the aisle. However, grandchildren may be included in the procession by walking down with their grandparents. A lovely alternative is to have them escort Grandma down the aisle as Grandpa waits at the altar.

❑ Consider including a bridal bouquet of the same flowers that were carried in the original ceremony. You may prefer a smaller version of this bouquet, and have processing granddaughters carry an even smaller version of the bouquet, or just one flower of the same species. Another idea is that grandsons wear a boutonnière of the identical flower species.

❏ The use or re-giving of the original rings is customary; some couples opt to give another special anniversary ring to one another.

❏ Include traditions that correspond with your spiritual beliefs and convictions.

❏ Include as much family participation as possible, especially that of grandchildren.

❏ Though a candle-lighting ceremony may be a way of including children, be cautious. Consider the sand ceremony as an alternative.

❏ Try to include elements of your original wedding ceremony.

❏ Set up photographs of your original wedding.

❏ Include some of the music from your original ceremony; for example, the hymn, the original processional anthem, or the song that you danced to.

❏ Some elements of a vows renewal ceremony (particularly the vows themselves) really should be personalized. Therefore, think of what you would like to say to one another and write it down.

❏ Finally, if you are planning on a commitment ceremony or a vows renewal ceremony, read and review the appropriate chapters specific to the special requirements and preparation for these unique rituals.

Chapter Eleven:

Weaving it All Together

So for you dears, who plan to be wed
Gather now thoughts of love in your head
From your lips must impart
Words of love in your heart
Poured forth into your vows to be said.

The Final Step: Joining All The Pieces

The final process of ceremony construction is unbelievably simple. Once you understand the basic steps and principles: voila! You've created your ceremony. So, let us begin the final process of ceremony creation by reviewing your preferences and finalizing decisions.

Decide on the religious or spiritual tone that you want your ceremony to take by reviewing the following categories:

- Religious

- Spiritual—nonreligious

- Spiritual—religious

- Universally spiritual

Revisit and review the ceremony questionnaire on page 27 and answer the questions. Decide on elements you wish to incorporate, if you have not already done so.

Consider possible readings and readers that you may wish to include.

Ask yourself if there are there any specific traditions you would like to include in the ceremony. If the answer is yes, think clearly about whether it is realistically feasible to incorporate them. You may wish to consult with your celebrant.

Review the section on ceremony timelines and determine—logistically and realistically—if the length of the outline you plan on creating is realistic and practical. Review the section on timelines of creative and unusual ceremonies on page 138 to determine if there are ideas and elements that inspire you. Decide whether or not it is possible to incorporate some of these ideas without compromising your and your partner's unique joint vision for your customized ceremony.

Remember that your choice of celebrant will undoubtedly affect the outcome of your personalized ceremony, particularly if she or he is difficult and uncooperative. Remember to interview her or him, following the guidelines in Chapter 1 in the sections on interviewing the celebrant.

If you are planning an interfaith or multicultural ceremony, hold in mind the following points:

- Review the religious and cultural ceremonies that you wish to include and incorporate them.

- Try to simplify or abbreviate those elements that are more elaborate, complex, and lengthy when integrating two religious traditions in one ceremony.

- Be sure that the overall tone of the ceremony is not excessively religious (to avoid competing traditions).

- Be sure that there is a fair and equitable acknowledgement of both traditions.

- Decide on your preferences regarding ceremony officiating, either by two separate clergy members who represent two separate religious traditions, or by one single celebrant who is a representative of both traditions. Once the decision is made, interview each celebrant carefully and thoroughly.

- Finally, if you are planning on a commitment ceremony or a vows renewal ceremony, read and review the appropriate chapters specific to the special requirements and preparation for these unique rituals.

The Sample Six

Most of the six sample ceremonies covered in this chapter are drawn from the material offered in Chapter 8: The Text: Words for Your Ceremony. Each ceremony contains:

- A brief description to assist couples in finding the fitting and compatible ceremony outline.

- An outline worksheet to help couples locate the elements in each sample ceremony. This makes easy work of cross-referencing all the sample ceremony components, particularly if the couple wishes to change and modify their selected ceremony.

- Suggestions for suitable and compatible readings and poems.

The core substance of a wedding ceremony is the wording. The words create the style and tone, and words, like poetry and music, can be either harmonious or discordant. Chapter 8, the core of this guide, lays out the wedding wording choices for each couple to help them create their own ceremony. The selections are extensive enough to afford sufficient choices and combinations to ensure couples a unique ceremony. Of course, it is in the hands of the bride and groom to make selections that resonate with their own special beliefs and values and to express in words their special union.

The following six sample ceremonies illustrate how a completed ceremony looks and flows after the selecting and "weaving together" process is complete. The first four ceremonies were created from the material in the wedding words sections of Chapter 8. Note the distinct style and feel of these ceremonies. Each is woven of many elements yet each is singularly unique. One of these six may be a perfect expression of the traditions and style of some couples; it may be the ideal fit for them. If that is the case, their ceremony is custom-made. To personalize it further, a favorite reading or song could be added.

The sample six are:

• Ceremony #1: Lightly Christian Nondenominational

• Ceremony #2: Lightly "From The Heart" Ecumenical

• Ceremony #3: Religious Christian Nondenominational

• Ceremony #4: Interfaith Christian-Jewish

• Ceremony #5: The Commitment Ceremony

• Ceremony #6: The Vows Renewal Ceremony

Ceremony #1:
Lightly Christian Nondenominational

This ceremony outline offers the perfect solution for couples of different Christian denominations, who tend toward less religious formality. This may also be ideal for those couples who are religiously "lopsided," where only one member is a practicing Christian. For these couples, a lightly Christian nondenominational and heartfelt ceremony may offer a good compromise.

Outline Worksheet:
Dedication 1 (specific)

Opening Benediction and Invocation 5

Opening Welcome 9

Marriage Foundation Address 10

Universal Ecumenical Wine Ceremony 3

Offering of a Scriptural Reading or Poem (suggestions)

Pre-Vows Charge/Statement

    (From "Joseph and Kerri," Chapter 7)

The Ring Blessing 3

Question and Agreement 1

Declarations and Promises 17

The Exchange of Rings 10

Closing Benediction 11

Final Pronouncement 2

Dedication 1 (specific):
Celebrant: "The bride, groom and their families have requested that this ceremony be dedicated to the memory of (name). Our love for him (her) (them) and the precious memories that we hold sacred in the depth of our hearts will live on eternally. May he (she) (them) abide in the loving light of the Eternal and Ever-living God. Amen."

Opening Benediction and Invocation 5:

Celebrant: "Holy Power of Infinite Love: We gather together before God as we witness, honor, and celebrate the joining together of (name) and (name) in marriage, which is a blessed and honorable estate, and from time immemorial considered the most intimate and noble of human relationships.

"As we stand firmly in the presence of all that is Holy and Divine, we ask that this union be blessed, protected, sanctified, and guided by Your Infinite Love. May each one gathered as witnesses to this sacred covenant know in their hearts, that this ceremony is but an outward sign of something inner and deeper, a union of hearts that already exists, and which we now formalize and sanction before each one gathered. Your role as witnesses is to unify and join in your well wishes and blessings for the bride and groom. May all that is showered forth upon these two this day be returned and double as gifts and blessings for each who offered them.

"In the name of the Father, Son, and Holy Spirit. Amen."

Opening Welcome 9:

Celebrant: "We are gathered here as loving friends and family to witness and support the joining in marriage of (name) and (name). They have opened their hearts and futures to one another, and today they will share their vows of marriage. We, as witnesses, are deeply thankful to them for opening their hearts to us, also, and inviting us to share in these precious moments.

"To this union they bring the fullness of their being as a treasured gift to share with one another. They invite each other to share in a joined life, acknowledging this union is born of love.

"For what greater joy is there for two human souls than to unite and support one another in all of their endeavors? Loving another person is the greatest and most precious gift we can ever wish for. The joining of two is not the diminishing of each individual, but the acknowledging and enhancing of the two in the creation of a marriage. Marriage is the joyful uniting of two unique and separate individuals who add their own special gifts and qualities to the union. It is into this state that bride and groom wish to enter, and each one of us gathered here has been chosen and honored to be witness to this union."

Marriage Foundation Address 10:

Celebrant: "A union based in love is the most holy and sacred of all loving relationships. Two people committed to one another who share this unique love are truly blessed. And the growth and development of this love does not begin with this ceremony. The wedding ceremony is the public affirmation and testimony to what already exists between the two of you that you have already built together, through your love and respect for one another. This ceremony blesses and affirms the sacredness of this union. It is the love you share that holds the two of you in this sacred bond. It is love itself that is truly sacred. As love grows greater, it becomes a great shield and stronghold that protects each of you from all of the distractions and difficulties that can erode the preciousness of this union. Always remember that your marriage is woven of the fabric of deep love, and it is this love that will hold, nurture, sustain, and protect your union as the years go by."

Offering of a Scriptural Reading or a Poem (suggestions):

Adapted from First Corinthians, Chapter 13:

"Love is patient and kind; love is not jealous or boastful; it is not arrogant or rude. Love does not insist on its own way; it is not irritable or resentful; it does not rejoice at wrong, but rejoices in the right. Love bears all things, believes all things, hopes all things, endures all things.

"Love never ends; as for prophecies, they will pass away; as for tongues, they will cease; as for knowledge, it will pass away. For our knowledge is imperfect and our prophecy is imperfect; but when the perfect comes the imperfect will pass away. So faith, hope, love abide, these three; but the greatest of these is love."

Adapted from "How Do I Love Thee?" (Sonnet 43) by Elizabeth Barrett Browning:

How do I love thee? Let me count the ways.
I love thee to the depth and breadth and height
My soul can reach, when feeling out of sight
For the ends of being and ideal grace.
I love thee to the level of every day's
Most quiet need, by sun and candle light.
I love thee freely, as men strive for Right;
I love thee purely, as they turn from Praise.
I love thee with the passion put to use
In my old griefs, and with my childhood's faith.
I love thee with a love I seemed to lose

With my lost saints,—I love thee with the breath,
Smiles, tears, of all my life!—and, if God choose,
I shall but love thee better after death.

Universal Ecumenical Wine Ceremony 3:

Celebrant: "It is fitting in this moment of celebration that the bride and groom now take their first sip of wine together to celebrate all that has taken place in their lives up to this point. This is also a symbol and expression of all hope and faith in the harvest of their lives from this point forward. As you participate in the wine ceremony and drink from this cup, may you, under God's guidance, draw contentment, peace, strength, and solace from the cup of life. May you find life's joys doubled and life's bitterness a little sweeter, because you share them together, and may all things be blessed and sanctified by companionship and love."

Celebrant to bride and groom: "(Name) and (name), may your lives give forth abundance, health, joy, and blessings."

Pre-Vows Charge/Statement:

Celebrant: "It is now time to state your wedding vows to each other. These promises are solemnly and truthfully made before God and this company who witness the choice you have made to enter the portal of marriage today, to walk forward together hand in hand, joining together your hearts, your destinies, and your lives. As you embark upon the sacred and noble path of marriage, remember to cherish and honor the love that brought you together. Together you are about to formally affirm the love and respect that you already hold for one another. Therefore, (name) and (name), before you repeat your vows to one another, I offer you this charge: May you always remain friends. May you laugh together and be joyful. Be a source of strength and comfort."

The Ring Ceremony and Blessing 3:

Celebrant: "The ring is a symbol of the sincerity and permanence of a couple's love for one another. The circle is also a symbol of eternal love that, like a circle, is without beginning and without end. *(Rings are handed to celebrant.)* Bless these rings, O Lord, and the two who will exchange them in the spirit of endless and eternal love. Amen."

Question and Agreement 1:

Celebrant: "Do you, (name), take (name) as your wife (husband)?"
Groom (Bride): "I do."

Declarations and Promises 17:

Groom (Bride): "I am blessed to receive you as my cherished wife (husband). I treasure you as my beloved life companion and dearest friend. As we embark upon our life's journey together today, I pledge to you these promises: To love, honor, respect, encourage, and listen to you. I will uphold you in all your endeavors. I will rejoice at your successes. Throughout the sunshine and shadows of life, I will do my utmost to be a tower of strength for you. I will offer you a soft shoulder to lean on, a warm embrace to comfort you, and a strong hand to support you. These promises I make to you this day before God and these witnesses."

The Exchange of Rings 10:

Couple (repeated after celebrant prompts): "You are my deepest and most beloved friend. Accept this ring as a token of my unending devotion, love, and commitment to you. With this ring I offer to you this day, I wed my lifetime companion and my dearest friend."

Closing Benediction 11:

Celebrant: "May all that you have already become—through your separate life journeys, which have brought you to this moment of the joining of the two—and all that you will become—as a consequence of the promises you have made and the life that you will now continue to develop—expand and grow in love for all of your days together. Amen."

Final Pronouncement 2:

Celebrant: "(Name) and (name), though I have officiated your ceremony, it is beyond my power to sanctify your relationship—because the two of you have already done so, in your hearts, through the love you share with one another. Since love is a direct attribute of God, only God alone can truly and fully bless this marriage. Therefore, in the name of Almighty God before these loving witnesses, it is my legal right and my greatest privilege to pronounce that you are, indeed, husband and wife."

Ceremony 2:
Lightly "From the Heart" Ecumenical

This is probably the most versatile of ceremonies. It is an excellent fit for numerous couples, including those who practice their spirituality outside the doctrinal definitions of organized religions; those who consider themselves nondenominational, non-religious, or non-practicing interfaith couples; and those who are universally spiritual or Unitarian/Universalist.

Outline Worksheet:

Acknowledgement 1 (general)

Opening Benediction and Invocation 2

Opening Welcome 1

Marriage Foundation Address 2

Bride and Groom Candle-Lighting Ceremony 5

Offering of a Reading or Poem (suggestions)

Pre-Vows Charge/Statement

The Ring Blessing 2

Question and Agreement 7

Declarations and Promises 18

The Exchange of Rings 8

Closing Benediction 4

Final Pronouncement 7

Acknowledgement 1 (general):

Celebrant: "We acknowledge those friends and family members who could not attend this ceremony today due to the great distance between us. Their love and support is carried to us over the miles, as on the wings of love. For love transcends all barriers, obstacles, time, and space. We acknowledge our love for them and hold them deeply in our hearts."

Opening Benediction and Invocation 2:

Celebrant: "Divine Spirit, Font of All Blessings: We gather here today in joy and awe as we stand in Your Presence and enter into quiet prayerfulness. As family and friends of (name) and (name), we celebrate their joining in marriage. We offer up our deepest gratitude to You and we rejoice that these two have been blessed to have found this love that they share. We ask that the love between them grows broader and deeper with the passing years. May this union be filled with mutual trust and genuine affection. May these qualities of spirit stand them in good stead when difficulties and challenges assail them. May the sheer strength of their loving union forge a great shield of power and courage that they both can share. May this love that they share double their joy. May each of us here share this exquisite moment and as witnesses may we also be blessed. Amen."

Opening Welcome 1:

Celebrant: "Welcome. We gather here today as witnesses to celebrate the joining in marriage of (name) and (name). This ceremony is but an outer ritual of that which is deeper and real; a union of body, mind, and spirit, which religion may sanctify and the state may authorize, but which neither can create. Marriage is a public recognition of the personal experience of two in love. It is the dedication of two, to one life fully shared. It is not intended for happiness alone, but for the personal inner growth of each one, who dedicate their life to a union of mutual support and respect, through the joining of a life fully shared, through life's tests and trials given and returned and forgiven.

"We, as witnesses, are asked to hold foremost in our minds and hearts the greatest and loftiest potential and possibilities for the bride and groom, so that they may fully know the wonder of a shared life of committed loving and caring.

"May they each, as a couple joined in love, come to know both the great power and the gentle tenderness of the love they share, as they walk together through the portal of this ceremony into a new life, a new beginning as husband and wife."

Marriage Foundation Address 2:

Celebrant: "Today is your wedding day, a day you will always remember. This is one of the greatest and most important days in anyone's life. You begin this day as two people in love and end it as husband and wife—a team of two, united in one life. This is the beginning of a new journey, a new chapter in your lives. All of your individual hopes and dreams will now be joined. Some are different and some are the same. But they become woven together for the greater good of your union. You now become a team who together build a marriage requiring the very best that you each can be. As the marriage begins to take form, so do your individual characters. You two are the authors of this life that you share and build. Yet the very process of committing to the creating of this marriage will in fact build *you,* will build your inner strength and character. Most importantly, this will deepen and open your hearts. For the greatest attribute in this union is love. Love is what will support and sustain you over the years."

Offering of a Reading or Poem (suggestions):

"In One Another's Souls" by Rumi (adapted)
The moment I heard my first love story I began seeking you, not realizing the search was useless.
Lovers don't meet somewhere along the way.
They are in one another's souls from the beginning.

The Navajo Prayer. (Author unknown)
When you were children, you talked like children
But now that you've grown, be done with childish things
And put them away.
When you were children you looked into a mirror
That gave only a blurred reflection of reality
But with love and maturity,
    be not afraid to look into that mirror
And see each other face to face.
Be swift like the wind in loving each other.
Be brave like the sea in loving each other.
Be gentle like the breeze in loving each other.
Be patient like the sun who waits and watches
The four changes of the earth in loving each other.
Be wise like the roaring of the thunderclouds and lightning
    in loving each other.
Be shining like the morning dawn in loving each other.
Be brilliant like the rainbow colors in loving each other.
Now forever, forever there will be no loneliness
Because your worlds are joined together forever, forever.

Bride and Groom Candle-Lighting Ceremony 5:

Celebrant: "The center column candle has been lit, symbolizing the unity of love, which binds and unites. Love is what created us and is what sustains us throughout our lives. Love impels us to tap the deepest place within our own hearts. Love builds and creates the depth and strength of the best that we can be. These individual candles symbolize the two distinct lives of two in love."

Celebrant to bride and groom: "As you light these candles from the unity candle, you draw to you the fire of infinite love. Hold your individual flames together to form the one greater flame of your union in marriage and of the inextinguishable love that brought you—and will hold you—together. Amen."

The Pre-Vows Charge/Statement:

Celebrant: " I offer you this charge: 'From this day forward walk together fearlessly upon the path of marriage. Respect one another's dream and aspirations. Laugh together, play together, celebrate your similarities yet respect your differences. Offer your hands to support and encourage, offer your love to enfold and to comfort, and be gentle and kind. But most of all, always love and honor one another.'"

The Ring Ceremony and Blessing 2:

Celebrant: "From time immemorial, a circle of metal has been a symbol of the durability of a couple's love for one another and their union. As these rings of precious metal encircle upon themselves, so do those who commit their lives to one another encircle each other with their love, throughout the years of a lasting marriage. As precious metal is solid and strong, so is a committed marriage pledged in love solid and strong."

(Rings are handed to celebrant.)

Celebrant: "May these rings be blessed and the two who will wear them. May they stand together steadfast in a circle of unbreakable love. Amen."

Question and Agreement 7:

Celebrant: "(Name), do you promise to share your life with (name) as her (his) husband (wife), to live together in all honesty and faithfulness? Do you promise also to join together in the spirit of tolerance, sharing your hopes and dreams, your joys and sorrows?"

Groom (Bride): "I do."

Declarations and Promises 18:

Groom (Bride): "I, (name), choose and accept you, (name), as my wife (husband). I promise to be a kind and loving friend to you, to be true to you and to respect you, to stand by you when you need comfort and understanding. I will continue to respect and care for you. When you are assailed with discouragement, I will offer you encouragement. When you are blessed with life's successes, I will celebrate and rejoice with you. Together the strength of our love will help build a solid marriage. A marriage built on love is unshakable, as the bonds of this love are unbreakable."

The Exchange of Rings 8:

Couple (repeated after celebrant prompts): "As a token of my deepest and eternal love, I give you this ring and pledge my constant faith and abiding love. Wear it forever as a symbol of my endless and eternal love."

Closing Benediction 4:
(A Native American Wedding Blessing, Version 1)

by Maureen Burwell Pollinger

Celebrant: "May the healing sun that watches over the earth warm you,

May the soft breeze that whispers over the plains cool you.

May your home give you shelter from the storm and may the soft rain nourish your pastures.

May the stars in the heavens be your blanket of blessings and may the silver moon light your way over the long night's waters.

Let your words to one another be as sacred as the songbird's song and clear as call of the loon.

May your hearts shine as brilliantly as the northern lights over the mountain peaks and as beautifully as the summer rainbow.

May your embrace be as gentle as the morning dove and your love as mighty as the roaring buffalo.

May blessings linger above you as the humming bird hovers over the cobweb thistle, and may abundance rain upon you.

May your love be as powerful as the mountain thunder, as

vast as the endless sky and as deep as the greatest ocean.

Be a soft pillow for your beloved to fall upon in times of sadness and celebrate together in times of gladness.

Proclaim your union, from the highest mountain to the deepest valley, that those who hear may also be so blessed.

Rejoice at sunrise, for one more day with your beloved and when the sun sets deeply over the plains offer a prayer of gratitude, for another day together.

Walk together hand-in-hand upon life's unpredictable journey.

For your two lives are now woven together as one life and your love will live forever in the heart of The Great Spirit."

Final Pronouncement 7:

Celebrant: As your joined life stretches out before you, know that you are committed and dedicated to each other because of the vows you have exchanged this day, born of the love you share. Therefore, because of these promises you have made to one another today, before God and these witnesses, it is my legal right, and my greatest pleasure, to pronounce that you are now married."

Ceremony #3:
Religious Christian Nondenominational

The following ceremony offers a perfect fit for unions where one or both partners are divorced Catholics. Many of the ceremonies I officiate include unions where one partner is Catholic. Often a religious ceremony officiated by a nondenominational or ecumenical minister is the only option available to divorced Catholics, as they are not candidates for a marriage in the Catholic Church due to their divorce status. In addition, this somewhat neutral Christian ceremony will serve many moderately religious, mixed and same-denomination couples.

Outline Worksheet:

Opening Benediction and Invocation 4

Opening Welcome 10

Marriage Foundation Address 14

The Rose Ceremony (for the mothers)

Offering of a Scriptural Reading or Poem (suggestions)

The Ring Blessing 6

Presbyterian Vows

Closing Benediction 3

Universal Hand-Joining Ritual 6

Final Pronouncement 1

Opening Benediction and Invocation 4:

Celebrant: "Dearly beloved, we come together in the presence of Almighty God the Father, Son, and Holy Spirit, to witness and bless the joining together of (name) and (name) in holy matrimony. The bond and covenant of marriage was established by God in creation. It signifies to us the mystery of the union between Christ and His Church, and Holy Scripture commends it to be honored among all people. Therefore, marriage is not to be entered into unadvisedly or lightly, but reverently and in accordance with the purposes for which it was instituted by God. Amen."

Opening Welcome 10:

Celebrant: "Each of us gathered is privileged to witness this union sanctioned by God. We are given the opportunity to be fully inspired by the commitment of (name) and (name) and by their shared love that has brought them to this moment. Today the bride and groom will declare their love for one another, before each of you as witnesses. As they make this covenant today before God, they do so fully knowing that He is the creator of this life that they share from this day forward, and He is the creator of the special and unique love that bonds and unifies their lives. May each of you gathered here hold them in your prayers; pour forth your blessings and special benedictions upon them and upon this union. Affirm in your hearts that this love that they share will continue to expand, intensify, and grow with the passing of the years. May God bless and sanctify this union and by His Love may all things be hallowed. Amen."

Marriage Foundation Address 14:

Celebrant: "A strong and loving marriage is a spiritual journey of profound inner growth and selflessness. It requires the willingness to admit to being wrong, even when a stubborn mind tells you differently. It requires the ability to forgive the unimportant issues while having the conviction to steadfastly support and defend the important issues. The commitment to marriage is a noble path that impels us to develop selflessness and consideration. As love grows and expands deeper and fuller, we fully recognize how precious our chosen partner is. As we grow in our love for each other, we grow in wisdom.

The glorious Presence of Divinity resides within the human heart. Here lies the inborn gift of deep wisdom; the wisdom to see ourselves reflected in our partner. We become mirrors for one another, helping one another to develop and grow. In wisdom we recognize that the difficulties and conflicts that arise in a marriage can serve to inspire and set in motion the necessary and required growth of character that must be developed to ensure that a marriage will endure and remain whole.

"Working through these difficulties can be the perfect motivation for turning inward and tapping those inner reservoirs of love that lie deep in the heart. This is our most profound connection with one another, because it is here that we connect with the ever-loving God.

"With God all is possible."

Offering of a Scriptural Reading or Poem (suggestions):

"Love Is a Mighty Power"
by Thomas à Kempis (priest, monk, and writer)
Love is a mighty power, a great and complete good.
Love alone lightens every burden,
    and makes rough places smooth.
It bears every hardship as though it were nothing,
    and renders all bitterness sweet and acceptable.
Nothing is sweeter than love, nothing stronger, nothing higher,
    nothing wider, nothing more pleasant, nothing fuller or
    better in heaven or earth; for love is born of God.
Love flies, runs and leaps for joy. It is free and unrestrained.
    Love knows no limits, but ardently transcends all bounds.
    Love feels no burden, takes no account of toil, attempts

things beyond its strength.

Love sees nothing as impossible, or it feels able to achieve all things. It is strange and effective, while those who lack love are faint and fail.

Love is not fickle and sentimental, nor is it intent on vanities. Like a living flame and a burning torch, it surges upward and surely surmounts every obstacle.

Adapted from St. Paul to the Ephesians

Give yourself to one another completely. Be generous in your giving and make no conditions for these gifts. Love one another constantly and fully. Be humble in your acceptance of your partner's love. Be honest with each other. Be thankful for each other's love and strive to develop its richness day by day. Respect each other in every way. Be patient with each other's weaknesses and accept each other for what you are, not what you wish one another to be. Communicate constantly with one another. Be calm, patient, tolerant and reasonable in your communication. Be capable of good listening. Share with one another misfortune and fortune alike. Be compassionate and express your love for one another constantly. Know your limitation and be honest with yourself as you are with one another. Fuse your souls into one another and be happy for the love you have been so fortunate to find in one another.

The Rose Ceremony for the Mothers

Together the bride and groom offer the mothers private thanks and hugs as they present each of them with a long-stemmed red rose.

The Ring Ceremony and Blessing 5:

Celebrant: "The circle is a symbol of wholeness, holiness, perfection, and peace."

(Rings are handed to celebrant.)

Celebrant: "Almighty God, we ask for Your blessing upon these rings and upon the bride and groom who will wear them. May they be blessed with wholeness of body and mind. May they be blessed with holiness, perfection, and peace of spirit. May these rings symbolize the eternity of their love. Amen."

Presbyterian Vows

Celebrant: "(Name), wilt thou have this woman (man) to be thy wife (husband), and wilt thou pledge thy faith to her (him), in all love and honor, in all duty and service, in all faith and tenderness, to live with her (him) and cherish her (him), according to the ordinance of God, in the holy bond of marriage?"

Groom (Bride): "I will."

Groom (Bride): "I, (name), take thee, (name), to be my wedded wife (husband), and I do promise and covenant, before God and these witnesses, to be thy loving and faithful husband (wife); in plenty and in want, in joy and in sorrow, in sickness and in health, as long as we both shall live."

(Rings): "This ring I give thee, in token and pledge of our constant faith and abiding love."

Closing Benediction 3:

Celebrant: "The Lord bless you and keep you, the Lord make His face shine upon you, and be gracious to you. The Lord lift up His countenance upon you, and give you peace. Amen."

Final Pronouncement 1:

Celebrant: "As you have each made this commitment to one another in the holy bond of marriage before God and this loving community of witnesses, it is my legal right as a minister by the powers vested in me—and it is also my greatest joy—to pronounce you husband and wife."

Ceremony #4:
Interfaith Christian-Jewish

Generally interfaith ceremonies flow more easily when the tone of the ceremony is not excessively religious.

The following ceremony outline for the Christian-Jewish couple offers a fair acknowledgement and representation of both Christianity and Judaism. My suggestion to the Jewish member of the union is that she or he asks a beloved family member or elder to participate in ceremonial elements that require the reading of Hebrew.

Outline Worksheet:

The *Shehekhianu* as an Opening Prayer
Opening Benediction and Invocation 7
Opening Welcome 4
The Hebrew Blessing of the Wine
Universal Ecumenical Wine Ceremony 1

Marriage Foundation Address 12 (optional)

Offering of a Scriptural Reading or Poem (suggestions)

Quote from Baal Shem Tov

Bride and Groom Candle-Lighting Ceremony 6

Unitarian Universalist Vows 2

The Ring Blessing 6

The Exchange of Rings 5

Closing Benedictions 1 and 3

Final Pronouncement 6

The *Shehekhianu* as an Opening Prayer:

Transliteration: Barukh atah Adonai, Eloheynu, melekh ha-olam she-hekheeyanu v'keey'manu v'heegeeyanu la-z,man ha-zeh.

Translation: Blessed are you, Lord, our God, ruler of the universe, who has kept us alive, sustained us, and enabled us to reach this season.

Opening Benediction and Invocation 7:

Celebrant: "Divine Power of Love and Light: We call upon Your blessings as we gather together in the presence of Your eternal love to witness the joining of (name) and (name) in marriage. We pray that each of them find deep and profound gentleness, joy, and caring in this union that will provide a loving sanctuary as they journey through their shared life together. Through this union, may they each bring to the other positive, loving challenges, inspiration, wisdom, and joy. As the depth of their love expands and grows, may they come to know You more fully as the Loving Presence who resides within the purity and stillness of their own hearts. Inspired by their love, as witnesses may each of us gathered here offer up our own prayers of gratitude, not only for the privilege of being present at this union, but also for the blessings You bestow upon us as witnesses. Amen."

Opening Welcome 4:

Celebrant: "We gather here today in joy to witness a celebration of marriage. The bride and groom, in their mutual respect, dedication, and devotion to one another, now wish to unite in the commitment and bond of marriage.

"For each of us gathered here, our most sincere hopes and wishes are that bride and groom be always encouraged and motivated by that radiant power of mutual love that first brought them together. The power of love is stronger and greater than the conflicts they may face. It is bigger than life's unpredictability and challenges. It always invites each of them to learn, to blossom, to grow, and to evolve. It is always to love that we must return. May each gathered here send forth their wholehearted blessings and support for the bride and groom, for the fulfillment of a life committed to love and mutual married joy."

The Hebrew Blessing of the Wine:

Transliteration: Bar-uch' A-tah' Adonai El-o-hei-nu me'-lech ha-o-lam' bo-re' pe-ri' ha-ga'-fen.

Translation: Blessed are you, Lord, Our God, King of the universe. You created the fruit of the vine.

Universal Ecumenical Wine Ceremony 1:

Celebrant: "Throughout history, in many traditions, the sharing of a cup of wine has symbolized the central moment of sharing during significant celebrations. In ancient cultures, wine has symbolized the fruit of our labors and the gathering of the harvest after the years of work, dedication, and sacrifice. It is fitting in this moment of celebration that the bride and groom now take their first sip of wine together to celebrate all that has taken place in their lives up to this point. The sharing of the wine also serves as a symbol and expression of all hope and faith in the harvest of their lives from this point forward."

Celebrant to bride and groom: "As you each sip from this single cup of wine, you partake in an ancient ritual of sharing. From this moment on, your two lives have become as one. Drink from the cup of life and may your lives be sweet and full, and may they bring forth abundance."

Marriage Foundation Address 12:

Celebrant: "(Name) and (name), you each hold a strong belief in God and his magnificent creations that so often go unnoticed and taken for granted. Remember, always, that God is the creator of this life that you share. He is a source of guidance and comfort, not only throughout every living moment of your lives, but during those special moments of celebration. The Divine presence and guidance is central to this wedding ceremony. We call upon God to guide you through both the joys and the disappointments of this life you will both share. May your faith in the Divine Presence help each of you to recognize how precious and unique your chosen partner is. Within each of us lie inherent gifts and qualities that can often be discovered and unveiled within ourselves by seeing them reflected in our partner. When we recognize the very best in our beloved partner, we also see the inner Divinity within ourselves. Each marriage then, is an opportunity to develop and achieve the highest and best we can ever hope to be. Each witness gathered here is a vital part of this ceremony and offers the bride and groom a powerful gift—the gift of encouraging thoughts, wishes, and prayers for their future lives together from this moment on."

Offering of a Scriptural Reading or Poem (suggestions):

A note about including a reading: Typically various elements are incorporated into an interfaith ceremony. Adding a reading can lead to "ceremony overload." For those whose hearts are set on including a reading, I suggest they choose one that is short and religiously neutral.

The following readings fit the criteria of neutrality, though the first sample works better as a closing benediction or wedding charge which could be included directly after the exchange of vows and rings.

"A Wedding Charge"
by Reverend Maureen Burwell Pollinger:

May you always be friends, confidants and playmates.
May you laugh together,
Support each other's dreams and aspirations.
Celebrate your similarities, respect your differences.
Be a source of strength in times of sadness,

A joyful friend in times of gladness.
Share your thoughts yet don't inflict.
Support and comfort yet don't constrict.
But most of all beyond all other,
Love and honor one another.

From *Twelfth Night* by William Shakespeare:

A contract of eternal bond of love,
Confirm'd by mutual joinder of your hands,
Attested by the holy close of lips,
Strengthen'd by interchangement of your rings;
And all the ceremony of this compact
Seal'd in my function, by my testimony

From the *I Ching:*

When two people are at one in their inmost hearts, they shatter even the strength of iron.

Quote from Baal Shem Tov:

From every soul there is a light that reaches straight to heaven.
When two souls who are destined to be together find one
    another,
Their streams of light flow together
and a single, brighter light flows forth from their united being.

Bride and Groom Candle-Lighting Ceremony 6:

Celebrant to bride and groom: "This unity candle flame is a symbol of the oneness of this union and the eternal flame of love that burns within your two hearts. (Name) and (name), please light your candles from the unity candle. The individual candles represent your lives before today, the love and the care that nurtured you as you grew. They represent all that you can be from this day on, all of your possibilities as individuals. As you light your candles from the unity candle and join the separate flames together, your individual hopes, dreams, and futures will now be entwined and united. May the sacred and eternal flame of love continue to burn within your hearts."

Unitarian Universalist Vows 2:

Celebrant: "(Name), will you take (name) to be your wife (husband)? Will you love, honor, and cherish her (him) now and forever more?"

Groom (Bride): "I will."

Groom (Bride): "I, (name), joyfully receive you, (name), into my life as my wedded wife (husband), to live together and work together, to create a marriage built on love and mutual respect. I promise to honor, comfort, and cherish you, in sickness and in health, in sorrow and in joy, from this day forward."

The Ring Blessing 6:

Celebrant: "The ring is a circle, a symbol of love and eternity. Like the infinite universe, love is endless. May you enter into the circle of married love. May your devotion to each other grow ever stronger, building a sanctuary of love that expands and grows with the passing years."

(Rings are handed to celebrant.)

Celebrant: "Lord, may these rings be blessed and may this bride and groom stand steadfast and secure in a circle of ever-growing love. Amen."

The Exchange of Rings 5:

Couple (repeated after the celebrant prompts): "This ring is a circle, unbroken, just as my love for you is unbroken and complete. I offer you this ring as a token of the promises that I have made to you this day. Wear it as a symbol of our eternal commitment to one another."

Closing Benediction 1:

Celebrant: "May your hearts be open, your love be full, your lives be joined, your fates be sealed, your union be strong, your home be sheltered, and your marriage be blessed. Amen."

Closing Benediction 3:

Celebrant: "The Lord bless you and keep you, the Lord make His face shine upon you, and be gracious to you. The Lord lift up His countenance upon you, and give you peace. Amen."

Final Pronouncement 6:

Celebrant: "You have chosen each other to love, you have given your solemn vow to one another for all of your days together, therefore before Almighty God and before this community of loving witnesses, it is my legal right by the powers vested in me—and it is my greatest blessing and privilege—to pronounce that you are now husband and wife."

Ceremony #5:
The Commitment Ceremony

Though the following ceremony outline text is designed for a commitment ceremony, it serves equally for a legally binding same-gender civil union or same-gender marriage ceremony. In these situations, couples in love want the same sentiments expressed in their ceremony as do all couples who are getting married. Included are ten innovative rewordings of the final pronouncements that avoid the phrase "husband and wife."

Outline Worksheet:

Opening Benediction and Invocation 9 (adapted)

Opening Welcome 8 (adapted)

Foundation Address (adapted)

Offering of a Scriptural Reading or Poem (suggestions)

Candle-Lighting Ceremony 3 (adapted)

Pre-Vows Statement

Exchange of Commitment Vows

The Ring Blessing

The Exchange of Rings 3

Closing Benediction 1

Final Pronouncement

The Kiss

Opening Benediction and Invocation 9 (adapted):

Celebrant: "Spirit of Eternal Love: We unite our hearts and minds as we come together to witness and celebrate the union of (name) and (name) as these two are united as one in a life commitment of undying love. May all that is noble, righteous, and lovely abide within each of them as they embark upon the path of a lifetime union. May their lives be filled with blessings and may they gain strength, stamina, and the courage to overcome life's adversities and challenges as the years advance. Help them to keep their love alive and precious by their compassion for and their commitment to one another. These prayers and petitions we offer you that each gathered here will empower and uphold these benedictions by the mere depth of their prayerful intentions for this couple. Let us remember that an unselfish wish is a prayer that will draw blessings back into our own lives as witnesses to this union. Amen."

Opening Welcome 8 (adapted):

Celebrant: "Welcome all who gather here. As each of us evolve and grow through our own personal and unique life journey, we eventually come to the realization that love is much more than romance. We begin to fully know that true love is a guiding force and the most important thing in our lives.

"Love is the creator of our deepest dreams and highest aspirations. Love gives us the courage to forge ahead in times of difficulties. Love restores and revives us when life becomes discouraging.

"Love impels us to share our joys and celebrations with those we love. Love is an extension of all that is good and great. Love is Divine.

"As we witness this commitment ceremony, I ask each of you to hold in your hearts the very best wishes and highest good for (name) and (name) and for the creation and continuation of a union based on the power of Divine Love."

Foundation Address
(adapted from Marriage Foundation Address 3):

Celebrant: "A true committed union of souls in love is the deepest of all human relationships and bonds. It offers us the magnificent opportunity to open our heart to another in nurturance, comradeship, and understanding. It challenges us, offering us limitless opportunities to grow and expand our minds and our hearts to one another. It necessitates a commitment to selflessness, sensitivity, openness, honesty, and compassion.

"A union that is based on loving another fully and completely requires that we each tap the deepest place within, the very heart of compassion where God resides within us. Thus, a truly conscious and sacred partnership of love is an instrument and a vehicle for spiritual development and self-realization. Loving another and having that love reflected back is life's greatest, most cherished, and most sacred gift anyone could ever wish for.

"Let each of you, now and forever, always treasure—and be eternally thankful for—the gift of this special love that you share."

Offering of a Scriptural Reading or Poem (suggestions):

A note about readings: For the commitment ceremony, one must be careful to avoid readings with references to the term "marriage." Similarly, while researching readings for civil unions, choose those that are gender-neutral.

"In One Another's Souls" by Rumi (adapted)

The moment I heard my first love story I began seeking you,
not realizing the search was useless.
Lovers don't meet somewhere along the way.
They are in one another's souls from the beginning

"A Sacred Space" by Lau Tzu

Your love requires space in which to grow. This space must be
safe enough to allow your hearts to be revealed.
It must offer refreshment for your spirits and renewal for your
mind
It must be a space made sacred by the quality of your honesty,
attention, love and compassion.
It may be anywhere, inside or out, but it must exist.

"A Native American Wedding Blessing" (Version 1):

by Maureen Burwell Pollinger.
May the healing sun that watches over the earth warm you.
May the soft breeze that whispers over the plains cool you.
May your home give you shelter from the storm and may the
soft rain nourish your pastures.
May the stars in the heavens be your blanket of blessings and
may the silver moon light your way over the long night's
waters.
Let your words to one another be as sacred as the songbird's
song and clear as call of the loon.
May your hearts shine as brilliantly as the northern lights over
the mountain peaks and as beautifully as the summer rainbow.
May your embrace be as gentle as the morning dove and your
love as mighty as the roaring buffalo.
May blessings linger above you as the humming bird hovers
over the cobweb thistle, and may abundance rain upon you.

May your love be as powerful as the mountain thunder, as vast as the endless sky and as deep as the greatest ocean.

Be a soft pillow for your beloved to fall upon in times of sadness and celebrate together in times of gladness.

Proclaim your union, from the highest mountain to the deepest valley, that those who hear may also be so blessed.

Walk together hand-in-hand upon life's unpredictable journey.

Rejoice at sunrise, for one more day with your beloved and when the sun sets deeply over the plains offer a prayer of gratitude, for another day together.

For your two lives are now woven together as one life and your love will live forever in the heart of The Great Spirit."

Candle-Lighting Ceremony 3 (adapted):

Celebrant: "'From every human being, there rises a light that reaches straight to heaven. And when two souls who are destined, to be together find one another, their streams of light flow together and a single, brighter light goes forth from their united being.' Baal Shem Tov. A candle flame is a symbol of the light of infinite and eternal love, born of all that is Divine. Love is what brought you together. Love is what will sustain you throughout your lives together. From love you are created, to love you will return."

Celebrant to each partner: "Please light your individual candles from this center candle. Now, bring your lighted candle flames together, acknowledging and symbolizing your union. You are both joined in a union and bond of eternal love and as the two flames merge into one, your love for one another grows even stronger and brighter. Always remember the radiant light of your union represents your connection to God, the source of all light. Amen."

Pre-Vows Statement:

Celebrant: "(Name) and (name), I offer you these timeless sentiments, which I quote from the I Ching: 'When two people are at one in their inmost hearts, they shatter even the strength of iron.'"

Exchange of Commitment Vows:

Celebrant: "Will you, (name), take (name) to be your committed partner in love and in life? Will you love, honor, and cherish her (him) now and forever more?"

Partner: "I will." (Speaking to partner) "I (name) joyfully receive you (name) into my life as my beloved life partner to live together and work together to create a fully committed union built on love and mutual respect. I promise to honor, comfort and cherish you in sickness and in health, in sorrow and in joy, from this day forward, bonded together as lifetime lovers and faithful partners in a union of eternal love."

The Ring Blessing:

(Rings are handed to celebrant.)

Celebrant: "May these rings be blessed and may the wearing of them be a reminder, from this day forward, to stand together at the center of the circle of your lives; to be a source of reliability, dependability, and constancy with and for one another, throughout your lives together. Amen."

The Exchange of Rings 3:

Couple (repeated after the celebrant prompts): "This ring I give you is a circle that has no beginning and no end and is unbroken, as is our love. Wear it as a token and symbol of my love for you and of this sacred union of two beloveds joined as one and blessed by God."

Closing Benediction 1:

Celebrant: "May your hearts be open, your love be full, your lives be joined, your fates be sealed, your union be strong, your home be sheltered, and your commitment be eternally blessed. Amen."

Final Pronouncement:

Celebrant: "(Name) and (name), you have each spoken from the depth of your hearts, where the loving God resides. Therefore, having witnessed your promises and your mutual avowed commitment to one another for life this day before all assembled here as witnesses and as a community of loving friends and family members, on behalf of all that is Sacred and Divine, it is my greatest honor to pronounce, make known, and declare publicly and before God that you are now two beloved souls who are united for a lifetime commitment of mutual love and support."

Or:

- Committed to one another in a lifetime union of love

- Joined together as partners for life

- Life mates and partners joined in a bond of love

- Life partners joined in a pledge of unending love

- Sacred union of two beloveds joined as one and blessed by God

- Two united as one in a life commitment of undying love

- United and joined for a lifetime of love and commitment

- United companions and lovers joined unbreakably for life

- United in a lifetime partnership and bond of love

- United life partners

The Kiss

You may seal your union with a kiss.

Ceremony #6:
The Vows Renewal Ceremony

I purposely designed the following "ecumenical" vows renewal ceremony to convey certain adaptability, in order to accommodate the needs of most, if not all, couples planning to renew their vows. Included are a number of sample readings, which may be substituted with ones which convey the appropriate religious or cultural expression for that particular couple. My hope (and my gift to them) is that this outline will serve those blessed couples whose love and dedication have endured the passing of the years.

Outline Worksheet:

Opening Benediction

Opening Welcome

Offering of a Scriptural Reading or Poem

The Ring Blessing
Pre-Vows Statement
Exchange of Renewed Vows
Reading by Bride and Groom
The Closing Benediction (The Celtic Blessing)
The Final Pronouncement
The Kiss

Opening Benediction:

Celebrant: "We thank you, Lord, for the great love and continuing joy that has brought—and held—(name) and (name) together in the union of lasting marriage. We ask for your continued blessings upon them and support as they reaffirm their lasting commitment as partners in love and life. May they continue to treat this love with deep gratitude and awe, and may each of us gathered here as witnesses be overjoyed and encouraged in our own lives and relationships, that this may be an inspiration for each of us gathered here."

Opening Welcome

Celebrant: "(Name) and (name), we are gathered here today to celebrate (number) years of marriage and your continuing love for one another. Each of us gathered is truly privileged to witness the possibilities that a union can offer. We are indeed inspired by the strength and deep commitment that has brought you to this moment. Today, on this momentous anniversary, you will re-declare to one another that, despite life's challenges and difficulties, you will continue to love and be faithful to one another. Once again, you commit yourselves to one another in marriage. This time each of you is blessed to have amassed the wisdom of experience of a life spent together.

"As you once again make this covenant today before God, do so with the knowledge that He is the creator of this life you share together and He is the creator of the special and unique love you hold and have held for each other. May this special love continue to expand, intensify, and be ever sustained by God."

Offering of a Scriptural Reading or Poem (suggestions):

From the *Brahma Sutra*
When the one man loves the one woman and the one woman loves the one man, the very angels desert heaven and sit in that house and sing for joy.

From Sonnet 18 by William Shakespeare (adapted)
Shall I compare thee to a summer's day?
Thou art more lovely and more temperate;
When in eternal lines to time thou grow'st
So long as men can breathe or eyes can see,
So long lives this, and this gives life to thee.

From the Book of Ruth:
Where thou goest I will go, and where thou livest I will live. Your family is my family and your God, my God.

The Ring Blessing
Celebrant: "The ring is a token of your love and, like a circle,

is a symbol of peace. It also symbolizes unity and infinity. This circle is beginningless and endless, as is love. As this ring is created from precious gold, so your love is created, nourished, and sustained by the precious love of God.

"Once again, as you exchange rings, you affirm that, like a circle, your love is without beginning and without end. Your lives are held within the circle of a union that is unbreakably joined by God, the source of all love. May these rings be blessed and the two who wear them. May they continue to stand together steadfast in a circle of Divine protection and love. Amen."

Celebrant Pre-Vows Statement

Celebrant to bride and groom: "(Name) and (name), years ago, you each stood together and made your vows to one another. As you stand here today, reflect back to those two people who loved and trusted in that shared love. At that time, your love had not yet stood the test of time. Now, as you stand together, you have shared your dreams and deepest aspirations through the ups and downs of life. The years have passed and time has brought you even closer. The promises that you are about to make reaffirm, acknowledge, and pay tribute to the depth of that love and respect that has continued to develop, blossom, mature, and grow over these years. These promises declare your continuing love to be a special gift that you two have honored and treasured, which will strengthen your lives for whatever situations you may face with strength and courage forever."

Exchange of Vows Renewal
(Ecumenical/Interfaith/Non-denominational)

Celebrant to groom: "Therefore I ask you, (name), after the passing of these years, do you receive (name) as your beloved wife?"

Groom: "I do."

Celebrant to groom: "Will you continue to love, honor, respect, and cherish her? Will you give thanks to her and for her—not only in your words, but also in your actions? Will you continue to honor and support her growth and aspirations?"

Groom: "I will."

Celebrant to bride: "Therefore I ask you, (name), after the passing of these years, do you receive (name) as your beloved husband?"

Bride: "I do."

Celebrant to bride: "Will you continue to love, honor, respect, and cherish him? Will you give thanks to him and for him—not only in your words, but also in your actions? Will you continue to honor and support his growth and aspirations?"

Bride: "I will."

Reading to be read by the Bride and Groom (suggestions):

Eskimo Love Song (Author unknown)
(The bride and groom recite to one another in turn)

You are my wife
My feet shall run because of you
My feet shall dance because of you

My heart shall beat because of you
My eyes see because of you
My mind thinks because of you
And I shall love because of you
You are my husband
My feet shall dance because of you
My heart shall beat because of you
My eyes see because of you
My mind thinks because of you
And I shall love because of you

Celtic Blessing (adapted from ancient Gaelic runes)
Deep peace of the running wave to you.
Deep peace of the flowing air to you.
Deep peace of the quiet earth to you.
Deep peace of the shining stars to you.
Deep peace of the Son of Peace to you.

Final Pronouncement:
Today you have renewed the promises and vows you made to each other on your wedding day. As you walk forth together today, you are joined in love and bonded in marriage through the vows and promises you gave to one another years ago and the renewal of those shared promises once again today, before these loving witnesses. I am overjoyed before all that is Sacred and Divine to conclude this ceremony with the greatest blessings upon the two of you. I therefore pronounce that you are forever joined in love as husband and wife.

The Kiss:
Please celebrate and seal this renewed union with a kiss.

EPILOGUE

Our lives speed by at a dizzying pace. One predictable constant for each of us is change. Change is inevitable. We are truly privileged to have those precious loved ones in our lives who enrich each moment of each day, caring, supporting and loving us throughout the ups and downs of life. When we find that special partner to share our love and our life with, we are doubly blessed, for we are given the opportunity to grow rich in blessings and gratitude.

In the end, when the ceremony is over and your honeymoon is a magical memory revisited on those dim, dreary winter days, remember that your ceremony was a symbol of a deep and committed union which only two people in love can truly create. Now you two begin the real work; the creation of your marriage. And keep in mind, it requires work and commitment. Be creative in finding ways to keep your love nourished, fresh, and alive. Also remember that love is not stagnant, but grows not only through the joys but through the pains and difficulties the two of you will share; drawing you both ever closer.

Continue to foster and maintain gratitude and forgiveness. Give thanks for the love you share. Your marriage will shape you in ways that you never imagined were possible. You will never be the same.

May God bless each and every one of you as you embark on the noble and spiritual path of marriage.

Closing Words

Some final thoughts on creativity and inspiration or "A lesson from a five-year-old":

Each of you working with this guide and planning your ceremony has already been blessed for having met your beloved partner. Working with this book offers abundant ideas and guidance collected and written over the years of my ministry. Yet few of us really work alone. My ministry, and this book, were not created by one, but by a team of many. The hundreds of couples I have worked with have inspired me, motivated me, and helped me build my inventory of information and knowledge that I can now offer back to every couple whose ceremony I officiate. However helpful this guide may be, in the end it is the couple themselves who decide on the ceremony style and wording, even if their decision is based on one of the enclosed pre-created six sample ceremonies; the final choice is still theirs and they add to it their own distinctive style. For those of you still working on your overall ceremony, the following exercise may be helpful:

While designing your wedding, visualize your ideal ceremony from the perspective of a director producing a film. Watch it play out in your imagination like the scene of a movie. Be inspired, and if you wish, be outrageous. For the moment, don't censor, just unleash your inspiration and creativity as you produce your imaginary ceremony and let your heart be the director. Now replay the same scene, only this time become the actor rather than the observer. Become the bride or groom (the leading lady or leading man). Feel and experience your ceremony: the location, the ceremony site, the participants, the procession, the theme, the music and most of all, the ceremony words. Take note of what feels right and wonderful and what feels flat and empty. Be fully inspired. In the end, we need to be realistic, but the impractical and unrealistic can be reined in and modified later, begin with being creative. There is much in our lives to inspire, open, or soften our hearts. Without a doubt, one of the most inspirational events in our lives is our own wedding. Inspiration and creativity are all about listening to the words and wisdom of the heart.

And finally, an example of an unforgettable moment of inspiration from my five-year-old grandson, Liam:

Liam was walking with his mother, my daughter Penelope, during that magical moment directly after a thunderstorm. The luminously edged clouds had parted, opening a swath of clear silver-gold sky. Rays of sun shone through the opening like fingers of God. The whole scene was otherworldly. Liam looked up at the sky and said: "Mommy, when I look at the sky after a thunderstorm it looks so beautiful, I hear chimes in my heart."

I end this book with the following benediction I was inspired to write, which I dedicate to those who are blessed to have found their beloved life partner with whom they commit to the path of marriage. *May they hear chimes in their hearts.*

A Universal and Ecumenical Benediction (which flows out from The Divine Heart, through this little human heart, onto the pages of this book):

> We call upon all that is Holy, Sacred, and Divine to
>   guide us on life's unpredictable journey.
> May we each walk forward in grace and dignity,
> In strength and fearlessness,
> In clarity and wisdom,
> In gratitude and humility,
> May our hearts be full.
> May fullness empower us,
> May our minds be strong,
> May strength softly humble us,
> May life's discouragements build determination,
> May determination build courage,
> May courage build tenderness,
> And may tenderness build compassion.
> When life blesses us with a partner to joyfully share this
>   journey,
> May we walk together hand in hand upon the path of life
>   joined in devotion.
> For two souls who love deeply and whose destinies are
>   entwined, are held sacred by the fire of Divine Love,
>   whose light shines ever brighter in the world because of
>   their union.
> And so it is. Amen.

BIBLIOGRAPHY

Thomas Merton:
The Seven Story Mountain. Harourt Brace, 1948.
Fiftieth anniversary printing: Houghton Mifflin Harcourt, 1998.
Information on Thomas Merton can be found at:
The Thomas Merton Center-Bellarmine University
2000 Norris Place Kentucky 40205-1801
Phone: 502-452-8187
http://www.merton.org/

Baal Shem Tov:
Rabbi Yisroel (Israel) ben Eliezer (August 27, 1698-May 22, 1760), often called Baal Shem Tov or Besht, was a Jewish mystical rabbi. He is considered to be the founder of Hasidic Judaism. Besht was born in a small village that over the centuries has been part of Poland, Russia, and is now part of Ukraine. He died in Medzhybizh, which had once been part of Lithuania, then Turkey, Poland and Russia, and is also now in Ukraine, in the Khmelnytskyi Oblast.
Websters on-line-dictionary
Information on Baal Shem Tov can be found at:
Baal Shem Tov Foundation
http://www.baalshemtov.com/index.php

John O'Donohue:
John O'Donohue (1956-2008) was a priest, poet, philosopher and writer. He was best known as the author of *Anam Cara: A book of Celtic wisdom.* John O'Donohue's vision brought together various strands of wisdom, including European and Christian mysticism, and the deep spirituality and mythology of the Celtic lands. He was once described as "a poetic priest with the soul of a pagan."

He was a wonderful speaker with an enthusiasm and freshness that listeners found compelling. He had a degree in philosophy and English literature. His dissertation for his PhD was on Hegel. Information on John O'Donohue can be found at:

The John O'Donohue website:

http://www.johnodonohue.com/

http://www.johnodonohue.com/about

The Seven Blessings:

Sheva Brachot (Hebrew: ברכות שבע) literally "the seven blessings" also known as *birkot Nesuim*. Immediately following the reading of the ketubah (the marriage contract), the second ceremony begins. This ceremony involves the recitation of seven blessings and hence is commonly referred to as the Sheva Berakhot.

My Jewish Learning:

http://www.myjewishlearning.com/life/Life_Events/Weddings/ Liturgy_Ritual_and_Custom/Nissuin.shtml

The Seven Blessings are a key part of a traditional Jewish wedding ceremony. The blessings are adapted from ancient rabbinic teachings, beginning with the blessing over the wine and ending with a communal expression of joy. In many ceremonies the prayers are read or chanted in both Hebrew and English. There are also numerous modern English variations on the blessings. Many couples also ask friends or relatives to read some or all of the blessings, or they may ask all the guests in attendance to read the blessings from a wedding program. Some couples create their own blessings, or ask honored guests to create their own.

InterfaithFamily:

http://www.interfaithfamily.com/life_cycle/weddings/The_ Seven_Blessings.shtml

Acknowledgments:

Gratitude is such a beautiful thing. I find that it's a healing force unto itself, like a blanket of silver blessings enveloping us in love…It wants nothing *from* us, just an open and grateful heart for us. *For only through the eyes of the heart can we truly see.*

The order of the following acknowledgements has no bearing on the level of importance of each. I am indebted and grateful to each person listed below.

The endorsements for this book were so graciously gifted. I am deeply thankful to:
The Reverend Dr. Jon Mundy
John Michael Heuer
Jamie Kiffel-Alcheh
Father Aristide Bruni
Bruce Littlefield
To each of you: May your generosity and kindness be fully returned one thousand-fold as blessings and abundance.

My amazing Editor, Alice Peck for seeing and sifting out the 'jewels'. I thank her for jumping in feet first and wholeheartedly taking on this project. She plied her expertise, intuition and special touch to a 'behemoth' of a manuscript. She shaved and sculpted it while keeping the essential core text practically unchanged. No one else could have brought to it her unique magic.

Julie Favreau Schwartz of Wyndjammr Design for her genius and creativity, for reading my mind and for the beautiful design of this book.

All of my wedding clients, for whom this book was—and is—created. Each of their special stories is deeply inspirational and without which this book would have been incomplete.

Maryellen and John: Spiritual siblings. For their loving recognition, guidance, nurturance and friendship...beyond words.

Jamie Kiffel-Alcheh: Author, editor and friend, for her vision, support, belief, friendship and wisdom beyond her years.

The Reverend Dr. Jon Mundy: My spiritual 'Sherpa' and friend who guided me through seminary into my ministry and for his delightful—and infectious—humor.

The late Reverend Cannon Ernest W. Southcott: My first spiritual teacher, for his guidance all those years ago. In quiet moments I still hear his booming laughter as it echoed joyfully through the spire and rafters of St. Wilfrid's Church, Halton, Leeds, England.

Barbara Kestenbaum: Former Yoga goddess, editor and organizational dynamo, for her help and for believing in this project from its infancy.

My sister Penelope: For her friendship, for always being as dependable and solid as a rock. Her actions bear out her depth and speak volumes.

My husband Kenneth: Life partner and dear friend, for suggesting that I write this book, for supporting, encouraging and respecting all of my varied endeavors, (even those that leave him clueless and befuddled). I thank him for walking this life path with me and for his love.

My children and their families: For just being who they are and whom they are destined to be; for what more can I wish?

Penelope, Steven and Liam

Rosalisa, Mark and Rachel

Joseph and Kerri

My family in England: (My roots and kinfolk) For their love and welcoming kindness, which transcends the miles. My sister Penelope, my brother John and my sister-in-law Mary, and their families.

For my stepchildren and their families. Each is a gift and a bonus.

For my friends: For being there.

Nancy

Nietta

Diana

Violet, and so many more.

To Those who watch over me, who want only my greatest and highest good. They are my beacon.

Made in the USA
Charleston, SC
03 February 2013